New Casebooks

REVENGE TRAGEDY

EDITED BY STEVIE SIMKIN

palgrave

First published 2001 by
PALGRAVE
Houndmills, Basingstoke, Hampshire RG21 6XS and
175 Fifth Avenue, New York, N. Y. 10010
Companies and representatives throughout the world

PALGRAVE is the new global academic imprint of
St. Martin's Press LLC Scholarly and Reference Division and
Palgrave Publishers Ltd (formerly Macmillan Press Ltd).

ISBN 0-333-92237-9 hardback
ISBN 0-333-92236-0 paperback

This book is printed on paper suitable for recycling and
made from fully managed and sustained forest sources.

A catalogue record for this book is available
from the British Library.

Library of Congress Cataloging-in-Publication Data

Revenge tragedy/ edited by Stevie Simkin.
        p. cm. – (New casebooks)
    Includes bibliographical references and index.
    ISBN 0-333-92237-9
    1. English drama–Early modern and Elizabethan, 1500-1600–History and crit-
icism. 2. English drama–17th century–History and criticism. 3. English drama
(Tragedy)–History and criticism. 4. Revenge in literature. I. Simkin, Stevie. II.
New casebooks (Houndmills, Basingstoke, England)

    PR658.R45 R48 2000
    822'.051209–dc21   00-065209

10   9   8   7   6   5   4   3   2   1
10   09 08 07 06 05 04 03 02 01

Printed in China

New Casebooks

(continued overleaf)

REVENGE TRAGEDY Edited by Stevie Simkin
SHAKESPEARE: *Antony and Cleopatra* Edited by John Drakakis
SHAKESPEARE: *Hamlet* Edited by Martin Coyle
SHAKESPEARE: *King Lear* Edited by Kiernan Ryan
SHAKESPEARE: *Macbeth* Edited by Alan Sinfield
SHAKESPEARE: *The Merchant of Venice* Edited by Martin Coyle
SHAKESPEARE: *A Midsummer Night's Dream* Edited by Richard Dutton
SHAKESPEARE: *Much Ado About Nothing* and *The Taming of the Shrew*
    Edited by Marion Wynne-Davies
SHAKESPEARE: *Romeo and Juliet* Edited by R. S. White
SHAKESPEARE: *The Tempest* Edited by R. S. White
SHAKESPEARE: *Twelfth Night* Edited by R. S. White
SHAKESPEARE ON FILM Edited by Robert Shaughnessy
SHAKESPEARE IN PERFORMANCE Edited by Robert Shaughnessy
SHAKESPEARE'S HISTORY PLAYS Edited by Graham Holderness
SHAKESPEARE'S TRAGEDIES Edited by Susan Zimmerman
JOHN WEBSTER: *The Duchess of Malfi* Edited by Dympna Callaghan

GENERAL THEMES

FEMINIST THEATRE AND THEORY Edited by Helene Keyssar
POSTCOLONIAL LITERATURES Edited by Michael Parker and Roger Starkey

New Casebooks Series
Series Standing Order
ISBN 0-333-71702-3 hardcover
ISBN 0-333-69345-0 paperback
(outside North America only)

You can receive future titles in this series as they are published by placing a standing order. Please contact your bookseller or, in case of difficulty, write to us at the address below with your name and address, the title of the series and the ISBN quoted above.

Customer Services Department, Macmillan Distribution Ltd
Houndmills, Basingstoke, Hampshire RG21 6XS, England

Contents

Acknowledgements

The editor and publishers wish to thank the following for permission to use copyright material:

Deborah G. Burks, for '"I'll Want My Will Else": *The Changeling* and Women's Complicity with Their Rapists', *English Literary History*, 62 (1995), 759–90. Copyright © the Johns Hopkins University Press, by permission of the Johns Hopkins University Press; Karin S. Coddon, for '"For Show or Useless Property": Necrophilia and *The Revenger's Tragedy*', *English Literary History*, 61 (1994), 71–88. Copyright © the Johns Hopkins University Press, by permission of the Johns Hopkins University Press; Jonathan Dollimore, for material from *Radical Tragedy: Religion, Ideology and Power in the Drama of Shakespeare and his Contemporaries*, pp. 139–50. Copyright © Jonathan Dollimore 1984 by permission of Pearson Education Ltd; J. W. Lever, for material from *Tragedy and State*, 2nd edition, Routledge (1987), pp. 1–17, by permission of Taylor and Francis Books Ltd; Ania Loomba, for material from *Gender, Race, Renaissance Drama*, Oxford University Press, India (1989), pp. 93–118, by permission of the author; Christina Luckyj, for 'Gender, Rhetoric, and Performance in John Webster's *The White Devil*', from *Enacting Gender on the Renaissance Stage*, ed. Viviana Comensoli and Anne Russell, pp. 218–32. Copyright © 1999 by the Board of Trustees of the University of Illinois, by permission of the University of Illinois Press; Cristina Malcolmson, for '"As Tame as the Ladies": Politics and Gender in *The Changeling*', *English Literary Renaissance*, 20:2 (1990), 320–39, by permission of *English Literary Renaissance*; Katharine Eisaman Maus, for material from *Inwardness and Theater in the English Renaissance* (1995), pp. 55–71, by permission of the University of Chicago Press; Michael Neill, for '"What Strange Riddle's This?": Deciphering' *'Tis Pity She's a Whore*' from *John Ford: Critical*

Re-visions, ed. Michael Neill (1988), pp. 153–80, by permission of Cambridge University Press; Molly Easo Smith, for 'The Theater and the Scaffold: Death as Spectacle in *The Spanish Tragedy*', *Studies in English Literature, 1500–1900*, 32 (1992) 217–232. Copyright © *Studies in English Literature, 1500–1900*, by permission of The Johns Hopkins University Press; Susan J. Wiseman, for ''*Tis Pity She's a Whore*: Representing the Incestuous Body', from *Renaissance Bodies*, ed. Lucy Gent and Nigel Llewellyn (1990), by permission of Reaktion Books Ltd.

Every effort has been made to trace the copyright holders but if any have been inadvertently overlooked the publishers will be pleased to make the necessary arrangement at the first opportunity.

General Editors' Preface

The purpose of this series of New Casebooks is to reveal some of the ways in which contemporary criticism has changed our understanding of commonly studied texts and writers and, indeed, of the nature of criticism itself. Central to the series is a concern with modern critical theory and its effect on current approaches to the study of literature. Each New Casebook editor has been asked to select a sequence of essays which will introduce the reader to the new critical approaches to the text or texts being discussed in the volume and also illuminate the rich interchange between critical theory and critical practice that characterises so much current writing about literature.

In this focus on modern critical thinking and practice New Casebooks aim not only to inform but also to stimulate, with volumes seeking to reflect both the controversy and the excitement of current criticism. Because much of this criticism is difficult and often employs an unfamiliar critical language, editors have been asked to give the reader as much help as they feel is appropriate, but without simplifying the essays or the issues they raise. Again, editors have been asked to supply a list of further reading which will enable readers to follow up issues raised by the essays in the volume.

The project of New Casebooks, then, is to bring together in an illuminating way those critics who best illustrate the ways in which contemporary criticism has established new methods of analysing texts and who have reinvigorated the important debate about how we 'read' literature. The hope is, of course, that New Casebooks will not only open up this debate to a wider audience, but will also encourage students to extend their own ideas, and think afresh about their responses to the texts they are studying.

John Peck and Martin Coyle
University of Wales, Cardiff

Introduction

STEVIE SIMKIN

I

Whenever issues of justice have preoccupied our culture, the question of revenge has always followed close behind. The thirst for revenge is revived every time reports surface of the terrible hurt and destruction humans regularly wreak upon one another, from the mass slaughter of war to the private domestic cruelties committed from day to day, and debates about retribution and fitting the punishment to the crime remain current, even if the terms of those debates have shifted significantly over the past four hundred years.[1]

History and anthropology reveal revenge to have been fundamental to the customs and practices of primitive societies.[2] Fredson Bowers notes that 'the modern theory of crime presupposes the existence of a State', and in a society with no state, there could be no crime in this strict sense: the only recourse for the wronged party was direct revenge upon the one who had inflicted the injury.[3] In England, we can trace a gradual shift away from privately exacted revenge and the tradition of feud (wars between families) towards a centrally organised justice system, as the state becomes more firmly established. By the sixteenth century, a serious crime against any subject of the crown is being interpreted as a crime against the monarch's own person, and the state is required to respond.[4] The Elizabethan state, however, did not countenance acts of private revenge; Bowers quotes a number of sources (including a treatise by James I and various legal documents) that make it very clear that an avenger was liable to be punished by law as severely as the one who had committed the first murder.[5] Bowers also shows how this strong line militating against revenge had already been maintained for some time by the Church.

As we might expect, changes in state laws were not immediately and universally accepted in a society as disparate as Elizabethan England. The frequent condemnations of acts of revenge in religious, legal and other discourse of the time prove that established customs died hard, and suggest that the lawlessness of the principle of revenge was profoundly unsettling for those in authority. Many who had inherited a tradition in which families settled scores for themselves at a local level were no doubt frustrated by the introduction of a centralised legal bureaucracy and, under these conditions, revenge tragedies may have provided some kind of pressure valve release. Furthermore, with the state acting on behalf of the monarch (the recipient of any injury against a subject), the decision to circumvent the law had serious implications. Anyone who felt compelled to enact private revenge was expressing, implicitly or explicitly, dissatisfaction with the state's ability to intervene in an effective manner. 'Blood vengeance', as Katharine Maus remarks, 'almost automatically subverts the power of the crown.'[6]

In Western culture, the revenge plot has been one of the linchpins of narrative structure. Revenge is central to much Greek tragedy: the story of Orestes and Electra, as told by the dramatists Aeschylus, Sophocles, and Euripides, pivots on a revenge plot.[7] Agamemnon, king of Mycenae, is murdered by his wife Clytemnestra. Responding to the bidding of the god Apollo, their children Orestes and Electra wreak vengeance on Clytemnestra and her lover Aegisthus. Orestes is subsequently pursued and driven mad by the Furies. The Greek influence filtered down into early modern drama primarily via the work of the Roman playwright Seneca (writing in the first century AD, some five hundred years after the Greek dramatists); Seneca's work was generally taken as an authoritative paradigm of the classical tradition.[8] Ironically, it is probable that Seneca (unlike his Greek forbears) did not write his plays for performance. The Elizabethan and Jacobean dramatists, however, found their audiences eager for spectacles staging the kind of extravagant violence that was only described as off-stage action in Seneca's work. Revenge tragedies proved immensely popular in Elizabethan and Jacobean theatres: the five plays discussed in this volume are only representative. The revenge theme is familiar, too, in other European countries at this time – the plays of Racine and Corneille in France, and Calderon in Spain, are the most obvious examples. During the Romantic era, generally considered a fallow period for dramatic works, a number of writers well known for their poetry wrote 'closet drama' – plays written to be read rather than performed. Byron's *Manfred* (1817), Keats's *Otho the Great* (1819), and Shelley's *The Cenci* (1819) are the most familiar, and the latter stands firmly within the tradition of the revenge genre. Elsewhere, at roughly the same time, revenge plots were cropping up in operatic works (most famously in Mozart's *Don Giovanni* [1787]) and had passed into other literary contexts, especially the novel. During the nineteenth century, the massive popularity of melodrama led to a proliferation of revenge-oriented plots.

In our own time, the revenger figure, that man or woman who takes the law into his or her own hands, has been a stock character in mainstream Hollywood film, and the commercial success of many of these films is an indicator of the drawing power of the revenger. Over the past thirty years, the popularity of series like the *Death Wish* and *Dirty Harry* films in the 1970s and 1980s, and of movies like *Se7en* (1996) and *Double Jeopardy* (1999) in the 1990s, is a sign that revenge remains a reliable box office draw.[9] Are audiences attracted to the spectacle of violent retribution by their own impatience with the cumbersome apparatus of legal justice? Is their interest aroused by frustration with a state system that is ill-equipped to do the job effectively, or by a conviction that close connection with the business of punishment has been removed from the hands of those to whom it matters? With the revenge abstracted into a depersonalised legal process, aggrieved individuals (and all those who identify with them and their cause) may be left feeling cheated, and more inclined to glamorise those who do take matters into their own hands in the 'safe' environment of theatrical or cinematic fantasy.

II

For many years, revenge tragedies were largely neglected, consigned to a dark corner of the map of Renaissance culture, despite their obvious prominence.[10] At a time when the Shakespearean era was identified in theatrical terms as the golden age of English drama, and in literary terms as the distillation of the finest insights into the human condition, revenge tragedies were embarrassing blemishes best ignored. To take John Webster and his critical fortunes as a representative example, we find George Bernard Shaw famously dismissing him as 'Tussaud Laureate', and in the 1940s and 1950s, influential critics such as Ian Jack and L. G. Salingar regularly describing his work as 'decadent'. According to Jack, Webster has 'no deeper purpose than to make our flesh creep', and Salingar, while conceding that Webster is 'sophisticated', qualifies his judgement by adding that 'his sophistication belongs to decadence', remarking how in the plays 'every sensation is inflamed, every emotion becomes an orgy'.[11]

In terms of literary genealogy, however, it is difficult to separate revenge plays from other early modern tragedies such as *Hamlet* (clearly in the revenge tradition, and owing a sizeable debt to Thomas Kyd's *The Spanish Tragedy*), *Othello* and *King Lear*. Moreover, simply dismissing the plays as decadent, sensationalist and, by implication, beneath serious critical attention, has provocative consequences: Shakespeare's *Titus Andronicus*, for instance, is as bloody and barbaric as anything Webster or Ford devised and has, as a result, frequently been seen as an embarrassment by some editors. The consensus in the eighteenth century was that it must have been the work of another writer. When *Titus* is rehabilitated, as in Jonathan Bate's Arden edition (third series, 1995), this is achieved by clawing back its high cultural status: Bate argues that the play has been misjudged by dismissive critics, and that it is in fact 'one of the dramatist's most inventive plays, a complex and self-conscious improvisation upon classical sources'.[12] Again, a further indicator of cultural status can be gleaned from a consideration of the place of these plays in the context of the theatre industry. Occasionally they may crop up in the margins of fringe theatre, and a high profile (or school syllabus) work can once in a blue moon earn itself a commercial run, particularly if a fashionable star can be secured for a key role (such as Juliet Stevenson, who appeared in Webster's *The Duchess of Malfi* in the West End of London in 1995). However, these plays for the most part are revived only by state-subsidised theatre companies (usually the Royal Shakespeare Company or the National Theatre), or by ambitious student groups. Consequently, they are (with some reluctance) permitted to join the established canon of classical works, occasionally dragged out like exotic creatures for a season to be observed by curious audiences and often patronising theatre critics, and then locked securely away again for another ten years.

In both literary and theatrical terms, then, revenge tragedies are conventionally to be understood as belonging to the category of high culture. At the same time, the genre's taste for episodes of extreme (and endlessly inventive) violence has, as we have already seen, earned it the casual and dismissive labels 'decadent', 'exploitative' and 'gratuitous'. In recent years, a number of critics have noted in passing that revenge tragedies share a certain amount in common with contemporary violent cinema, a self-evidently popular (as opposed to elite) cultural phenomenon.[13] These debates about cultural status quickly become complex when we start to consider them using either philosophical terms of reference, or paradigms imported from cultural studies.[14] Strictly speaking, mainstream film is an instance of mass culture, since it is produced 'for the people' rather than 'by the people', and it is disseminated globally. Early modern theatre evidently works on a scale (in terms of audience exposure) that is incommensurate with the Hollywood industry. However, it is probably true to say that, in some respects, the plays themselves would feel more at home in this popular, or mass culture context, given that the original audiences for these plays would undoubtedly have been much more socially heterogeneous than the middle-class audiences that patronise subsidised theatre in Britain today. It is worth noting that even in the context of violent cinema, however, there are finer degrees of differentiation analogous to the attitudes mentioned above. Just as Jonathan Bate argues that Shakespeare's *Titus* is a complex work (and so clearly set apart from a 'slasher movie'),[15] so Kerrigan, for instance, refers to Clint Eastwood's bloody western *Unforgiven* (1992) as 'thoughtfully violent', an intriguing distinction.[16] Interrogation of the revenge tragedy genre's cultural status is one way in which it may be opened up to scrutiny from current theoretical perspectives. In the same way that, in film studies, a movie like *Dirty Harry* may be of interest for the way in which it intervened in American culture, politics and society in the early 1970s, so we may choose to analyse a play like *The Changeling* not primarily in aesthetic terms (which may, depending on taste and fashion, lead us to denigrate it), but in order to consider it primarily as a cultural artefact.[17]

Contemporary critical theory of every cast has, in fact, found the revenge genre a rich source of ideas about Renaissance society and politics: recurrent issues include sexuality, the complex relations of gender and power, and the relationship between the individual and the state. There are, too, other matters that are perhaps more specific to the genre: court corruption is a particular preoccupation (especially for Webster), and the fact that revenge tragedies frequently feature violence that is more explicit and extreme than the norm has led to increased interest in an age where body politics has been a fashionable field of study for poststructuralist critics of all allegiances. In view of all this, it is not surprising to find feminist critics, psychoanalytic critics, new historicists and cultural materialists all drawn to plays such as *The Duchess of Malfi*, *The Revenger's Tragedy* and *'Tis Pity She's a Whore*. This volume samples a wide range of critical positions, with the rest of this introduction providing an overview of the issues surrounding revenge tragedy as they are reflected in the selection of essays.

III

The extent to which religious orthodoxy was challenged or endorsed in Elizabethan and Jacobean culture in general, and the drama in particular, has long been a preoccupation of literary critics, but has taken on a new importance in recent criticism influenced by Marxism and left-wing political ideas. In the past, seeking to find a way of redeeming the alleged decadence and sensationalism of a playwright like Webster, some critics made vociferous claims for his strict moral sense. Lord David Cecil, for instance, writing in 1949, saw Webster's plays as rigidly Calvinist, with the villain of the piece always finally caught in traps he has laid for others.[18] The titles themselves of two important works published in the 1960s, Irving Ribner's *Jacobean Drama: The Quest for Moral Order* (1962) and Robert Ornstein's *The Moral Vision of Jacobean Tragedy* (1960), act as testimony to an abiding obsession at this time with moral criticism.[19] There was, however, no consensus on the moral or religious standpoint of Webster, even less of shadowy figures like Thomas Kyd or the author of *The Revenger's Tragedy*, whoever he may have been.[20] Indeed, Jonathan Dollimore, in his book *Radical Tragedy* (an extract from which is included in this volume as essay 5), proposes that 'in the Renaissance God was in trouble; "he" was being subjected to sceptical interrogation, not least in the theatre'.[21] Dollimore's essay presents *The Revenger's Tragedy* as a 'parody of the providential viewpoint, the *caricature* of the vengeful god', and argues a convincing case that the playwright's determination to underline his playful use of theatrical conventions is radically subversive in this respect.

Perhaps more surprising is Katharine Maus's suggestion that *The Spanish Tragedy* can be read as a challenge to religious orthodoxy (essay 4). In the play, Kyd draws, unabashed, on pagan religions as well as Christianity, an indication of his indebtedness to the Roman dramatist Seneca. The Roman influence is firmly established from the opening moment of the play: the ghost of Don Andrea recounts for the audience his journey to the underworld of Greek and Roman mythology. Maus's argument is subtle and provocative, however, in her description of how the play interrogates the specific target of providential belief – faith in a God that guides and directs our actions. Maus reveals how providence removes itself from the action of the play, exposing a 'divine justice machine' that is 'all too human'.[22] As a result, a new reading of Kyd emerges that puts him intriguingly close to dominant readings of his contemporary Christopher Marlowe and to Dollimore's understanding of the author of *The Revenger's Tragedy*.

Elsewhere, satire on churchmen is common currency in the plays, perhaps reaching its apotheosis in *The Duchess of Malfi*'s Cardinal, described in the play by Antonio as a 'melancholy churchman' who 'strews in his way flatterers, panders, intelligencers, atheists, and a thousand such political monsters' (I.i.153–5).[23] Cardinal Monticelso, the equivalent character in *The White Devil*, is a prototype of the *Malfi* cleric: we learn in Act IV, scene i of his 'black book' of criminals, which Francisco borrows to seek out an assassin to serve in his murderous plot against Bracciano and Vittoria. The Cardinal of *Malfi* is undoubtedly the greater villain; he takes a married woman as his lover, and later murders her with a poisoned bible in an attempt to conceal his involvement in the death of the Duchess. All this is enacted by a man who, according to Antonio, 'should have been Pope', and was only prevented from taking office by too blatant deployment of bribes along the way.[24] This is satirical stuff, but we need to remember exactly what Webster is satirising: to take it as an attack on Christianity *per se* is to miss the particular political and religious context. Webster's target here is specifically the Catholic church, and in an England still firmly entrenched in Protestantism (despite James I being more conciliatory than his predecessor), it would most likely have been interpreted as nothing more radical than fashionable anti-Catholic propaganda.

The worlds of the dead and the living often overlap in the genre: *The Spanish Tragedy* ends with the 'character' Revenge promising to 'begin [the] endless tragedy' of the characters lying slain on stage once they have been transported to the underworld (IV.v.48) – another instance of pagan cosmology in the play.[25] The fact that ghosts are familiar figures in revenge tragedies is further evidence of the blurring of the boundary between mortality and eternity in the drama. In terms of cultural practices, the ghosts act as reminders of the ancient principle of vendetta, where revenge is a duty and not a right. The undead inhabit revenge tragedies in a variety of forms. Webster haunts his villains with apparitions, often of their victims – Flamineo sees a vision of Bracciano in *The White Devil* (V.iv.120); the Duchess's spirit haunts both Bosola (V.ii.340–1) and her husband Antonio in *Malfi* – a ghostly echo of the Duchess's voice warns her husband of impending danger (V.iii.19–45). In the same play, the Cardinal talks of his visions of 'a thing armed with a rake / That seems to strike at me' (V.v.6–7). In *The Changeling*, the ghost of Alonzo appears to his murderer De Flores in the dumb-show preceding the fourth act. These are not mere Gothic trappings, however; in most cases, such apparitions are instrumental to the movement of the narrative. John Kerrigan talks of how revenge wakes the dead, or, as he puts it, 'makes the "undead" come to life'.[26] The most familiar examples are the Ghost of Old Hamlet, and Andrea in *The Spanish Tragedy*, a ghost who introduces and watches the drama with the personification of revenge squatting beside him. Gloriana in *The Revenger's Tragedy* is in a sense awakened by Vindice (whose name of course means Revenge): having been poisoned by the lecherous Duke for resisting his sexual advances, Gloriana is 'resurrected' by her lover Vindice, who dresses her skeleton as a prostitute, and arranges a midnight encounter with the Duke. The 'undead' character, her skull poisoned, kisses the Duke, and Vindice finishes him off with his dagger (III.v.144, 216).[27]

Robert N. Watson suggests that 'the world of revenge tragedy is primarily a human world, and the bloody rule is do unto others as you have been done to'.[28] While a play like *Hamlet* does engage with the revenge theme in terms of its implications for damnation or salvation, most other revenge tragedies are in line with Watson's analysis. In *'Tis Pity She's a Whore*, for instance, Ford stages disputes between the hero Giovanni and his spiritual adviser, a friar, but these arguments are over Giovanni's erotic desire for his sister, and consequently dispute the sin of incest, not the morality of revenge. Elsewhere, characters seem to leave religious coordinates out of account altogether. The dying speeches of Webster's protagonists are notable for their apparent failure to envisage their imminent fates, or to determine anything of value in their lives and deaths: in *The Duchess of Malfi*, Julia, poisoned by her lover the Cardinal, dies with the words 'I go, / I know not whither' (V.ii.284–5); Bosola declares 'We are only like dead walls, or vaulted graves, / That, ruined, yields no echo' (V.v.96–7); his victim the Cardinal asks, 'let me / Be laid by, and never thought of' (V.v.88–9); Ferdinand declares, 'I do account this world but a dog-kennel' (V.v.66); in *The White Devil*, Flamineo finds himself 'in a mist' (V.vi.259), and Vittoria despairs that 'My soul, like to a ship in a black storm, / Is driven I know not whither' (V.vi.248). Religious scepticism is most acute, it seems, when these characters are *in extremis*, caught in the agonising and prolonged death throes that are the inevitable fate of so many of them.

IV

I have already noted how explicitly staged violence is a vital constitutive feature of revenge tragedy. Furthermore, there is a general tendency in the invention and representation of such acts of violence to accentuate the grotesque, the macabre, and the horrific. Carol Clover notes that 'all that lies between the visible, knowable outside of the body and its secret insides is one thin membrane, protected only by a collective taboo against its violation.'[29] Nowhere is the fragility of the body more evident than in revenge tragedy. 'What's this flesh?' asks Bosola in *The Duchess of Malfi*; 'A little curded milk, fantastical puff-paste; our bodies are weaker than those paper prisons boys use to keep flies in' (IV.ii.120–2). Time and again, the body is violated, punctured, caused to bleed, mutilated. Characters have limbs and other body parts removed at the drop of a hat – Hieronimo bites his own tongue out to ensure that torture will yield no secrets in *The Spanish Tragedy* (IV.iv.191); in Shakespeare's *Titus Andronicus*, Lavinia, Titus's daughter, is raped, has her tongue cut out and her hands cut off (II.iii).[30] Later, Titus's enemy, Tamora, is served her own sons baked in a pie (V.iii.59–61). Probably drawing on the same Greek legend as Shakespeare, Marston, in *Antonio's Revenge*, depicts the revenger murdering

Julio, Piero's young son, and serving up the boy's limbs at a banquet; the strangely moving and disturbing stage direction states that Piero, who has had his tongue cut out, 'seems to condole his son' (V.iii.81).[31] In 'Tis Pity She's a Whore, Annabella, the central female character, has her heart cut out by her incestuous brother and presented to her husband at a banquet celebrating his birthday (V.vi.31–4).[32] Murders are varied and imaginative in their planning and execution. The Duchess of Malfi is garroted (IV.ii.229); in the same play, another character kisses a poisoned bible (V.ii.284). In The White Devil, Isabella kisses a portrait of her husband that has been coated with poison (II.ii.23), while Bracciano has a corrosive poison spread on the inside of his helmet which, eating away at his skull, sends him mad (V.iii); he dies at the hands of his enemies, who have disguised themselves as monks come to offer him comfort in his final hours (V.iii.173).

While the violence depicted in, for example, 'Tis Pity She's a Whore seems to remain resolutely straight-faced (this being no guarantee, incidentally, that an audience will be so obliging), the author of The Revenger's Tragedy is more adventurous. The death of the Duke strikes sparks by clashing the blackly comic and the horrific, in an analogous fashion to the ironic horror movies of the 1980s and 1990s (such as the Nightmare on Elm Street and Scream series).[33] Stealing the idea of a play-within-a-play from Kyd's The Spanish Tragedy (also recycled by Shakespeare in Hamlet), The Revenger's Tragedy enacts its revenge plot via a masque – a dramatic performance that heightens further the sense of ritualised violence. The pile-up of murder upon murder, revenge upon revenge, mounts towards a farcical pitch in the final scene, where the second group of revengers arrive after the masque only to find their job already done, their intended victims already slain.[34]

The Revenger's Tragedy seems to offer a direct invitation to the audience to indulge in laughter, and certainly the fine line between the comic and the horrific in the play has been one traditional concern of criticism. More recently, critics have concerned themselves with the close juxtaposition of death and eroticism in plays such as The Revenger's Tragedy and 'Tis Pity She's a Whore – Karin Coddon examines the former in essay 6, and both Susan Wiseman (essay 10) and Michael Neill (essay 11) devote a considerable amount of space to close study of the violence inflicted on Annabella by her brother and lover Giovanni in Ford's play. Poststructuralist theory has been preoccupied with debates about the status of the human body and what it signifies, and the recurrence of the body depicted *in extremis* in these plays marks them out for special attention.

V

A number of the essays that follow approach the texts from a feminist perspective: Ania Loomba's contribution (essay 2) is particularly useful as an overview of the issues of gender and power that are central to so many plays in the genre. The development of revenge tragedy runs to some extent on a parallel line with the evolution of a new kind of performance space in early modern England, and a shift of venue from the open spaces of so-called public playhouses such as the Swan, the Rose and the Globe, to the indoor private playhouses such as Blackfriars, Whitefriars and the Phoenix.[35] The private playhouses were smaller, totally enclosed, and featured the innovation of artificial lighting. Admission prices were higher, and as a consequence it is likely that a split started to open up between the popular open-air theatres and the more exclusive, bourgeois audiences attending the private theatres.[36] The relative intimacy of the acting space at the indoor theatres offered the potential at least for what we could term a greater naturalism in acting technique – voice projection would have been less of a problem, and there would presumably have been less temptation for players to telegraph their emotions by physical and facial gesture. Although we should be wary of imposing twentieth-century understandings of psychology on 400-year-old characters, some critics have claimed to see a growing psychological complexity in creations such as Ferdinand and the Duchess in *Malfi*, Beatrice-Joanna and De Flores in *The Changeling* and Giovanni in *'Tis Pity She's a Whore*.[37]

There is an analogous shift from the public to the private sphere that can be traced in the texts themselves. Whilst Elizabethan tragedy tends to centre around royalty and figures of political significance, domestic settings feature much more prominently in the drama as we move into the Jacobean and Caroline eras. Of course, the courtly, or at least aristocratic settings for the tragedies remain, since the tragic register is necessarily the domain of the elite, but increasingly the focus is on personal, rather than state politics. For example, while *The Duchess of Malfi* centres very much around Italian court life, and the corrupt workings of state power, the central concerns of the play are sexual jealousy and intrigue, an affair between a lady and her servant, hints of incestuous desire between brother and sister, a sexually corrupt priest, sexually motivated revenge and so on. *The Duchess of Malfi* is concerned with one woman's sexual desire set against her society's expectations for her in terms of love and marriage, and Middleton and Rowley's *The Changeling* finds Beatrice-Joanna in a similar predicament. This interrelation of public and private spheres conveniently foregrounds that shift from politic to domestic, from public to private. *'Tis Pity She's a Whore* is another primarily domestic tragedy, a world of brother and sister, widowed father and children, a gossipy nurse, a betrayed husband, petty intrigues and back alley stabbings.

One consequence of the move away from matters of royalty and state politics, and a corresponding shift towards the domestic, the social, and the private, is in the representation of women in the drama, and especially the foregrounding of sexual politics. For the most part, women figure as minor players in dramas about affairs of state, since their roles at court tended to be limited (the irony of a female monarch around this time notwithstanding). However, with interest moving towards the private, domestic sphere, women begin to take centre stage, so that it is in the tragedies of Webster, Middleton and Ford that we find some of the most fascinating heroines of early modern drama. The emergence of sexuality as a frequent, central issue in the drama can also be associated with the move into the private and domestic sphere. We shift from debates around patriarchal power in matters of state politics to the exercise of patriarchal power in personal sexual politics, and the way that power is threatened and subverted or reinforced. Such debates are central to the essays by Cristina Malcolmson (essay 7) and Deborah Burks (essay 8) in this volume.

Sexual relationships are represented with surprising frankness in some of the plays; the scene depicting Antonio and the Duchess of Malfi before retiring to bed is one instance (III.i.1–57), as well as the Duchess's invitation at the end of their wooing scene that they should 'go to bed together', while she jokes about 'Lay[ing] a naked sword between us, keep us chaste' (I.i.491). In *'Tis Pity She's a Whore*, we see Giovanni teasing Annabella the morning after they have consummated their relationship (II.i.1–20). These sexual relationships are often seen to transgress contemporary codes of behaviour, and in some cases our own, the incestuous bond between

Annabella and Giovanni being the most striking example. Incestuous desire is also hinted at in the relationship between Ferdinand and his sister the Duchess in *Malfi*. If incest is the ultimate taboo in society, then it can be seen as 'a vehicle for the expression of illicit desire, a challenge to the fundamental conventions of society' – social, political and religious.[38] In *Malfi*, the fact that the Duchess, as a widow, chooses to remarry, may have shocked Jacobean audiences. The fact that her second husband is her servant would have made matters worse. Similarly, the relationship between Beatrice-Joanna and De Flores in *The Changeling* is presented very much in terms of deviancy, partly because of De Flores' lowly status, partly because of his physical disfigurement. The early modern conviction that a beautiful exterior should mirror a morally beautiful interior is evident in the dynamics of their relationship, and Beatrice-Joanna finally inspires so much horror because of the striking disjunction between her physical beauty and apparent moral, spiritual degeneracy. When he discovers her affair with De Flores, Alsemero exclaims to Beatrice, 'O, thou art all deformed!' (V.iii.77).[39] Moments later, confronting the servant, he cries 'oh cunning devils! / How should blind men know you from fair-faced saints' (V.iii.108–9). Ania Loomba (essay 2) analyses the 'logic' and political significance of the familiar binary that determines Beatrice's position in the play. 'Woman to man is either a god or a wolf', declares Bracciano in *The White Devil* (IV.ii.88–9), and even if the moral complexities of figures like the Duchess in *Malfi* or Beatrice in *The Changeling* eschew such clear-cut categorisation, the men in the plays can rarely see past the binary of goddess and whore.

The roles women adopt in these plays, the way they are treated, and in particular the ways in which they are punished for transgressive behaviour (almost always sexual) are abiding preoccupations in contemporary criticism of the genre. Cristina Malcolmson's study of *The Changeling* (essay 7) looks closely at these issues, with specific reference to the trial of Frances Howard, which had caused a sensation some seven years before the first performances of the play. Female sexuality is strictly policed by the patriarchy: Ferdinand and the Cardinal watch their sister the Duchess of Malfi like hawks; Beatrice-Joanna in *The Changeling* is similarly observed by her father and her intended husband. The use of potions in order to test whether or not Beatrice is still a virgin is perhaps the most striking manifestation of this male obsession with women's sexuality. In the subplot, meanwhile, Alibius, expecting to be cuckolded, locks up his young, attractive wife. In *'Tis Pity She's a Whore*, Annabella is caught between her violent husband and the plots of her jealous brother who is also her lover. Such women have little or no sexual autonomy, and when they attempt to assert sexual independence, retribution is swift and brutal. Significantly, the punishments, executions and deaths of transgressive women tend to carry sexual overtones. In *'Tis Pity*, the fatal violence inflicted upon Annabella is given a sexual accent by Giovanni's declaration that 'this dagger's point ploughed up / Her fruitful womb' (V.vi.32–3). In *The Changeling*, Beatrice-Joanna is dispatched by her lover De Flores after the two of them have been locked in a closet by her cuckolded husband. Her cries from behind the door, 'Oh, oh, oh!' (V.iii.139) and then 'Oh, oh!' (l.140) could be interpreted as orgasmic, as cries of pain as De Flores stabs her, or else as both simultaneously.

Women's sexual lives, and particularly their virginities, are seen as the possessions of men – their fathers' before marriage, their husbands' after. Women therefore have no right to determine partners for themselves, something that is at the root of many of the tragedies: in *The Changeling*, Beatrice-Joanna speaks for all these heroines when she wishes she had been born a man, able to choose her own partner: 'Oh, 'tis the soul of freedom!' she exclaims (II.ii.109). Beatrice pursues her desire for Alsemero, and is strangely and irresistibly drawn to De Flores, who becomes 'a wondrous necessary man' to her, as if to suggest her inevitable dependence on men (V.i.91). Vittoria (in *The White Devil*), the Duchess of Malfi and Beatrice all conform to the early modern notion that women are sexually insatiable; what we may interpret as a feisty heroine, a Jaocbean audience may well have seen as something monstrous. De Flores, weighing up his chances as he fantasises over Beatrice-Joanna, takes heart as he observes her with Alsemero. For if a woman proves unfaithful once, he muses, 'She spreads and mounts then like arithmetic, / One, ten, a hundred, a thousand, ten thousand' (2.2.63–4). Ferdinand in *Malfi*, warning his widowed sister against taking a second husband, notes how 'women like that part which, like the lamprey, / Hath ne'er a bone in't' (I.i.327–8). The centrepiece of *The White Devil* is the arraignment of Vittoria. In a rigged trial, she is cross-examined by her judge the Cardinal, branded a whore, and sentenced to imprisonment in a house of convertites (Act III, scene ii).

Tellingly, both Beatrice and Vittoria internalise patriarchal ideology at the point of death: Beatrice pursues her desire for both Alsemero and De Flores, and finally dies shamed. In her last speeches, Beatrice-Joanna explicitly locates the pollution in blood that she acknowledges as belonging to her father (V.iii.149–53). Gail Kern Paster describes how Beatrice is represented as having polluted the pure royal blood which is her inheritance. In death she becomes 'that blood "taken" from the patriarchal body in order to purge it, to relieve it from a plethoric disease ... [a disease caused by having too much blood in the body] ... this blood has been poured into a common "sewer", a drain, where it will mix with all forms of filth and waste.'[40] In *The White Devil*, Vittoria cries, 'O my greatest sin lay in my blood; now my blood pays for't' (V.vi.239–40).[41] In *Malfi*, the Cardinal, having heard that his sister has had a child by her secret lover, rages, 'Shall our blood, / The royal blood of Aragon and Castile, be thus attainted?' (II.v.21–3). Just before she dies, the Duchess remembers her brothers and tells Bosola that 'I have so much obedience in my blood, / I wish it in their veins, to do them good' (IV.ii.160–1).

There are a number of reasons why there is such a great deal of anxiety surrounding female sexuality in plays of this period, the most obvious being the crucial issue of legitimacy. A mother can always be sure a child is hers – a father cannot, and 400 years ago, with no way of testing for legitimacy, that anxiety must have been more acute than we can possibly imagine. Furthermore, with inheritance and lines of descent much more significant then than they tend to be in Western society today, male control over female sexuality gave the men power over the stability of the family and the legitimacy of heirs. Women's sexuality, once let off the leash, is seen as potentially catastrophic for the social infrastructure. Deborah Burks's essay (8) explores the connected issues of property, status and gender, as well as examining in detail early modern rape laws, in order to analyse the sexual and social dynamics of *The Changeling*, an analysis that has implications for all the plays discussed in this volume.

The Duchess of Malfi is deprived of her children, the offspring of her socially 'impure' alliance with Antonio. The line of succession in *Malfi* has been disrupted by the injection of base, servant-class blood and Ferdinand and the Cardinal seek to sever that line – in vain, as it turns out, since the eldest son survives. The same threat arises in *The Changeling* as a result of the relationship between

Beatrice-Joanna and De Flores. Annabella is due to suffer· at the hands of Soranzo for fathering the child of her brother, but Soranzo is pre-empted by Giovanni, who consumes all three of them (as well as the unborn child) in a murder / suicide pact. Transgressors such as the Duchess of Malfi, Vittoria and Beatrice-Joanna are seen to pollute the purity of the blood of the aristocratic body and, according to the logic of this ideology, they purge that body of its pollutants by their deaths. The punishment of the women is spectacular – a spectacle, something to be observed – because display is crucial as a demonstration of the extent of the state's legal control. As Foucault suggests in *Discipline and Punish*, 'If torture was so strongly embedded in legal practice, it was because it revealed truth and showed the operation of power'.[42] Foucault's writings about punishment and the body remain central to contemporary readings of early modern tragedy. Michael Neill's essay (11) provides a provocative Foucauldian reading of the death of Annabella and its aftermath, and Molly Smith (essay 3) considers the violence of *The Spanish Tragedy* (and in particular its preoccupation with the hanged man) in the context of the justice system, noting how both stage plays and executions functioned as 'entertainments' in Elizabethan London, and how they intersect with the state's preoccupation with the display of its power.

VI

I mentioned at the beginning of this introduction how the principle of revenge has persisted as a preoccupation of Western society, and a familiar plot structure on which to hang narratives. J. W. Lever, in the second chapter of *The Tragedy of State*, suggests that revenge tragedy typically follows a set pattern, with certain stock figures: the virtuous ruler (the Ghost of Old Hamlet in *Hamlet*, the character Antonio who restores order at the end of *The Revenger's Tragedy*); the anti-ruler, or tyrant – Claudius in *Hamlet*, the lecherous and corrupt Duke *in The Revenger's Tragedy*; and of course the revenger himself (or herself – Bel-imperia in part adopts that role in *The Spanish Tragedy*, although she operates under Hieronimo's direction).[43]

To some extent, as Lever explains in an endnote, this reflects a genuine response to the political scene in England at the time, and the familiar setting of the courts of Italian city states (famed for their corruption) can be seen as a kind of analogue for the court of

King James I. Tales of the king's excess are legion; Lever notes the fact that meals regularly consisted of 24 dishes – 30 or more on special occasions. Drunkenness and debauchery, somewhat inevitably, were frequent features of these court events. Sexual promiscuity was widespread. A figure like Spurio the bastard in *The Revenger's Tragedy* (or Edmund in *King Lear*) would have been a familiar sight at court.[44] The use of the masque in *The Revenger's Tragedy* is itself suggestive of James's regime – James was particularly fond of lavish court masques that celebrated his power, royalty and wealth. *The Duchess of Malfi* opens with a conversation between two courtiers who engage in a lengthy discussion comparing the order, harmony and purity of the French court with the corruption of the Italian court. Antonio notes:

> In seeking to reduce both state and people
> To a fixed order, their judicious king
> Begins at home. Quits first his royal palace
> Of flatt'ring sycophants ...
>
> (I.i.5–8)

This recalls James's patronage of his own favourite courtiers, a habit that stirred resentment amongst established members of the court. James, though he had to have a wife, and father children, had a number of male lovers whom he patronised. On being crowned king in London (he was already James VI of Scotland), he brought a large number of Scottish noblemen with him, distributing titles liberally, and taking little account of how the established English aristocracy might respond.

Vindice, the anti-hero of *The Revenger's Tragedy*, evidently sees himself as some kind of scourge of a corrupt society, but as the play gathers momentum, he surrenders to the joy of the violence he perpetrates in the name of justice. This is particularly evident at the two climactic moments of the play, the murder of the Duke, and the multiple deaths at the performance of the masque in the final scene. He becomes fanatically committed to the aptness of his revenge – note the detail with which he plans and carries out the murder of the Duke, and his insistence on the quality of the performance in the final masque. There are many reasons why Vindice might feel frustrated by the process of the law (or its failure). We witness a biased legal system in action in the second scene of the play, when the Duchess manages to reprieve her son, a rapist, from execution by pleading with her husband; we are left in no doubt about the need for some kind of action to restore true justice. Vindice himself has been waiting nine years for an opportunity to enact his own revenge upon the Duke.

The figure of the revenger has remained a stock character in contemporary fiction, drama and cinema. Some of Hollywood's most memorable (and controversial) screen *personae* have been revengers: as well as the Dirty Harry and *Death Wish* films mentioned above, numerous so-called 'exploitation' movies such as *The Exterminator* (1980), *Ms. 45: Angel of Vengeance* (1981) *I Spit on Your Grave* (1977) and *Last House on the Left* (1972) feature revenger protagonists.[45] The critically acclaimed thriller *Se7en* (1996) finds a young police officer, Mills, provoked to an act of revenge on John Doe, a serial killer who has meticulously planned a series of murders to mirror the seven deadly sins: the victim of his sixth killing is Mills's wife. The satisfaction the audience experiences in being permitted to witness swift retribution in action as Mills shoots Doe, is problematised by a recognition that Doe has, by provoking Mills to commit the final deadly sin (wrath), brought his murderous 'work of art' to completion. Hieronimo, the hero of *The Spanish Tragedy*, is in a position analogous to Mills's. Hieronimo is outraged at the state's failure to redress the injustice of the murder of his son – a failing he feels all the more acutely on account of his own position as knight marshal, a civil servant 'charged in the English court with maintaining the peace within twelve miles of the royal presence'.[46] Seeking revenge for his son's death, Hieronimo goes insane, driven to distraction in part by the conflicting principles represented by his public role (as one who administers justice) and his role as bereaved father (one desiring swift and direct retribution).

Of course, all these texts, both films and plays, need to be situated socially, politically and historically, and the contexts are going to be different in each case: the disturbingly fascistic overtones of the first two movies in the Dirty Harry series reflect an era of social crisis in the United States, and a politically conservative agenda. *Se7en*, exhibiting a moral complexity that is mirrored by its dark, oblique visual style, belongs to an era where the desperate grasping at ethical imperatives has given way to relativism and a surrender of the supposed certainties of the old order. Early modern revenge tragedies emerged from a culture very different from our own. As we have already seen, changes in the legal system may well have caused frustration and dissatisfaction in some social fractions, where individuals were more accustomed to bloodying their own hands in the pursuit of justice. Robert Watson notes that the Senecan model of revenge tragedy 'could hardly have proliferated so rapidly unless there were tensions in Elizabethan society to which it answered'.[47]

Both plays and films are preoccupied with the disjunction between what should be and what is in a fallen (or degenerate) world. In a society overfamiliar with corruption, and certainly for a public which has already supped its fill on horrors, perhaps the visions of excess that the two popular genres offer to their respective audiences constitute a logical next step. It is here that we may draw parallels between contemporary society and the early modern world, as we puzzle over the extreme violence of revenge tragedy and the increasingly graphic, recurrent and protracted violence in contemporary cinema. It may be that a film like *Se7en* comes closest to a play like *The Revenger's Tragedy* in its deep scepticism, both texts feeling the lack of a secure moral centre. Revenge tragedies, now so infrequently staged, still have the capacity to shock, and their power inheres in something greater than mere spectacles of death and cruelty. As J. W. Lever notes, 'drama ... [is] inseparable from life, life from politics, and politics from a sense of the past'.[48] Time after time, revenge tragedies invite us to reassess the links between justice and revenge, violence and the social order. In so doing, they continue to challenge audiences and readers to engage directly with the politics of the past and the present, and the ways in which they interrelate.

NOTES

1. *Lex talionis* (the law of repayment in kind) is, as John Kerrigan notes, rooted in philosophical, religious and legal discourse, and in the West it has been inherited via both classical Greek heritage and Judaeo-Christian tradition (John Kerrigan, *Revenge Tragedy: Aeschylus to Armageddon* [Oxford, 1996], pp. 21–3). Kerrigan traces the evolution of this law of reciprocity via Plato's *Laws*, Aristotle's *Rhetoric*, and, in the Bible, via the teaching in Exodus 21:23–5 of 'eye for eye, tooth for tooth'. Set against this is Jesus Christ's teaching of 'turn the other cheek' (Matthew 5:38–9), although other verses in the New Testament advocate retributive justice (Romans 12:19: 'Vengeance is mine, I will repay, says the Lord'). For more in-depth discussion of the issue of revenge in early modern society, see Fredson Bowers, *Elizabethan Revenge Tragedy 1587–1642* (Princeton, NJ, 1940), ch. 1; and Lily B. Campbell, 'Theories of Revenge in Renaissance England', *Modern Philology*, 38 (1931), 281–96.

2. Fredson Bowers provides a good summary of this scholarship in the opening chapter of his *Elizabethan Revenge Tragedy*.

3. Bowers, *Elizabethan Revenge Tragedy*, p. 3.

4. Katharine Eisaman Maus (ed.), *Four Revenge Tragedies* (Oxford, 1995), Introduction, p. xiv.

5. Bowers, *Elizabethan Revenge Tragedy*, pp. 10–11.

6. Maus, *Four Revenge Tragedies*, p. xiv.

7. See Aeschylus, *Agamemnon*; Sophocles, *Electra*; Euripides, *Orestes*.

8. See Seneca's *Agamemnon* in particular, which is based on Aeschylus's play of the same name.

9. Clint Eastwood's Dirty Harry made his first appearance in the film of that name (1971); the sequels were *Magnum Force* (1973), *The Enforcer* (1976), *Sudden Impact* (1983) and *The Dead Pool* (1988). Charles Bronson's *Death Wish* franchise ran from 1974–94, with rapidly diminishing returns in both artistic and box office terms. *Se7en* was a huge success, both critically and commercially. *Double Jeopardy* was, at the time of writing, the most recent box office phenomenon to incorporate a revenge plot, grossing over $100 million in the US alone.

10. Revenge tragedies not covered in this volume include a lost *Hamlet* play by Thomas Kyd (c. 1589), Shakespeare's *Titus Andronicus* (1591) and *Hamlet* (1600), Marlowe's *The Jew of Malta* (1589), Marston's *Antonio's Revenge* (1600), Chettle's *Hoffman* (1602), Mason's *The Turk* (1607), Chapman's *The Revenge of Bussy D'Ambois* (1610), Tourneur's *The Atheist's Tragedy* (1611), Middleton's *The Maiden's Tragedy* (1611) and *Women Beware Women* (1621), Beaumont and Fletcher's *The Maid's Tragedy* (1611), Fletcher's *Tragedy of Valentinian* (1614) and *The Bloody Brother* (1619), Drue's *The Bloody Banquet* (1620), Massinger's *The Duke of Milan* (1621) and *The Unnatural Combat* (1621), Goffe's *Orestes* (1623), D'Avenant's *Albovine* (1626), Heminge's *The Jew's Tragedy* (1628) and *The Fatal Contract* (1630), Shirley's *The Maid's Revenge* (1626), *The Traitor* (1631) and *The Cardinal* (1641), and Henry Glapthorne's *Revenge for Honour* (1640).

11. Ian Jack, 'The Case of John Webster', *Scrutiny*, 16 (1949), 43; L. G. Salingar, 'Tourneur and the Tragedy of Revenge', in Boris Ford (ed.), *The Age of Shakespeare*, The Pelican Guide to English Literature (Harmondsworth, 1955; revd edn 1982), p. 451.

12. Jonathan Bate (ed.), *Titus Andronicus*, Arden 3rd series (London, 1995), p. 3.

13. For instance, John Kerrigan, *Revenge Tragedy*, pp. 1, 25, 321, 328; Katharine Eisaman Maus (ed.), *Four Revenge Tragedies* (Oxford,

1995), p. xi; Jonathan Bate (ed.), *Titus Andronicus*, p. 2; Robert N. Watson, 'Tragedy', in A. R. Braunmuller and Michael Hattaway (eds), *The Cambridge Companion to English Renaissance Drama* (Cambridge, 1990), p. 317.

14. For a very full and accessible philosophical engagement with these debates, see Noel Carroll, *A Philosophy of Mass Art* (Oxford, 1998). For more discussion of popular culture in relation to early modern drama, see Michael Bristol, 'Theater and Popular Culture' in John D. Cox and David Scott Kastan (eds), *A New History of Early English Drama* (New York, 1997), pp. 231–48.

15. Bate (ed.), *Titus Andronicus*, p. 2.

16. Kerrigan, *Revenge Tragedy*, p. 25.

17. Noel Carroll argues that the film *Dirty Harry*, in presenting the criminal Zodiac as 'evil incarnate', and offering him 'as a paradigm of the urban criminal, [...] has favourable implications for authoritarian police practices' (*A Philosophy of Mass Art*, pp. 406–7).

18. Lord David Cecil, *Poets and Storytellers* (London, 1949), p. 34.

19. Mark Stavig also reads Ford as a strict moralist in his *John Ford and the Traditional Moral Order* (1968).

20. The authorship of the play remains in dispute; it has traditionally been assigned to Cyril Tourneur, although a case for Thomas Middleton as author, in circulation for some time, is probably now the more dominant view. For discussion of the authorship question, see Samuel Schoenbaum, *Internal Evidence and Elizabethan Dramatic Authorship* (Evanston, IL., 1966); D. J. Lake, *The Canon of Thomas Middleton's Plays: Internal Evidence for the Major Problems of Authorship* (Cambridge, 1975); the introduction to the Penguin *Thomas Middleton: Five Plays*, edited by Bryan Loughrey and Neil Taylor (London, 1988) and Martin White, *Middleton and Tourneur* (Basingstoke, 1992), Appendix I, pp. 166–71.

21. Jonathan Dollimore, *Radical Tragedy: Religion, Ideology and Power in the Drama of Shakespeare and his Contemporaries* (2nd edn, Hemel Hempstead, 1989; first published 1984), p. xxix.

22. The phrase 'divine justice machine' is, Maus notes, G. K. Hunter's epithet (G. K. Hunter, 'Ironies of Justice in *The Spanish Tragedy*', *Renaissance Drama*, 8 [1965], 101).

23. Quotations from Webster's works in the introduction are taken from the Oxford World's Classics edition of *The Duchess of Malfi And Other Plays*, ed. René Weis (Oxford, 1996).

24. See *Duchess*, I.i.155–8.

25. Citations from Maus (ed.), *Four Revenge Tragedies*.

26. Kerrigan, *Revenge Tragedy*, p. 38.

27. Citations from Maus (ed.), *Four Revenge Tragedies*.

28. Robert N. Watson, 'Tragedy', p. 318.

29. Carol Clover, *Men, Women, and Chainsaws: Gender in the Modern Horror Film* (London, 1992), p. 32.

30. Citations from Jonathan Bate (ed.), *Titus Andronicus*.

31. Citations from Keith Sturgess (ed.), *The Malcontent and Other Plays* (Oxford, 1997). The human banquet motif recurs in the genre; it also appears in William Heminge's *The Jew's Tragedy* (1628) and Thomas Drue's *The Bloody Banquet* (1620). The story originates in the Greek myth of Thyestes, dramatised by Seneca in the play of the same name.

32. Citations from Simon Barker (ed.), *'Tis Pity She's Whore* (London, 1997).

33. *Scream* (1996), *Scream 2* (1997), *Scream 3* (2000); the *Nightmare on Elm Street* films appeared in 1984, 1985, 1987, 1988, 1989, 1991 and 1994.

34. For a full survey of this phenomenon, see Nicholas Brooke, *Horrid Laughter in Jacobean Tragedy* (London, 1979).

35. For more detailed discussion, see John Orrell, 'The Private Theatre Auditorium', *Theatre Research International*, 9 (1984), 79–94; Keith Sturgess, *Jacobean Private Theatre* (London, 1987), esp. chs 1–4; Andrew Gurr, *The Shakespearean Stage 1574–1642* (3rd edn, Cambridge, 1992), esp. pp. 154–64; Peter Thomson, *Shakespeare's Professional Career* (Cambridge, 1999; first published 1992), pp. 101–3.

36. This has been hotly debated: see W. A. Armstrong, 'The Audience of the Elizabethan Private Theatres' in *Review of English Studies*, n.s. 10 (1959), 234–49; Andrew Gurr, *Playgoing in Shakespeare's London* (2nd edn, Cambridge, 1996); Ann Jennalie Cook, *The Privileged Playgoers of Shakespeare's London, 1576–1642* (Princeton, NJ, 1981); Martin Butler, *Theatre and Crisis 1632–1642* (Cambridge, 1984); Keith Sturgess, *Jacobean Private Theatre* (London, 1987); J. Leeds Barroll, *Politics, Plague and Shakespeare's Theater* (Ithaca, NY, 1991); Ann Jennalie Cook, 'Audiences: Investigation, Interpretation, Invention', in Cox and Kastan (eds), *A New History*, pp. 305–20.

37. For debates about early modern acting styles in relation to 'naturalism', see R. A. Foakes, 'The Player's Passion: Some Notes on Elizabethan Psychology and Acting', *Essays and Studies*, n.s.7 (1954), 62–77; Andrew Gurr, 'Who strutted and bellowed?', *Shakespeare Survey*, 16 (1963), 95–102; B. L. Joseph, *Elizabethan Acting* (2nd edn, London, 1964); Michael Hattaway, *Elizabethan Popular Theatre*

(London, 1982); Joseph R. Roach, *The Player's Passion: Studies in the Science of Acting* (London, 1985); Martin Buzacott, *The Death of the Actor: Shakespeare on Page and Stage* (London, 1991); David Mann, *The Elizabethan Player: Contemporary Stage Representation* (London, 1991); Andrew Gurr, *The Shakespearean Stage*; Bert O. States, *Hamlet and the Concept of Character* (Baltimore, MD, 1992); Peter B. Murray (Basingstoke, 1996).

38. Alexander Leggatt, *English Drama: Shakespeare to the Restoration, 1590–1660* (London, 1988), p. 229.

39. Citations from Richard Dutton (ed.), *Women Beware Women and Other Plays* (Oxford, 1999).

40. Gail Kern Paster, *The Body Embarrassed – Drama and the Disciplines of Shame in Early Modern England* (1993), p. 89.

41. Menstrual blood in early modern society was one of a series of signifiers that apparently 'proved' that women were naturally predisposed to 'leak'. Furthermore, this series of signs together 'proved' that women did not have control over the workings of their own bodies. For a full discussion, see Paster, *The Body Embarrassed*, esp. ch. 2.

42. Michel Foucault, *Discipline and Punish*, trans. Alan Sheridan (first published London, 1977; 1991 reprint), p. 50.

43. Lever, *Tragedy of State*, pp. 18–19.

44. Ibid. pp. 35–6.

45. The last three mentioned belong to another subgenre, that of the rape-revenge film. It is interesting to note the ways in which these films invert or endorse the sexual politics that structure plays like *The Duchess of Malfi* and *The Changeling*. See Carol Clover's extensive discussion of these films in her *Men, Women and Chainsaws*.

46. C. L. Barber, 'Unbroken Passion: Social Piety and Outrage in *The Spanish Tragedy*' in his *Creating Elizabethan Tragedy* (Chicago, 1988), p. 135.

47. Watson, 'Tragedy', p. 318.

48. See essay 1, p. 24–5.

1

Tragedy and State

J. W. LEVER

The first question a teacher of literature faces today is summed up in the needling word 'relevance'. What is the relevance of his subject, his period, his theme? If he doesn't ask himself, his students will certainly ask him, in no deferential tone. The question is not of course new: replies to it have been formulated since the time of Plato. One convenient reply is that what is interesting must be relevant; if not to our practical needs, then to our mental growth. The proper study of mankind is man; literature is the stuff of human experience; hence its interest, and hence its relevance. All the same, priorities must be reckoned with. In the present-day world, alienated in poverty and affluence, dehumanised by state bureaucracies and military machines, the most urgent study of mankind would seem to be not the eternal human condition, but the prospect of survival in the face of impersonal power drives. What priority can be staked out for the literature of another age – or, to be quite specific, for Jacobean tragedy? While turning this over in my mind, I happened to read an article by *The Times* drama critic describing some current theatre productions in Prague.[1] The writer began by stating his initial sense of embarrassment at visiting Czechoslovakia at this point in her history for no better reason than to report on plays. Very soon, though, he became aware that this was an insular reaction, due mainly to the assumption of most English-speaking people that the theatre is a minor luxury to be forgotten in times of stress. In fact, he found audiences more responsive, even more explosive in their response, than he had ever known before. Drama was clearly felt to be inseparable from life, life from politics, and

24

politics from a sense of the past. He reported an interview with Ottomar Krejca, the director of Prague's 'Theatre Behind The Gate', who described the theatre as 'a political arena that has the strongest effect when it fulfils its purely artistic intentions to the utmost ... It moves away from everyday life in order to embrace it.'

A striking example of this function of the theatre may be seen in the much-acclaimed Prague production of de Musset's *Lorenzaccio*, a drama of the eighteen-thirties, set in the Florence of the fifteen-thirties. The time is soon after the defeat of the last Florentine republic, which had held out for three years of siege against the professional armies of Austria and Spain. When the play opens, the city has been brought under the rule of a Medici tyrant who serves as the puppet of the occupying powers. Imperial troops keep guard, while disaffected students roam the streets. Political arrests and banishments are the order of the day. Lorenzino, the young hero, is a secret revolutionary who has pledged himself to free Florence by killing its ruler. He wins his way into Duke Alessandro's confidence by acting as his spy and procurer, knowing well that his inner self is being corrupted in the process. At last his opportunity comes. The Duke is lured to a secret rendezvous where he hopes to find a new mistress, and is assassinated in private. But having gained his objective at a terrible price to his soul, Lorenzino finds that nothing positive has been achieved. The people fail to revolt, and a student uprising is easily put down. A new puppet ruler is appointed, as useful to his masters as the one who was slain. The lasting validity of the play is finely expressed in the recent production, where the murdered Duke Alessandro is wrapped in a red robe, from which the same actor steps out in the coronation scene to act the new Duke Cosimo, with Lorenzo's double crouching at his side, ready, as the reviewer puts it, 'for another fruitless round in the endless cycle of oppression and revolt'.

It is easy to understand why this play, set in sixteenth-century Italy by a French writer living in the revolutionary currents of the eighteen-thirties, should have an electrifying effect upon Czech audiences in the winter of 1969–70. However, *Lorenzaccio* is only one example of an approach to drama which views immediate issues as part of a vast continuum and evokes history as an extension of the individual memory. De Musset's play bears a generic resemblance to many Jacobean tragedies, with their court settings, their pervasive atmosphere of idealism and corruption, their ambivalent finales. On the Jacobean stage contemporary issues constantly lurk below the surface of historical or fictitious settings. The events of the play may be taken, as in Chapman's *Bussy* tragedies, from recent political happenings in France; they may, as in Jonson's *Sejanus* or Chapman's *Caesar and Pompey*, be dramatisations of Roman history; or they may present, as in plays of Marston, Tourneur and Webster, incidents inspired by the court intrigues of Renaissance Italian despotisms. But for audiences of the time, the relevance was sufficiently clear. Chapman explicitly drew attention to the parallels between his protagonist Byron and the Earl of Essex, executed for treason in 1601. Less direct, but unmistakable in their tenor, are the recurrent allusions to royal favourites, scheming politicians, sycophants, and the network of informers and secret agents through which the contemporary state controlled the lives of its nationals. As Jonson's character Silius observes in *Sejanus*,

> These can lie,
> Flatter and swear, forswear, deprave, inform,
> Smile, and betray; make guilty men; then beg
> The forfeit lives, to get the livings; cut
> Men's throats with whisperings ...
> (I.27–31)

Jonson knew well what he was talking about. He was cited before the Privy Council in connection with this same play. Already in 1597 he had been imprisoned for his share in the comedy *The Isle of Dogs*, described as containing 'very seditious and slanderous matter'; care was taken that no trace of this play should survive. In 1598 he was in prison again, where, as he later told Drummond, he was set upon by 'two damned villains to catch advantage of him' – in other words, to trap him into some statement of opinions that could be used for a charge of treason. In 1606 Marston was driven to hide away from London for approximately two years because of his share in the play *Eastward Ho*. Chapman's two-part play *Byron* led, as a result of protests by the French ambassador, to the arrest of three of the actors. Chapman himself managed to escape, but scenes from *The Tragedy of Byron* were cut out and never appeared in print, while most of Act IV in *Byron's Conspiracy* has similarly vanished. Even closet dramas not intended for public performance, or publication, might endanger the author. Fulke Greville mentions that, following the advice of friends, he destroyed his *Antony and Cleopatra*, written during the Queen's reign, rather than run the risk of parallels being found in it to the relationship of Elizabeth and Essex. It seems to me a fair surmise that Shakespeare for similar reasons put off the writing, or at least the performance, of his own *Antony and Cleopatra* – the historical sequel to *Julius Caesar* – until some five years after Queen Elizabeth's death.

That the theatre should be intensely concerned with politics was inevitable in a time of acute tension. Through the fifteen-nineties the tracking down of Catholic recusants and the suppression of Puritan groups imposed a strait-jacket of religious orthodoxy. Then in the last years of Elizabeth's reign and the first years of James I a series of shocks assailed the body politic. The rebellion of Essex and his followers, including Southampton, the patron of Shakespeare and Chapman, was followed in 1603 by the tangle of conspiracies known as the Main Plot and By-Plot, in which Cobham and Raleigh with many other noblemen were implicated. In 1605 came the Gunpowder Plot which nearly succeeded in blowing up King and Parliament together. Two years later again, in 1607, peasant disorders and riots against enclosures of the common land swept the Midland counties, to be put down by ruthless repression. Catholics and Puritans, noblemen and peasants, intellectuals with heterodox opinions, had their various, ultimately related grounds for discontent. Over against them stood a governmental system supported by its state church, its lawyers and secret agents, which farmed out monopolies to favoured courtiers and encouraged the nobility to ruin themselves and their estates by conspicuous spending.[2] In the words of Tourneur's Vindice,

> I have seen patrimonies washed a-pieces,
> Fruitfields turned into bastards,
> And, in a world of acres,
> Not so much dust due to the heir 'twas left, too,
> As would well gravel a petition.
> (*The Revenger's Tragedy*, I.iii.50–4)

Beyond these immediate issues, the serious playwrights of the age were aware of a wider transformation of society taking place throughout Europe and undermining all traditional human relationships. It consisted in the growth and concentration of state power, the destruction of the Italian city republics, the conversion of English, French and Spanish noblemen into court parasites, the absorption of petty despotisms by great monarchies, and the concomitant suppression of a wide range of individual freedoms. The effect upon the victims was to promote a re-thinking of ancient assumptions. What had once been regarded as the privileges of noblemen or burghers or free peasants came to be seen in universal terms as the immemorial rights of what Chapman called 'man in his native noblesse'. In opposition to these stood a concept of absolutism which required that all loyalties, all personal obligations and human bonds be sacrificed to the interests of state. 'The commonwealth', wrote Montaigne, 'requireth some to betray, some to lie, and some to massacre.'[3] In *Sophonisba* Marston paraphrased these words and added the comment:

>   I am bound to lose
> My life but not my honour for my country;
> Our vow, our faith, our oath, why they're ourselves ...
>   (II.i.81–3)

Elsewhere in the same play a character remarks sardonically, 'Thou know'st, a statist must not be a man' (II.ii). The motivations of power are seen without illusions by Webster's Bosola:

> Some would think the souls of princes were brought forth by some more weighty cause than those of meaner persons; they are deceived, there's the same hand to the fist. The like passions sway them, the same reason that makes a vicar go to law for a tithe-pig and undo his neighbours, makes them spoil a whole province, and batter down goodly cities with the cannon.
>   (*Duchess of Malfi*, II.i.94–9)

Driven to these conclusions by the inescapable facts of their time, many thinking men would be prepared to echo Byron's cry:

> The world is quite inverted, Virtue overthrown
> At Vice's feet ...
> The rude and terrible age is turned again ...
>   *Byron's Tragedy*, I.ii.14–15,17)

All the less would they be inclined to give credence to that hotchpotch of antiquated science, fancy, and folklore dignified by some modern scholars as the Elizabethan World Order.[4] This medieval theory of static hierarchies, each dominated by a supposedly perfect specimen from the stars down to the plants and minerals, had long since declined from a philosophy to a political mystique.

> We see the sun ... as a monarch among the planets ... the moon as an empress ... the fire bearing the sovereignty over the other elements

... Among the beasts, the lion. Among birds, the eagle ... There is no
power but of God, and the powers that be are ordained of God ... It
is absolutely unlawful for subjects to rise against their prince, be he a
tyrant or a heretic.[5]

I have quoted from William Vaughan's stock compilation of received ideas, *The Golden Grove*; many another text would do as
well. Corresponding to nothing in the experience or speculative
thought of the age, this creed of absolutism served chiefly to bolster
up a precarious monarchy which lacked a standing army or an
efficient police force.[6] Asserted by Tudor apologists, preached in the
homilies officially prescribed for reading in church, reiterated in
popular books of universal knowledge for the tired shopkeeper, the
so-called 'chain of being' was in an advanced condition of rust by
the end of the sixteenth century. It may well be that a silent majority still nodded assent to these platitudes. For the critical, questing
minds of Raleigh and Fulke Greville, of Jonson and Marston and
Chapman and the mature Shakespeare, such arguments by un-
proved analogy bore no relation to the facts of nature, of history, or
contemporary politics.

What truly exercised these writers was the self-evident phenomenon of state. The word 'state' carried a range of connotations, most
of them challenging the traditional view of a divinely sanctioned
order. As the term for a commonwealth or polity it was a
Renaissance coinage, derived from the idiomatic Italian phrase *lo
stato*, which might be rendered in our own idiom as 'the set-up'.
The set-up, the system, the establishment, the *status quo*: no aura of
divinity, no moral sanction pertained to the actuality of state, by
implication subject to change. The same sense of impermanence and
flux was to be seen in the state of nature, the vicissitudes of history,
the whims of fortune, the pomp and display of kings and their
favourites.

> If my dear love were but the child of state,
> It might for fortune's bastard be unfathered,
> As subject to time's love, or to time's hate,
> Weeds among weeds, or flowers with flowers gathered.

Shakespeare's Sonnet 124 reflected a view of life and society subject
to continuous alteration and change. The writers of his age were,
like him, re-discovering and affirming from their own experience
the ideas of classical thinkers: Ovid, who in the last book of the
Metamorphoses brought in Pythagoras to declare that 'no species is

permanently itself, but nature the innovator continually produces one shape from another';[7] Polybius, who, anticipating Spengler by two milleniums, traced a pattern of the rise and fall of empires. Accordingly, Sir William Alexander's poem greeting the accession of James I, *A Paraenesis to the Prince*, expressed a bare tithe of the unquestioning loyalty the occasion might call for. It outlined a theory of kingship arising from the people's choice and dependent for its survival upon the people's consent. Man was originally born free, a dweller in woods and caves who recognised no master. With the building of cities came the establishment of laws and the choice of leaders. Later still, whether through fear of ambitious individuals, or for security in war, or through the advent of some much admired personality, thrones were set up, and the keys of life and death entrusted to one man. Kingdoms first started in small provinces and towns; subsequently, great monarchies swallowed up the small; in the end, the greatest destroyed themselves through overweening ambition.[8] Kings should therefore take heed, avoid the outward signs of glory and cultivate a sense of responsibility.

> This is a griefe that all the world bemones,
> Whilst those lacke iudgement that are borne to iudge,
> And like to painted tombes, or guilded stones,
> Are for th'afflicted people no refuge.
> Kings are their kingdomes hearts, which tainted once,
> The bodies straight must die, in which they lodge:
>   And those, by whose example many fall,
>   Are guiltie of the murder of them all.
>
>   (st.19)

Alexander welcomed the accession of King James as a safeguard against the danger of foreign rule; but he stressed the need for even lawful rulers to maintain their virtue and consult their people:

> O neuer throne established was so sure,
> Whose fall a vitious Prince might not procure.
>   (st. 39)

However, Alexander's conclusions were mild as compared with the tremendous implications of Fulke Greville's dramatic poems *Mustapha* and *Alaham*, which were not printed until 1632, four years after Greville's death. Writing of these in his *Life of Sidney* he set forth a new aim for tragedy: 'my purpose in them was not (with the Ancient) to exemplify the disastrous miseries of mans life ... nor yet (with the Moderne) to point out Gods revenging aspect upon every particular sin … but rather to trace out the high waies of ambitious Governours, and to shew in the practice, that the more audacity, advantage, and good successe such Soveraignties have, the more they hasten to their own desolation and ruine'.[9] As Greville's editor points out, by the tragedy of the ancients Seneca was meant, and by modern tragedy in all probability such works as *Dr. Faustus, The Jew of Malta, Richard III*, even *Macbeth*.[10] Instead, Greville offered a type of drama modelled on the Senecan form but devoted to a searching, impassioned analysis of the workings of state. Following Renaissance practice, he chose his subjects not from mythology but from history, whose contemporary relevance could easily be noted. Objectivity was gained by the Turkish settings, events taking place at the court of the Sultan, an absolute despot supported by the authoritarian creed of Islam. But Greville left no room for doubt that his concepts of state and the state church applied to the West as well as the East. As his Mahometan priests declare:

> The Christian bondage is much more refined,
> Though not in real things, in real names;
> Laws, doctrine, discipline, being all assigned
> To hold upright that witty man-built frame;
>   Where every limb, though in themselves distinct,
>   Yet finely are unto the sceptre linked.
>
> An art by which man seems, but is not free;
> Crowns keeping all their specious guiding reins,
> Fast in the hand of strong authority;
> So to relax, or wind up passion's chains,
>   As before humble people know their grief,
>   Their states are used to look for no relief.
>   (*Mustapha*, Chorus II, 109–20)

In the five headlong choruses of *Mustapha*, religion and law are seen as universal instruments of rule and means to secure the hold of despotism upon the people. The rise of great states and the growth of empires are characterised as a fatal disease of society. Ultimately it is the people themselves who must decide their future, for it is only with their acquiescence that absolutism prevails:

> Whence I conclude: mankind is both the form,
> And matter, wherewith tyrannies transform:
> For power can neither see, work, or devise,

Without the people's hands, hearts, wit and eyes:
So that were man not by himself oppressed,
Kings would not, tyrants could not make him beast.
(Chorus II, 205–10)

Greville and Alexander, like Daniel and other writers of the Countess of Pembroke's circle, did not intend their plays for public performance. While making them a vehicle for the ideas of the age, they modelled their form on the strict classical precedents they found in Seneca. The professional playwrights, on the other hand, had to accommodate their outlook to the complexities and fluidity of the living theatre. Yet for them too, Seneca was a potent, omnipresent influence. No amount of research into the survival of medieval stage traditions can wipe out this vast presence, which shaped the imagination of Renaissance Europe.[11] Nor should the spiritual reach of early Greek tragedy blind us to the fact that dramatists in the age of despotism found their true affinity in this Roman writer at the court of Nero. Seneca was the poet of the extreme situation; the projector of the terrible moment when the hammer-blows of tyrannical force bring man to the edge of endurance. Aeschylus and Sophocles had measured human suffering in the balance of divine justice: Seneca rejected any evidence of justice in the action of the gods, who were indeed hardly more than names for the destructive urges in the cosmos and in man himself. Against these blind, malignant forces he opposed the power of rationality, the Stoic affirmation of a kingdom of the mind, unshaken by tyranny, unmoved by horrors:

Not riches makes a king, or high renown ...
A king is he that fear hath laid aside,
And all affects that in the breast are bred ...
It is the mind that only makes a king.
(*Thyestes*, Chorus II).[12]

Hoc regnum sibi quisque dat: this kingdom each man bestows upon himself. Seneca's maxim strikes the keynote of Jacobean tragedy with its contrast between the state of outward seeming and the inner monarchy of man. 'I never was a prince till now', declares Marston's Andrugio as a fugitive in danger of death. 'Every inch a king', affirms Shakespeare's Lear at the height of his madness. Webster's tragic duchess preserves her integrity through mental torture with the words 'I am Duchess of Malfi still.'

Writing in a different civilisation for a different theatre, the Jacobean playwrights broke the classical mould of drama to offer a much wider range of characters and settings. Action was centred in the court life of the modern state, amid the swirl of political and sexual intrigue. Immediate precedents lay to hand in the spectacular melodramas of Marlowe and the intricate theatrical effects of Kyd. Clowning and comic relief, masques and disguises all made their contribution. Intermingled with them were Senecan devices creating what seem to us odd discrepancies. Ghosts and supernatural omens incongruously guide the actions of Italian dukes or French noblemen. But these are only the more superficial features. Far more important is the persistence of the Senecan view of life and its compelling vision of tragedy. The Senecan tyrant had not changed his character down the ages from the Roman empire to the Renaissance, though he and his agents had added to their ferocity a cold cynicism we may if we like call Machiavellian, remembering always that Machiavelli, at heart a republican patriot, only formulated the practice of the modern ruler.[13] As for the Senecan attitudes of resistance, defiance, or unflinching endurance of tyranny – whether it be the tyranny of earthly rulers, or of fortune and the stars – these too had not essentially changed. In the Rome of the Caesars an educated elite turned away from the official religion to seek a personal philosophy, and found their needs answered in the Stoic way of life. So in the late Renaissance age of despots thinking men abandoned the traditional world outlook with its fixed hierarchies and drew moral stamina from a revived Stoicism. This did not necessarily mean a total rejection of religious faith. Rather like modern existentialism, Stoic doctrines could be reconciled on a metaphysical plane with Christianity. But like existentialism, which exercised its maximum influence in the time of Nazi oppression, its appeal was less as an abstract philosophy than as a guide to conduct. Epictetus and Seneca were not systematic thinkers, but they offered a dignified response to the paradoxes and absurdities of the human condition; they supplied a stance for the alienated individual in a society and a cosmos drained of meaning. Renaissance Stoicism was not so much an academic theory as a practical discipline for men involved in the world of action, caught, whether they wished it or not, in the meshes of 'state'.

Most of the plays I shall be considering present us with modes of tragedy unrelated to Aristotle's familiar definitions. They are not primarily treatments of characters with a so-called 'fatal flaw', whose downfall is brought about by the decree of just if inscrutable powers. The heroes may have their faults of deficiency or excess; but the fundamental flaw is not in them but in the world they inhabit: in the political state, the social order it upholds, and likewise, by projection, in the cosmic state of shifting arbirtary phenomena called 'Fortune'.[14] For the most part, indeed, we are not greatly concerned with the characters as individuals. Generally their emotional relationships and psychological make-up are sketched in broad outlines which hardly call for a close-range scrutiny. What really matters is the quality of their response to intolerable situations. This is a drama of adversity and stance, not of character and destiny. The heroes vary a good deal in stature and in their respective claims on our admiration. Their attitudes range over the whole gamut from total commitment to the destruction of evil, even at the cost of destroying in the process their own integrity, to an opting out of the conflict by self-chosen death, or retreat into an impregnable kingdom of the mind. There are varying degrees of defiance and endurance: philosophical consistency is less important than the establishment of the individual stance. As for the powers that be, whether on earth or above it, at court or in the stars, the force they exercise is unrelated to what men understand by reason or justice. The rational man who remains master of himself is by the same token the ultimate master of his fate. In the words of Chapman's Byron:

> I am a nobler substance than the stars,
> And shall the baser overrule the better?
> Or are they better, since they are the bigger?
> I have a will, and faculties of choice,
> To do, or not to do; and reason why
> I do, or not do this; the stars have none ...
> (*Byron's Conspiracy*, III.iii.109–14)

I have suggested a community of outlook in Jacobean tragedy; but this does not of course imply a common dramatic method. It is only to be expected that in the theatre of the early seventeenth century, with its diversity of traditions and techniques, the tragedy of state should be enacted in diverse forms, operating through a variety of theatrical effects. Perhaps the most clearly defined form, the one we think of first when we speak of Jacobean tragedy, is the revenge play, or, as it is sometimes called, the tragedy of blood. Certainly blood is much in evidence in this class of plays, both on the stage and in the minds of the characters. It is liberally prescribed in the memorable stage directions at the beginning of Marston's *Antonio's Revenge*: '*Enter* Piero, *unbrac't, his armes bare, smear'd in blood, a poniard in one hand bloodie and a torch in the other,* Strotzo *following him with a corde*'.

And blood persists down to the hero's last entry in Ford's *'Tis Pity She's a Whore*, probably to be taken as the last play of this kind:

> *Enter* **Giovanni** *with a heart upon his dagger.*
>
> **Giovanni**   Here, here, Soranzo! trimm'd in reeking blood
> That triumphs over death; proud in the spoil
> Of love and vengeance! Fate or all the powers
> That guide the motions of immortal souls,
> Could not prevent me.
>
> (V.vi.10–14)

While Giovanni's defiance of fate strikes a Senecan note, the theatrical effect of his entry with a bleeding heart on his dagger does not derive from classical drama, where horrors are almost always intimated only by report. It belongs rather to the Elizabethan tradition which, like the modern 'theatre of cruelty', prided itself on its capacity to shock. Frequently the Jacobean revenge play also met the psychological need for compensatory laughter. Clowning, parody, black farce, were concomitant effects, a necessary counterpoint to horror which, if we only think of these plays as printed texts, may appear crude and bathetic. Again, in the treatment of revenge which underlies the action, we are faced with the Elizabethan tradition of complex intrigue and counter-intrigue, disguises and masques, which make a notable contrast to the simple plot-machinery of such classical revenge plays as *Orestes* or *Medea*. The question may be asked whether the word 'tragedy' is not a mere literary label we are attaching to a mode of 'pure' theatre which makes its appeal at the subliminal level and does not speak to the rational mind. Is the Jacobean revenge play, with its affinities to the 'theatre of cruelty', an anticipation of the doctrines of Artaud, who wished to offer the spectator what he called 'the truthful precipitates of dreams, in which his taste for crime, his erotic obsessions, his savagery ... even his cannibalism'[15] would be met? At the opposite extreme of interpretation, there is the didactic concept, which sees this class of play as the treatment of an important issue for the seventeenth-century moralist: whether, and to what extent, revenge may be justified. Fredson Bowers, in his pioneer study *Elizabethan Revenge Tragedy*

(1940), supplies a great deal of information, based on sermons, tracts, and other contemporary writings, concerning Elizabethan attitudes to revenge. The conclusion reached, which might have been guessed from the start, is that the normal respectable, God-fearing citizen in the time of Elizabeth or King James thought revenge was a very bad and impious course of action. Accordingly it is to be inferred that audiences regarded revenge plays as cautionary fables, and watched the unfolding of the intrigues with a mounting sense of disapproval and a growing conviction of the soundness of their own orthodox opinions.

In my view neither of these interpretations hits the mark. I do not see the Jacobean revenge play as so-called 'pure theatre' where the spectators are meant to peel off their rational minds, their political and social preoccupations, for a vicarious sauna-bath in the collective unconscious. Nor, at the other extreme, would I regard these plays as exemplary warnings on the evils of taking the law into one's own hands. What Bowers fails to allow for is that in Jacobean tragedy it is not primarily the conduct of the individual, but of the society which assails him, that stands condemned. Certainly the taking of private revenge was an evil of the age, and the extent to which the code of honour should be respected was a very live issue. But the typical situation of the revenge play is unrelated to the operation of the feud or the possibilities of recourse to law. The hero is faced with iniquity on high, with crimes committed by a tyranny immune to criticism or protest. His father may have been murdered, his mistress dishonoured, his friend ruined by the despot or his minions. Through personal wrongs the play dramatises the general corruption of state, and confronts the hero with the imperative necessity to act, even at the price of his own moral contamination. The treatment of these issues may be sensationalised, but the issues themselves involve the dramatist's preoccupation with objective reality. Concerned, in Greville's words, 'to trace out the high ways of ambitious governours', the Jacobean revenge drama evokes an authentic form of tragic experience.

[...]

In Webster's two late-Jacobean tragedies the Italian setting and relationships of the revenge play are recalled. After the work of Chapman and Jonson, however, there could be no return to the simple juxtapositions of Marston and Tourneur. While the Renaissance state is presented in a wealth of realistic detail, satirised in baroque conceits, castigated in sententious couplets, the old antitheses of tyrant and revenger, vice and virtue are overlaid. In *The White Devil* corruption is seen as a universal phenomenon, the ambience of an entire civilisation. As in Jonson's satires, the innocent evoke only a passing pity; the characters who dominate the stage differ as between cunning hypocrites and wrongdoers who are at least frank in their lust and pride. In *The Duchess of Malfi*, however, there is a shift of perspective; a focusing, as in Chapman, upon the individual predicament. Social and cosmic issues are viewed through the eyes of particular characters. Love is seen as the only possible mode of human existence; power recognised as self-destructive. The choice lies not between good and evil, but between reason and madness, ultimately between life and death. In this final analysis, the catastrophic ending of tragedy admits at least some modest hope of a better future, not only in an after-life, but even on earth. The insane criminals of the established order lie dead, as well as their victim and their dupe. But the son of a Duchess who preferred love and motherhood to the sterility of rank and power, and of her husband, an honest commoner, has survived. 'Let us make noble use / Of this great ruin', says Delio in the last speech of the play. The silent unnamed boy at the side of his father's friend is the modest token of another, more humanly acceptable order.

From J. W. Lever, *The Tragedy of State* (1971; London, 1987), pp. 1–15.

NOTES

[This extract, taken from J. W. Lever's influential book *The Tragedy of State*, is a useful and very accessible preface to the rest of this collection. Lever's style has none of the sometimes difficult terminology of writers working within an established mode of critical discourse. At the same time, his rejection of traditional preoccupations such as plot and character, in favour of the political dimensions of the texts he studies, is strikingly modern.

The Tragedy of State itself was first published in 1971, and was reprinted in 1987 with an introduction by Jonathan Dollimore. Dollimore owes a debt to Lever's work which he readily admits; they share the conviction that art in general, and perhaps theatre in particular, is inseparable from politics. On the first page of the extract, Lever refers to the drama critic Irving Wardle's report in *The Times* describing theatre performances going on in Prague in November 1969, just about the time Soviet troops crushed an attempt on the part of a newly installed Czech government to institute liberalisation in the country. In these politically volatile times (demonstrations by students and workers in Paris in 1968, and the civil rights movement and protests against the Vietnam war in America are the most obvious examples of global unrest), Lever's impatience with the prevailing critical trends is palpable in his preface: infuriated by the tendency to reclassify every challenging Renaissance dramatist as 'a pillar of orthodoxy', he declares that he 'cannot endorse a view of Jacobean drama which would turn it, like Miss Havisham's house, into a place of drawn curtains and stopped clocks, where tragedy sat for ever re-enacting man's primeval fall' (*The Tragedy of State*, p. xix).

Some of Lever's remarks, often relegated to footnotes, anticipate the influence of Marxist thinkers on critics such as Jonathan Dollimore, Graham Holderness, Francis Barker and Alan Sinfield: in particular, his reference to 'conditioning by mass media in modern states well equipped with riot police, para-military forces and a vast range of repressive techniques' (see note 6 below) recalls Louis Althusser's Ideological State Apparatuses, those organisations (such as education, law, politics and family) by which the ruling power, via consensus or by direct force (Repressive State Apparatuses such as the police), retains its control. In the extract, quotations have been checked against the versions of *The Revenger's Tragedy*, *The Duchess of Malfi* and *'Tis Pity She's a Whore* included in Colin Gibson (ed.), *Six Renaissance Tragedies* (Basingstoke, 1997), and edited accordingly. Some notes have been shortened. Ed.]

1. *The Times* (Saturday Review), 29 November 1969: 'The Czech Dream', by Irving Wardle. [Czechoslovakia was subject to a Stalinist government during the 1950s, and when in 1968 new Communist party leader Alexander Dubcek attempted to institute a programme of liberalisation – what he termed 'Socialism with a human face' – Soviet premier Leonid Brezhnev sent in 600 000 troops to restore political orthodoxy, removing Dubcek in the process. It would be twenty years before Czechoslovakia would see real political reform, with the popular uprising that swept the Communist government from office and saw Vaclav Havel (a dramatist by trade) elected President in December 1989 – Ed.]

2. For a detailed description of extravagance, waste, corruption and vice at the court of James I, see G. P. V. Akrigg, *Jacobean Pageant* (Cambridge, MA, 1962), chs XIV and XVIII.

3. Montaigne, *Essays*, trans. John Florio, III.I (Everyman edn, London and New York, 1965), vol. 3, p. 8.

4. [Presumably a swipe at E. M. W. Tillyard's *The Elizabethan World Picture* (first published in 1943), which had become a standard textbook for the study of Renaissance literature by the time Lever wrote *Tragedy of State*. Not until critical theory made inroads into university departments in the late 1970s and early 1980s would Tillyard's book

begin to lose its grip on generations of undergraduates. *The Elizabethan World Picture* is now routinely cited as an example of everything that is misguided about the 'old historicism' – Ed.]

5. William Vaughan, *The Golden Grove* (1600), ch. 3.

6. 'We must remember ... how much more serious a problem civil discord was in the Renaissance than it is now and how much more important was the myth of the God-ordered universe in keeping the state functioning. In a state with no police force and no standing army it is easy to understand why moralists never tired of repeating that the individual's passions were everyone's concern' (Franklin M. Dickey, *Not Wiseley But Too Well: Shakespeare's Love Tragedies* [Princeton, NJ, 1957], p. 96). Dickey clearly underrates the 'problem' of civil discord in our day, and overlooks the analogous conditioning by mass media in modern states well equipped with riot police, para-military forces and a vast range of repressive techniques for curbing 'the individual's passions'.

7. 'Nec species sua cuique manet, rerumque novatrix Ex aliis alias reparat natura figuras' (Ovid, *Metamorphoses*, XV, 252–3).

8. Robert Ornstein in *The Moral Vision of Jacobean Tragedy* (Madison and Milwaukee, 1962 [1965? Ed.]), p. 282, note 7, has pointed out the prevalence of the idea of natural equality. It was stated in Christian terms in Erasmus, *The Education of a Christian Prince*, and developed as a secular theory by Bodin, tracing the rise, expansion and fall of states and empires through military conquest. See *The Six Books of a Commonweal* (trans. Knolles, 1606). Alexander's account seems indebted to Bodin.

9. Geoffrey Bullough (ed.), *The Poems and Dramas of Fulke Greville* (1939), vol. II, p. 221.

10. Ibid., pp. 1–2.

11. Perhaps the most illuminating brief description of Seneca's influence is to be found in Hardin Craig's 'The Shackling of Accidents: A Study of Elizabethan Tragedy', *Philological Quarterly*, 19 (1940), 1–19, rpt. Ralph J. Kaufmann (ed.), *Elizabethan Drama: Modern Essays in Criticism* (New York, 1961), pp. 22–40.

12. Trans. Jasper Heyood, *Newton's Seneca*, Tudor Translations (1927), pp. 66–7.

13. 'In the seat of Lorenzo the Magnificent sat the petty poisoners and tyrants of Medicean degeneracy; and the Machiavelli who had died crying "Amo la patria mia piu dell' anima" became in men's memory only the devilish archetype of Iago and Barabbas [*sic*]' (F. L. Lucas, Introduction to *The Works of John Webster* [London, 1927, 1966], vol. I, p. 37).

14. 'Seneca's consolation for the blows of fate is different from that of Aeschylus. It is philosophic instead of religious. The naturalistic submission of Aeschylus is gone. Instead of a human behaviour controlled and directed within human limits and justified by veneration to the gods, Seneca introduces a stoical remedy against the badness of man's lot ... man was sure to be beaten, but Seneca proposed to build up something within the heart of man which would enable him to gain a pyrrhic victory over fate. This doctrine is inherent in the stories of Hercules and Prometheus and is closely allied with titanism' (Hardin Craig, 'The Shackling of Accidents' in Kaufmann [ed.], *Elizabethan Drama*, p. 32). Here Craig in effect bridges the disparity between Seneca's philosophic quietism and the aspirations of his tragic heroes. The responses of philosopher and man of action were alike induced by the alienating factor of tyranny, actual in the world empire of Rome conceptualised in the notions of fate and the gods.

15. Antonin Artaud, *The Theatre and Its Double*, First Manifesto; trans. M. C. Richards (New York, 1958).

2

Women's Division of Experience

ANIA LOOMBA

CREDULITY

'The greatest fault that remains in us women is that we are too credulous', wrote Jane Anger in her passionate protest against women's inferior status written in 1589.[1] The point remains central to feminism today: as Catherine Belsey asks, 'why, since all women experience the effects of patriarchal practices, are not all women feminist?'[2] The functioning of dominant ideologies hinges on their internalisation by the oppressed subject. Patriarchal discourses, which I have identified as heterogeneous, are not necessarily experienced as such by women, although they confer a dichotomy upon the latter which is not always stable; on the contrary, as we saw in the case of the Elizabethan world picture, they seek to efface contradictions and appear as 'natural' and 'obvious', as 'plain common-sense'. In the texts we have been looking at, women internalise the values conferred upon them, as did that early feminist Christine de Pisan. She was at first overwhelmed by the force of male disdain of women:

> And I finally decided that God had made a vile creature when He made woman ... a great unhappiness and sadness welled up in my heart, for I detested myself and the entire feminine sex, as though we were monstrosities in nature ... Alas, God, why did You not let me be born in the world as a man ... and in my folly I considered myself most unfortunate because God had made me inhabit a female body in this world.[3]

41

In Renaissance drama, women repeatedly express similar desires to be either men or to possess what Vittoria calls 'masculine virtue' (*The White Devil*, III.ii.135). Beatrice cannot express her solidarity with Hero, for womanhood robs her of the power to act – 'O God, that I were a man' (*Much Ado About Nothing*, IV.i.304); Isabella in *The White Devil* echoes her: 'O that I were a man, or that I had power / To execute my apprehended wishes' (II.i.242–3). Conversely, to assert this power is to deny femininity, and Cleopatra declares 'I have nothing / Of woman in me' (*Antony and Cleopatra*, V.ii.236–7). Desdemona wishes that 'heaven had made her ... a man' (*Othello*, I.iii.163); Beatrice-Joanna reiterates this, for to be a man is 'the soul of freedom' (*The Changeling*, II.ii.109). In the comedies, such wishes take physical shape as women step out of both gender-roles and costumes; Moll Cutpurse (in *The Roaring Girl*) adopts both male clothing and a single status permanently. As Belsey comments: 'predictably, these creatures who speak with voices which are not their own are unfixed, inconstant, unable to personate masculine virtue through to the end'.[4] Their very attempts to transgress their limitations rob them of a unified subjectivity and express their self-negation, so typical in the psyche of the colonised: with their female skins and male masks, they approximate the splitting of colonial subject whom Fanon describes as oscillating between black skin and white mask.

The point, however, is to assess the ideological effect of this split as represented in the drama. Recent Renaissance criticism has pointed out that while on the one hand contradictions are the very means by which power achieves its aims, on the other these also set in motion the process which undermines it.[5] Homi Bhabha has analysed the complexity of the terrain on which colonial authority and the colonised subject interact; he has suggested that the effectiveness of colonialist discourse is undermined not only by its internal fissures but by its (mis)appropriation by its native recipient.[6] In the case of patriarchal authority, an analogous process may be traced. The similarity is neither accidental nor fanciful, given the historical parallels and overlaps between patriarchal and colonial authority.

Patriarchal discourse invites women to inhabit spaces split by a series of oppositions (for example, between man and woman, goddess and whore, public and private). But as we saw earlier, such a discourse itself is heterogeneously composed, unevenly imposed and subject to conflicts with the lived reality of the oppressed subject. As in the case of the colonial subject, the divisions involve a constant shifting, a torturous but dynamic movement between two positions which it is impossible to occupy at the same time. To the extent that women have internalised patriarchal ideology, they live the divisions and contradictions imposed upon them and also the myth of their duplicity. As long as this ideology is not in crisis, the inherent opposition between women's lived experience and taught roles is kept in check. But when there is an ideological crisis, the various contradictions imposed on women serve to destabilise the supposed fixity of patriarchal notions. No longer reconciled within a fixed and static whole, these contradictions result in change, alienation, and finally resistance. What needs to be examined is whether women live the myth of duplicity exactly on the terms of the oppressors or whether it is altered, used against the intentions of the patriarchy.

It is important to remember, however, that we are speaking of female protagonists of male authors, not of living women. Neither are they psychologically 'whole' or real entities with the subjectivities we may assign to real women, nor are they even the products of a self-consciously feminist imagination. Time and again feminist critics have asked whether we are not simply investing the plays with our own concerns, expecting the male authors to rise above the limitations of their sex and time, in reading an emergent feminism in the plays. The answer will be discussed over the next two chapters.[7] As I have previously mentioned, women characters are scripted both by a male author and by men within the plays. But, as Alan Sinfield suggests, these texts repeatedly focus on issues, such as gender relations, and institutions, such as marriage, that were at a point of crisis during the early modern period. So the representation of women repeatedly produces a disruption in these scripts: 'we should observe and reflect upon the activity of scripting the plays, rather than simply helping the text into a convenient plausibility ... So Shakespearean texts need not be pinpointed as either conservative or radical; they are stories through which analysis and discussion can disclose the workings of power.[8]

To read these plays either as straightforward documents of women's liberation or elaborate patriarchal devices for containment is to erase the conflicts and complexities of the Renaissance politics, discourses on women, the position of the popular theatre and that of playwrights. Sinfield says that the scripting of women in Shakespeare suggests 'a sadly conservative body of stories', although these stories can be contested by us.[9] But we should consider *why* the drama becomes increasingly preoccupied with the disorderly woman; why woman can no longer be presented as a stable entity; and why the stories themselves become deeply contradictory and contestable. The individual author may not be 'feminist', but the ideological effects of his fragmented female protagonist are radical precisely because she is presented as a discontinuous being. If on the one hand, she is the product of a mobile and fast-changing society, on the other, she becomes the means of the interrogation in this drama of the series of boundaries induced by dominant paradigms: between male and female, private and public, emotional and political, natural and artificial, Europe and its others, which are not only interrelated but can be seen as concurrently produced and emphasised from the Renaissance onwards.

These boundaries are intensified by both patriarchal and colonial discourses at the same time as they are apparently erased, as was seen in the case of *Othello*. Institutionalised readings of Jacobean drama have legitimised such manoeuvres by emphasising either its supposed 'quest for moral order' or its spiritual chaos measured against such an order.[10] Thus, even as T. S. Eliot concedes that Middleton and Dekker's *The Roaring Girl* may be seen to illustrate 'the transition from government by landed aristocracy to government by a city aristocracy', he is anxious to add that 'as literature, as a dispassionate picture of human nature, Middleton's comedy deserves to be remembered chiefly by its real – perpetually real – and human figure of Moll the Roaring Girl'.[11] Moll is thus detached from the disturbing implications of the Jacobean controversy over female transvestism and cross-dressing; her questioning of gender boundaries is negated by invoking a timeless femininity and humanity.

Let us return to the question of internalisation and to the resultant schisms in female subjectivity. Beatrice-Joanna is taught to think of herself as both sublime and degraded. Her name indicates a dual personality: Beatrice is a Petrarchan name meaning purity and recalling Dante's chaste passion, and Joanna was apparently one of the commonest names among servant girls at the time. Her initial role is that of goddess: tragically unaware of her sexual vulnerability, arrogantly sheltering behind her spoilt and privileged upbringing that nourishes an illusion of power, and callous with all the innocence of her own distance from violence. Both naïvety and arrogance are stripped from her by De Flores' reminder that as a woman she is displaced from the privileges of her own class:

> Push! Fly not to your birth, but settle you
> In what the act has made you, y'are no more now.
> You must forget your parentage to me:
> Y'are the deed's creature; by that name
> You lose your first condition, and I challenge you,
> As peace and innocency has turn'd you out,
> And made you one with me.
> *(The Changeling*, III.iv.134–40)

Men appear to function beyond the reach of money as far as women are concerned and thus approximate Fate itself: 'Can you weep Fate from its determin'd purpose? / So soon may you weep me' (III.iv.161–2). [...]

Here I want to emphasise that these complexities are not just *reflective* of the conflicting positions women necessarily occupy in patriarchal societies, but are also experienced as painful confusions by the women themselves. Beatrice's split as a member of the 'superior' class but the 'inferior' sex is internalised and includes her various 'beliefs'. For example, her initial faith in romantic love was contrary to but coexistent with the new individualist ethic which had taught her that even love marriages are not made in heaven, but cruelly and coolly manipulated. She is not treated as goddess by any of the men – even Alsemero treats her as a potential whore whose virginity must be clinically proved. Yet till the end she cannot relate to the word 'whore', for she retains a sense of her own being as a woman who only desires a loving husband and is therefore innocent:

> What a horrid sound it hath!
> It blasts a beauty to deformity;
> Upon what face soever that breath falls,
> It strikes it ugly: oh, you have ruin'd
> What you can ne'er repair again.
> (V.iii.31–5)

As the product of patriarchal myths and the victim of their judgement she continues to reiterate her 'love' for Alsemero: 'Forget not, sir, / It for your sake was done' (V.iii.77–8). She can lie to protect the dream of domestic bliss which she knows is illusory; 'Remember

I am true unto your bed' (V.iii.82). This is not just simple duplicity or deceit, for Beatrice conceives of herself both as innocent goddess and a degraded whore: she participates in her relationship with De Flores, and is not just its victim, so she is alienated from Alsemero; at the same time she also lives by the domestic ideal and continues to be repulsed by De Flores.

This is not to suggest, of course, that Middleton has some strange intuitive understanding of female psychology. Beatrice's relationship with De Flores at one level conveys shades of *Miss Julie, Lady Chatterley's Lover, A Streetcar Named Desire* and of *The Paradine Case*. As Hitchcock remarks in relation to that film, for a male audience there is a particular thrill in seeing an immaculately dressed, upper-class woman messed up by the end of the scenario, especially by a 'manure-smelling stablehand, a man who reeked of manure',[12] a thrill deriving from a fantasy of male power. Equally for women audiences there may be a pleasure in this situation, deriving from the idea of a double transgression. Middleton and Rowley's play exploits the first, maybe the second; but by allowing the contradictions of Beatrice's position to develop, posits her as a heterogeneous, split self, not as an aberrant sinner.

WOMEN BEWARE WOMEN

The experience of dichotomous existence results also in women becoming their own enemies. This is graphically portrayed by Middleton's *Women Beware Women* but not limited to that play. Both Dusinberre and Jardine have referred to the loneliness of the female tragic hero in the texts of the period.[13] Isolation is not simply the result of their confinement in a male world but indicates also the impossibility of these split beings realising female solidarity and companionship. On the one hand the attempts at female friendship constitute 'a secret space in the midst of male society, a haven where the normal modes of subjection are cancelled and where a version of traditionally male substantiality is annexed – what we might now hope to call human intimacy'.[14] In the context of Indian culture, Sudhir Kakar has suggested that the female companionship within the extended family can serve a similar purpose; this idea also crops up in Fatima Mernissi's analysis of Muslim *zenana*, or female quarters. Certainly women's folk songs, even marriage lyrics, jeer at men's notion of their own power, and female companionship affords a perspective on their own subordination; potentially even a subversive space.[15] On the other hand, I think that both in Indian society, and in the plays, these spaces are unable to be realised as female havens because they are subject to, not only the contradictions of class and race, but also the power relations resulting from women's patriarchal positioning – they manifest women's internal schizophrenia as well. Germaine Greer's idealisation of the extended family as opposed to the nuclear one is perhaps possible from the perspective of women's isolation in the Western family; it may be seen as a well-intended response to those who argue that such families are more 'developed' than other kinds of households. However, it ignores the tortuous reality of situations where mothers and sisters in-law provide no support to the young bride or mother, and instead connive in her murder for dowry or contribute to her daily harassment. Communities of women are not inherently free of, and may reproduce patriarchal power relations. For example, Beatrice and Diaphanta may be partners in conspiracy, but the relationship is essentially exploitative. Beatrice plays the male in it, testing Diaphanta's virginity and reproducing the structures of male legality:

> She will not search me, will she,
> Like the forewoman of a female jury.
> (*The Changeling*, IV.i.97–8)

Finally Diaphanta is destroyed by Beatrice and the secret space of their fellowship is violated by the rules that govern women in patriarchal class society. That the recurrent mistress–maid friendships in Renaissance drama are acts of desperate loneliness is evident in Beatrice's rather pathetic response to De Flores' question as to how she could ever trust her maid: 'I must trust *somebody*' (V.i.15; emphasis added). They are also based on the concept of feudal loyalty, which is now exposed to the tensions of a world where all 'natural' ties including those between servants and their superiors are fast eroding.[16]

Women often operate from what may crudely be defined as male positions. [...] Whereas in Shakespearean drama female solidarity is undermined by lack of power (Beatrice cannot defend Hero as a woman, Emilia defends Desdemona but both die anyway), Middleton's female changelings cannot even establish contact with each other. Their loneliness, isolation, and fissured relationships do not emerge as warnings against their depraved natures but indicate the contradictions imposed upon them within the patriarchal and class confine. [...] Beatrice-Joanna may betray Diaphanta, but she herself is hopelessly trapped between several men. By disallowing independent female agency in conditions of their subordination, the plays refuse the possibility of idealising the oppressed subject. Read in a situation where female participation, willing and unwilling, in the oppression of other women is a painful reality, these texts foreground the fissures of the honorary male, who is nevertheless both a victim and a potential rebel.

A 'GIDDY TURNING'

The discontinuity of Jacobean heroines has long presented a critical puzzle, as Belsey indicates,[17] but it had been ingeniously reconciled to the concept of a fixed human nature; for example: 'Middleton seems to have grasped the principle ... that the more generously a nature is endowed, especially perhaps a woman's, the more bitter is its corruption, if it is thwarted or maimed in the full course of its development.'[18] Nathaniel Richards, Middleton's first critic, observed that, 'he knew the rage / Madness of women *crossed*; and for the stage / fitted their humours'.[19] Despite their underlying assumptions of a unifying concept of female nature, even traditional readings acknowledge this repeated crossing and thwarting of female desires in Renaissance drama.

One significant movement in the plays is that restriction is increasingly accompanied by a fundamental dislocation of identity. Despite their appropriation of male clothing or even roles and despite their assertion of female independence, Rosalind or Portia do not approach the dichotomy of disorderly women of later drama such as the Duchess, Beatrice-Joanna, Vittoria or Bianca. The difference may in part be attributed to genre, but even within tragedy there is such a movement: no longer is it possible to posit the unified subject of liberal-humanism as the experience of survival becomes a discontinuous one. In short, there is no pure opposition of idealised subject and oppressive structures despite the increasing violence of their contact; the violence reaches out and slashes the psyche and self-conception of the woman and no longer remains simply an act committed upon her.

It has been pointed out that the title of *The Changeling* could apply to nearly every character in the play.[20] The heroine's near schizophrenia is therefore latent in those who regard themselves as stable. Repeatedly human relationships too emerge as changeable. De Flores reminds Beatrice that she is defined not by her birth but by her actions: 'Y'are the deeds creature' (III.iv.137), something that is constantly being made. However, recognition of change is resisted by the characters: Jasperino asks Alsemero if he has changed. Alsemero replies: 'No, friend / I keep the same church, same devotion' (I.i.34–5). Shakespeare's Parolles affirms 'Simply to be the thing I am / Shall make me live' (*All's Well That Ends Well*, IV.iii.310–11). The Duchess asserts that she is the 'Duchess of Malfi still', in spite of what has been done to her (IV.ii.139). Antony repeatedly affirms his identity even as it is constantly being eroded: 'I am / Antony yet' (III.xiii.92–3).

These are desperate attempts to sustain the eroding beliefs in the 'essential' selves which are being increasingly battered. Discontinuous identity in the drama has been previously analysed.[21] I want to suggest that such an interplay of stability and change in texts that foreground disorderly women has the effect of qualifying, indeed questioning, received notions of feminine identity. The plays move towards increasing female fluidity. Desdemona may be actually divided by her various positions in relation to the status quo, but she perceives herself as a unified person when compared to Beatrice-Joanna who acknowledges the 'giddy turning' inside her (I.i.152).[...]

Alsemero and Beatrice's relationship opens in a temple with reverberations of love as mystical and everlasting. Alsemero's 'inclinations to travels' have now paused. The lovers are transformed by their love; initially this transformation is evoked in the manner typical of romantic love conventions where passion leads to a new stability of self-conception. Romeo and Juliet's new identities are as firm and unchanging as their love. But with Alsemero and Beatrice, discordant notes are struck early: there is a constant play on verbal and conceptual change and terms related to these – 'will', 'judgement', 'eyes', 'seeing'. This makes for a sense that all perception is flawed, all relationships subject to change. To Alsemero's first declarations of love, Beatrice replies:

> Be better advis'd, sir.
> Our eyes are sentinels unto our judgements,
> And should give certain judgement what they see;
> But they are rash sometimes, and tell us wonders

Of common things, which when our judgements find,
They can then check our eyes, and call them blind.
(I.i.68–73)

[...] In patriarchal thought, the slide of woman from goddess to whore is premised simultaneously upon her potential for sexual activity, and upon her passivity as a receptacle for sin. Even when passive, the woman is irrevocably polluted by illegitimate sexual contact; therefore sin can be regarded as both outside of the female self and at the same time its most definitive constituent. In Renaissance tragedy, however, female propensity for sin is restructured: firstly, as socially induced rather than a moral attribute and secondly, as no longer static, but constituting a dynamic interaction between women's subjectivity and the social conditions of their existence. Therefore, in plays such as *The Changeling*, or *Women Beware Women*, female immorality is imposed upon the subject, but also *incorporated* into the individual's self-perception. It is no longer either alien or intrinsic to women, therefore it is no longer able unambiguously to carry the connotations of its patriarchal usage. The contradictions imposed upon women are internalised, but then they catalyse an alienation which radically disrupts all notions of social or psychic stability: the 'giddy turning' experienced by 'This changeable stuff' (*The Changeling*, IV.ii.46) is not containable within the dominantly defined notion of female dichotomy. [...]

Patriarchy and class power constitute the warp and the weft of violence against women in these plays. Middleton focuses on the grey area between seduction and rape; [...] Like Bianca in *Women Beware Women*, Beatrice-Joanna is 'forced' into submission. And like Bianca, the process of coercion is never outside her. If Bianca's seduction depends on an awareness of what is denied her in terms of wealth, glamour and freedom, Beatrice's transgression depends on an illusory perception of what is possible, by the combination of arrogance and naïvety that her class position confers on her. The effect of events upon character is reiterated. Beatrice changes twice – first she begins to love Alsemero, then De Flores. She had declared both undying love for Alsemero and her eternal hatred of De Flores; but then,

I'm forc'd to love thee now,
'Cause thou provid'st so carefully for my honour.
(V.i.47–8)

Each change does not simply negate the previous state of being; Alsemero notes that 'there's scarce a thing but is both lov'd and loath'd' (I.i.122). Beatrice is simultaneously attracted and repelled by De Flores, and both alienated from and attached to Alsemero. However, at no point does she stand neatly outside patriarchal ideology; she needs and exploits Diaphanta, she desperately lies to Alsemero, she is truly wretched at being called whore. Sigrid Weigel, in an interesting essay called 'Double focus', has argued that the latent schizophrenia of woman consists in the fact that those elements of the model of femininity which earn her *moral* respect (for example motherliness, understanding, sociability) are also the basis for her social subordination.[22] This is certainly true of women in the plays who necessarily experience themselves through male eyes, but even so their 'giddy turning' puzzles the men in the play for they are no longer the stable female subjects desired by dominant thought.

THE UNSTABLE DIVIDE

In Jacobean drama female transgression is no longer simply a spectre conjured up by the male imagination. Lisa Jardine is correct in protesting against the attempt of critics to exonerate the female heroes of these plays from the 'sexual slur'. The progression towards a dichotomous identity accompanies women's active sexuality which is no longer able to be expressed within patriarchal norms. Rosalind (*As You Like It*) or Portia (*The Merchant of Venice*) or Beatrice (*Much Ado About Nothing*) can step out of female clothing or roles, but their desires are reconciliable to the masculine will:

> Women are released from their usual habits, and the sexes from usual relations, in order to ... justify these customs ... Shakespeare's magnificient comic heroines thrive in facilitating marriages ... ones that restore the 'natural' sex roles. Shakespeare's women are at their best, then ... when they function to believe in or to deliver men from their own best selves or to die in trying.[23]

Finally the women choose perfectly acceptable lovers; in fact their selection often coincides with the will of the patriarch, as in *The Merchant of Venice*, although the process confers an illusion of free choice. They remain chaste until the marriage rites are formalised, and their defiance does not challenge the boundaries of either race or class. Even so, it is possible that the play on gender identity opens up the issue of women in a new way; on the whole, however, these are the texts (rather than *The Duchess* as Belsey suggests) where the liberal notion of marriage is glowingly evoked. In the case of Desdemona there is a radical conflict between her own perception of love, which is well within the limits of chastity and patriarchal transfer of woman from father to husband, and its political connotations, which clothe it with the implications of sexual impurity. In *The Duchess of Malfi* female sexuality hovers on the borders of acceptable limits: widow remarriage is licentious but technically permissible.[24] In *The White Devil*, Vittoria's desire is clearly unchaste, but she is faithful to her lover, as is Cleopatra; in Middleton's plays female sexuality makes a final break from the confines of romanticism as Bianca and Beatrice-Joanna oscillate between different men. In Ford, sexual transgression can only be expressed by incest, which is already evident in *Women Beware Women*. Therefore, the general distinction between Elizabethan and Jacobean drama is that in the latter the assertive woman does sexually transgress and is not only imagined to do so.

The shift is significant. As Woodbridge comments in relation to *The Duchess of Malfi*: 'Any defender of women could show a widow remaining chaste. But to turn a widow who does not remain chaste into a tragic hero was revolutionary.'[25] But precisely because of this, the ideological implications of female disobedience in the drama are still under debate, as the criticism of *The Duchess of Malfi* reveals. Lisa Jardine argues that in Webster's play male assessment of the Duchess is fraught with explicitly sexual innuendoes; that this controls the audience's judgement of her; that the Duchess's secret marriage would be regarded by them much as it is by her brothers – as a typically female act of cunning, duplicity and sexual waywardness, and that her punishment serves to exorcise the spectre of female rebellion.[26] Such a reading telescopes the ideological effect of the play into the attitudes of the male adversaries of the Duchess. There is an obvious emotional weightage accorded to the Duchess, but this only compounds the problems in assessing her, which Shepherd effectively sums up: 'If we indict her lechery we side with the vicious brothers; if we want a chaste heroine we share the credulous ignorance of Antonio.'[27]

Catherine Belsey avoids a simple equation of male positions within the play with the ideology of the text.[28] She points to the positive portrayal of the Duchess's relationship with Antonio and its deliberate contrast to the horrors of the brothers' wrath. This difference warns us that the sexual slur which the brothers confer upon the Duchess cannot be taken as the moral tone of the play itself, as Jardine seems to do. But precisely such a contrast between the Duchess and her brothers is located by Belsey in liberal-humanist oppositions between public and private, political and domestic. By marking the woman's place within the latter, 'the affective ideal which is so glowingly defined in *The Duchess of Malfi* collapses into the sad history of collaboration between liberalism and sexism which defines the western family from the seventeenth century to the present'. The play, concludes Belsey, 'is a perfect fable of emergent liberalism'.[29]

I would like to suggest firstly, that the Duchess's duplicity is handled very differently than in a medieval sterotype of female hypocrisy; and secondly, that the play does not subscribe to but questions the division between private and public – it exposes the ideological and political thrust of such a division. Whereas other defences of the period such as Anger's pamphlet or Middleton's *More Dissemblers Besides Women* argue that men, not women, are duplicitous, *The Duchess* – and *The White Devil, The Changeling, Women Beware Women,* and *Antony and Cleopatra* – offer an alternative examination of female duplicity which begins by *acknowledging* instead of denying it. In Painter's *Palace of Pleasure* (1567) which contained a translation from Matteo Bandello's original story of the Duchess, she is a 'fine and subtile dame', who lusts for Antonio in order to 'make hir way to pleasure, which she lusted more than marriage', and her marriage itself is a 'Maske and coverture to hide her follies and shameless lusts'.[30] Webster does not deny either the Duchess' duplicity or her active sexuality, but female pleasure is no longer a dirty word in the new text.

Its liberal connotations are questionable on the very grounds that Belsey uses to point to them. It is true that the Duchess remains firmly within the domestic arena. So do Vittoria, Bianca, Beatrice-Joanna, Desdemona, Annabella and Isabella; none of them overtly seeks to usurp male authority, they remain within the spaces that have been patriarchally defined as personal and assigned to women. I have already indicated the massive effort in early modern society to confine women, ideologically and physically, into domestic areas; we also have seen that it is not coincidental that the issue of absolutism arose at the same time as increased restrictions on women.[31]

The Duchess is literally enclosed in the male-dominated castle. Denied individual identity and even a name, she is merely 'the Duchess'. Not only are most Jacobean heroines banished to the domestic sphere (Cleopatra is an exception), but they often aim only for concessions patriarchally granted to them:

> Why might I not marry?
> I have not gone about, in this, to create
> Any new world or custom.
> (III.ii.110–12)

Despite their pitifully domestic urges, these women are thwarted, not merely within the family, but as in *The Duchess of Malfi* or *The White Devil*, by public authority, by all the institutions of feudal and mercantile patriarchy; their transgression evokes a political disarray, even a chaos of cosmic proportions. Instead of demarcating the private world from the public, the impossibility of the first isolating itself is underlined. Feminists have not invented the connection between the personal and the political; patriarchal thought recognises it and attempts to disguise it. Thus a dowry murder in India is officially referred to as a 'dowry death', which lifts it from the category of an ordinary murder and seeks implicitly to exclude it from the realm of common criminality and justice. It becomes a 'family problem', but of course the effort to hush it up is not merely familial, but requires the complicity of police, public opinion and legal structures. The most passive and confined of female lives works as a crucial link in the political and public hierarchies. Although the Duchess is a good wife and mother she violates some of the notions of ideal femininity, as indeed she must, for such notions are total only within a stereotype. Precisely because she is so compliant, she cannot be demonised as a totally deviant woman. Yet she is destroyed even as a witch would be. It is this combination of the normal and the radical, the domestic and the political, that makes the implications of the story so deeply disturbing, particularly in a situation where the most everyday normal woman is subject to the most violent fate.

The effect of a play like *The Duchess* is to highlight the violent underpinnings of the domestic. Active female sexuality is not merely a breach of decorum but also a flagrant breach of the public and political order, as feminists know and seek to reveal, and as patriarchy knows and seeks to hide. Precisely because most of these women do not conceive of or articulate their demands as political, the violent and public reaction to their aspirations serves, not to subscribe to, but to lay bare the division between domestic and political, personal and public, emotional and rational.

Again, in the 'sister-tragedy' of *The White Devil*,[32] Vittoria publicly confronts the judiciary as well as the Church, but only because her adultery, like the Duchess's remarriage, is not treated as a private issue. Vittoria recognises and exposes the attempt to divide the personal and the public by calling her trial a 'rape'; by claiming that the State and Church have 'ravish'd justice' (III.ii.271,273). Patriarchal legality conceives of female sexuality as criminal, so she seizes on its own analogy and inverts it by employing the language of sexuality to describe a legal procedure; thus she is the first to employ the connection between sexuality and power in favour of the woman. In a society where the nuclear family and its ideals are still evolving, as in India, the effect of Jacobean tragedy can be read as interrogation instead of closure. At the same time, such a reading is, I believe, not contrary to the sexual politics of the Renaissance, where the language of patriarchy is also the vocabulary of political control.

Vittoria *articulates* the connections between private and public; the Duchess does not. But the politics of these texts cannot be collapsed into the consciousness of the individual heroine: to search for a consciously political protagonist to carry the burden of an anti-patriarchal text would be to replicate the terms of idealist criticism. In searching for the perfect and unified female revolutionary, feminists may themselves be guilty of underlining the terms of heroic or liberal drama, which are denied by Jacobean tragedy. *The Duchess of Malfi* is not an elaborate patriarchal device to contain female rebellion; on the contrary, it takes a woman who is a misogynist's delight – duplicitous, sexually active, defiant – and then proceeds, not by defending her along the lines that misogynists are familiar with and know how to counter, but by asking questions which are hard to answer in the language of patriarchy. The fissures of the female changeling are patriarchally imposed upon her and yet serve to expose the politics of her subordination. It can be suggested that by rupturing the linkage of heroism and morality, these plays achieve for female identity what *Dr Faustus* or *Macbeth* had for the notion of man. But such a rupture becomes harder to acknowledge in the case of a woman, hence the dominant critical silence about its implications in these plays.

RESTRICTION AND RESISTANCE

[Earlier] I discussed the slide of meaning from physical and spatial to sexual and ideological mobility in Renaissance texts.[33] But the correspondence between them is not necessarily straightforward: for example, the most physically mobile female roles are those of Rosalind, Viola or Portia but here the mobility is dependent upon disguise and, I have shown, involves an ideological fixity of female behaviour. Moll Cutpurse is more mobile, more obviously defiant than the physically enclosed Duchess, or Beatrice-Joanna who is finally locked in a cupboard, or Vittoria who is confined to a reformatory; but she is not necessarily more resistant to patriarchy. Moll roams the city, resists the confine of marriage, but is also keeper of the law and, above all, doesn't raise the problem of uncontrollable female sexuality because she remains chaste. Partly, these differences can be related to those of the genre: generally speaking comedy foregrounds physical movement, while Renaissance tragedy increasingly concerns itself with its conceptual implications, resulting in duplicity and schizophrenia of the women. The tragic heroine is located within the estate, or castle, or home (Juliet cannot even consider running away with Romeo to Mantua, but must await him in the tomb of her forefathers) and her attempts at external or internal movement result in her violent end; her comic counterpart travels around, either into fictitious worlds like Arden or actual spaces of streets and shops of London, but is finally reinstated within the social order.

If Moll questions the spaces allotted to women by straying out of them physically, appropriating masculine dress that allows for more spatial freedom and refusing the confine of home and marriage, the Duchess interrogates social and sexual boundaries from within traditionally allotted female spaces and thus threatens their very separation from the masculine, the public, and the political arenas. Women's speech spans both physical and conceptual movement, but not all speech is disruptive – for example, *The Taming of the Shrew* involves not Kate's silencing but her schooling, so that her longest speech is a tribute to her husband; as a shrew she actually spoke less, but disobedience conferred the illusion of excess upon her words. But at other times, female speech epitomises rebellion (Cleopatra is the most verbose of Shakespeare's women), hence the injunction to women to obey *in silence*.[34]

In a society where stability was invoked to maintain monarchism and its attendant hierarchies, the interrogation of both physical and ideological boundaries is subversive. In the seventeenth century both sorts of movement threatened a status quo which had to accommodate the potential for literal movement in urban culture; so the ideology of privacy had to accomplish what the castle wall had hitherto done. Since the texts we have been looking at posit the division between private and public, inner and outer, emotional and political as constructed and unstable, such a divide is unable to serve its ideological function of keeping women 'in their place', and instead catalyses their movement away from their usual sphere. It becomes evident that on the one hand there is evidence of female resistance, and on the other, the slightest female movement is magnified by its political repercussions.

We are now in a position to consider the correlation between physical and conceptual mobility and coercion more fully, in order to approach further aspects of recurrent female duplicity in the texts. Men have a private as well as public existence, whereas women are taught to function within men's private lives only.[35] They lack a public life of their own – they are denied participation as producers and controllers of wealth or authority. But, correspondingly, they are denied a dimension comparable to men's private lives, since all aspects of their lives are controlled and in that sense public. It is significant that although 'private' dominantly refers to the sexual, woman's sexuality is publicly structured. Therefore, lacking both public and private space, physically as well as ideologically, woman has had to retreat further into her 'inner' being in order to find spaces that are not publicly controlled. We may identify the act of writing by women as an attempt to replace privacy with literary space. Such attempts may exist alongside the effort to find actual spaces, but are prioritised precisely when the former are not available. As such they are contradictory enterprises, doomed to failure because there are no free inner spaces in the absence of outer ones; creative writing is possible only when some realms of privacy are physically granted to upper-class women.[36] At the same time, secrecy and withdrawal can be seen as strategies to protect an inner life. It is in this context that the dissembling and duplicity of the Duchess and her sisters should be placed.

Let us return briefly to the example of Elizabeth I, who repeatedly attempted to appropriate a masculine identity in order to consolidate authority. In this she was not unique: for a latter-day female authority like Indira Gandhi also felt compelled to claim that she had been brought up as a boy and felt no different from a man: she thought it a compliment when referred to as 'the only man in the cabinet' and said that 'certain qualities are associated with men, such as decision making'.[37] No doubt the comparison can be extended to include other women, such as Margaret Thatcher, who rule as what Heisch has called honorary men and extend patriarchal rather than female power. Of course such assertions are strategic, but it is significant that Elizabeth simultaneously evoked her femininity, sheltering behind it to procrastinate on marriage, which her Parliament was pressuring her towards: 'The weight and greatness of this matter might cawse in me being a woman wantinge both witt and memory some feare to speake, and bashfulness besides, a thing appropriat to my sex ...'[38] Therefore she oscillated between her status as honorary male and weak female; while this may indicate at one level the internalisation of female inferiority, at another it was a brilliant strategy both to appropriate the public spaces denied to women and repudiate the 'private' realm allocated to them. Similar strategic employment of both masculine virtue and femininity will be noted in the case of Cleopatra's oscillation between 'president of my kingdom' (III.vii.17) and 'no more but e'en a woman' (IV.xiv.73).

These 'movements' allow us to consider the subversive aspects of female 'hypocrisy'. [...] For the men in *The Duchess of Malfi*, the Duchess is typed as duplicitous even before they know of her marriage. In the very first scene she is told that her 'darkest actions will come to light'; the Cardinal's fears anticipate, and perhaps contribute to the formulation of, her plans:

> You may flatter yourself
> And take your own choice: privately be married
> Under the eaves of the night.
>
> (I.i.316–18)

Beatrice-Joanna is assumed to be duplicitous by Alsemero even as he thinks of her as his goddess and the goal of his existence. By appropriating his virginity test, substituting Diaphanta for herself, Beatrice is attempting to protect herself but is also exposing the premises on which any marriage would be founded. The Duchess, Vittoria, Beatrice-Joanna merely adopt the dichotomy that patriarchal thought has conferred upon them anyway. The difference is that whereas women's anticipated duplicity or sexual activity is a patriarchal attempt to demonise and exorcise them, actual transgression is subversive of this control.

The increasing secrecy of rebellion also indicates the extent to which women are divided subjects whose public and private lives are forced apart and who are under male, public gaze. The fact that they are forced to experience themselves only in relation to men works like a knife, so that they can never be unified subjects in any sense, and experience the dichotomies of virgin / whore, intellect / body, reproductive vessel / decorative object. Male objectification is not only a placement of women in relation to men, but a specific female experience:

> To be born a woman has been to be born within an allotted and confined space, into the keeping of men. The social presence of women has developed as a result of their ingenuity in living under a such tutelage within such a limited space. But this has been at the cost of a woman's self being split in two·... her own sense of being appreciated as herself by another ... *Men act and women appear.* Men look at women. Women watch themselves being looked at. This determines not only the relations between men and women but also the relation of women to themselves. The surveyor of women in herself is male: the surveyed female. Thus she turns herself into an object.[39]

Women's criteria for self appraisal are male. Beatrice-Joanna thus experiences herself precisely as the combination of goddess and whore that she had been told all women are; she is at once the all powerful goddess whom all men desire and whose will is law, and the whore whom all men hate and who begs father and husband not to come near her for fear she will taint them.

Secondly, if 'male and female differences are seen as the product of symbolic structures encoded in the language of the pre-existing culture into which one is born, it can be argued that all women have suffered some degree of speech impediment in trying to communicate female experience with a phallocentric tongue.'[40] What Kristeva calls the 'hysteric's voice' is, according to Juliet Mitchell, 'women's masculine language talking of feminine experience'. Thus concludes Ecker, who quotes the others, 'Women are seen to speak from within the patriarchal discourse rather than from a source exterior to phallocentric symbolic forms.'[41]

Duplicity as a strategy is both born of and flawed by the dichotomies of women's own experience. It raises the question of false consciousness, which has also been asked in connection with women's crossdressing. Here it has been argued that women dressing as men only confirm male-imposed criteria of freedom, and that their rebellion is therefore not 'the real thing'.[42] The question takes us right back into the debates around ideology: Lenin, who needed to theorise the basis for the growing revolutionary consciousness in Russia, needed to go beyond Marx's definition of ideology as just 'false consciousness'. If ideology is necessarily rooted in material reality, and this reality is oppressive, then where are the sources of a revolutionary consciousness? Lenin extended the concept of ideology to a consciousness which is various, and includes different oppositional versions, such as the bourgeois or the socialist (*What is to be Done*). Althusser's further distinction between a general ideology (whose function is to ensure social cohesion) and specific ideologies (deriving from various class positions) is extremely useful here, for it allows us to see that cross-dressing, or women's dichotomies in the drama, are neither pure revolutionary consciousness nor merely false, but rather are representative of the powerful clash of ideas played out on the arena of subjectivity. In her notes on feminist theory, Joan Kelly concluded that an oppositional consciousness arises out of 'the discrepancy between the real and the ideal' experienced by those who stand on the boundary of the dominant culture: 'like Hegel's slave, woman experiences an "unhappy consciousness", a form of alienation that makes her at once a participant in the culture that oppresses her and a stranger to it':[43] such an unhappiness informs the duplicitous changeling of the drama.

RECEIVING THE DISORDERLY WOMAN

Dominant readings of Renaissance tragedy have moved towards a closure, a sealing off of its disturbances to authority and hence of its radical potential.[44] In the colonial context this has implied an effacing of the various contradictions experienced by the readers, both in relation to their own culture and to the colonial text. The binary oppositions imposed on women are analogous to and reinforce those of colonial discourse; thus in the case of Indian women the erasure extends to both powerfully interlinking sets of contradictions, each of which may otherwise serve as a vantage point for grasping the interrogation of various boundaries that I have traced in the texts, and vice versa.

It has been suggested that Indian women experience social space along the binary oppositions imposed by patriarchal thought – private / public, danger / safety, pure / polluted.[45] Instead of a static dichotomy, however, I suggest that the experience of Indian women is far more volatile. To begin with, Indian religions and culture contain powerful matriarchal myths, or myths of female power. Such myths, as we are repeatedly warned, may only confirm male superiority by either demonising female strength, or working as a safety-valve to let out anti-patriarchal steam. However, as Natalie Davis suggests, the image of the disorderly woman, *even when contained and demonised*, 'opens out behavioural options for women'.[46] Female strength and female disorder are not interchangeable; the images sometimes cited to glorify Indian traditions as proto-feminist in fact function to underline a male conception of female energy: 'The feminist movement has no relevance in India, none at all, because our whole background is different ... Take for instance Savitri – she is typically in the line of strong women. She challenged even death and persevered in doing so because she was exercising her natural feminine quality.'[47]

Savitri's power is derived from and is in the service of her husband. She had married Satyavan despite the knowledge that he was fated to die within one year. When the god of death Yama came to claim him, Savitri insisted on accompanying her husband since his wife's place was always with him. She refused to accept Yama's assurances that with her husband's death all her wifely obligations had expired. Finally Satyavan was returned to Savitri in acknowledgement of her devotion so that the two of them could beget 'a century of sons possessed of strength and prowess and capable of perpetuating our race'.[48] Here we have a powerful legitimisation of the ideologies that inform sati; and a woman's strength is as a wife and as a reproducer of the patriarchal family. Even in the evocation of the story to assert an indigenous tradition of female power (cited above), there is not only a rejection of feminism but, via the affirmation of wifely power as a 'natural' attribute of women, an implicit negation of a whole counter-tradition of powerful and disturbing femininity, subversive of precisely those norms upheld by Savitri.

This tradition has slowly begun to be uncovered, although large areas of it can be seen as assimilated into, demonised by, or clouded over by dominant histories, myths and cultures.[49] Liddle and Joshi suggest that this tradition, including worship of the mother goddess, constitutes 'a matriarchal *culture*, in the sense that it preserves the value of women as lifegivers and sources of activating energy, and it represents the acknowledgement of women's power by women and men in the culture'.[50] Although this concept is somewhat vague, and it is doubtful whether Indian culture today can be called matriarchal in any sense of the term, the presence of this counter-tradition makes available a powerful and potentially radical *ambivalence* and dichotomy, which is not so easily contained as dominant culture may suggest. In popular culture, the early figure of the powerful, malevolent, unmarried goddess is woven into images of everyday life female disobedience and vice versa; both are sought to be ritually exorcised but survive as powerful behavioural options. These may be bolstered by a wide array of contemporary images – for example, those provided by the growing women's movement; conversely, feminist movements or education may strategically seize upon the latent dichotomy of popular culture.

In the folk festival of 'Bandamma Panduga' in Andhra, for example, one may find a disturbance, an interrogation of desired female behaviour, through theatrical representation. The festival is designed to propitiate the goddess Bandamma, who is single, powerful and therefore evil. Her active sexuality is linked to fears of female authority in general and to widows, disobedient wives and promiscous women in particular. During the first four days of the festival, she is worshipped in her powerful and malignant aspect, and on the final day is represented as propitiated, tamed and domesticated. Two different kinds of theatrical performances are therefore held: the first are skits, which revolve around the theme of the world turned upside down and reversals of social, particularly sexual, hierarchy; the second is formal drama emphasising female loyalty, male protectiveness and social stability. As Tapper notes, the reversals in the skits are closely linked to actual fears of disorderly women:

> These skits are also interesting guides to the suspicions about female character which are a part of the ideological rationale for male dominance. Among the issues raised in them are the problem of the lack of male heirs, the role of female economic activity, the need for wives to respect their husbands, adultery and other aspects of marital breakdown.[51]

I will quote briefly from one such skit:

> **Wife** (brags, gossiping with another woman) Do you have a husband who is equal to mine? (Long pause) Well, perhaps our husbands are similar after all ... Your husband has a crooked mouth and mine has a crooked arse. (Enters the house and begins ordering her husband to help her take a heavy basket off her head.) Come on, help me take this basket off my head. Do it slowly, be careful. (As he helps her she uses the opportunity of his bending over to step on his head.) Due to my devotion to you as a loyal wife, if I put my foot on your head, I will go straight to heaven.
> **Husband** Hey! Are you putting your foot on my head?
> **Wife** Yes, doesn't every wife? Hold on, I'll take my leg down (said as she steps on him even more emphatically). Ah, I am so loyal to you. From the day I was born I never desired any other man. (Aside) Except Penta Rao![52]

The audience laughs at the reversals and these are finally 'righted' by the drama.

But as with the instances of disorder analysed by Davis, their containment is not complete; both the daily experience of oppression of women and the linkage with the power of the single goddess makes such images desired rather than totally negative. If Indira Gandhi encouraged representations of herself as Kali, the goddess of destruction, she was playing upon the ambivalence allowed by such an image. During the independence struggle, women's resistance was glorified and channelled into patriarchally accepted images of active women. For example, the legendary Rani of Jhansi, celebrated for her resistance to the British Raj during the 1857 uprising, is popularly represented as *mardani* or mannish; at the other end of the spectrum the Gandhian movement enlisted mass female participation, but on the premise that woman is 'a giver whose giving extends beyond the family but does not exclude it; a mother and sister not to a few individuals but to the country and to the world'.[53]

My point simply is firstly, that the ambivalence of such histories must be amplified. We must deny the supposed homogeneity of culture and position the Indian female readers as occupying diverse and contradictory heritages. Secondly, of course, the radical potential of such heterogeneity is not inherent but is catalysed in conjunction with subsequent developments – for example, growing articulation of female discontent and the women's movement. So one may suggest that the images of female disorder in Renaissance drama and in, say, Indian culture and contemporary reality, can be made to become mutually illuminating, can be made to interact in specific classroom situations.

We have spoken of the various contradictions which operate in the case of the Jacobean heroine. The final one is of course between the male author and the female creation. Whose voice do we hear? The woman protagonist or the male author? Do the heroines experience greater interiorisation of male behaviour than is usual because they are the products of the masculine pen? Or are they able to resist male domination more than real life women precisely because they do not suffer all the handicaps of the latter? Catherine Belsey's argument is that male actors playing women disguised as men produced a subject that is able to resist / transcend usual gender divisions.[54] Can we extend this, to suggest that because male writers speak as women who are trying to appropriate male prerogatives, there is even a greater disruption of the purely uni-gendered standpoint – such that the female subject is able to occupy the area between the real life woman and the conventional heroine, between the stereotypical woman and the monstrous one?

The question still remains as to why male writers should foreground the issue of female transgression. I have suggested that the idea of a patriarchal conspiracy reduces the complexities of the ideologies that inform the plays and and also ignores their political thrust. An author's attitude to gender relations is to be seen as part of his / her other politics, not simply coexisting with them; to use the sex of the author uncritically as an indicator of his / her feminism or patriarchalism would be as great a mistake as to accept the class background of an individual as sufficient for determining their politics – although we may grant that a feminist perspective is in principle far more readily available to women. On the other hand, the plays are far more contradictory and complicated than just simple defences of women.

Instead gender becomes also the metaphor (though not merely in a crudely representative sense) for a series of relationships between authority and its 'others'. Such metaphors are not limited for the use of those in power and it can be suggested that they are crucial for a drama which has increasingly been seen to focus on the complexity of power relations. As I shall suggest in the next chapter, women also become a vehicle for the theatre's exploration of its own complicated relationship to the status quo.

Finally, a constant harking back to the question of authorial intention may serve only to insist on a single and stable meaning; on the contrary to explore the different effects of the play is not only to uncover its meanings within specific situations, but also to amplify aspects of its inception which have been historically clouded by its dominant deployment. The radical interrogation possible via the duplicitous woman, then, may only be one meaning which attaches to Renaissance drama from the perspective of the situation obtaining in contemporary English studies in India; nevertheless it serves to focus both on Renaissance sexual politics and some of the subsequent histories of these texts.

From Ania Loomba, *Gender, Race, Renaissance Drama* (Manchester, 1989), pp. 93–117.

NOTES

[Ania Loomba's *Gender, Race, Renaissance Drama* is a groundbreaking study that seeks to bring together the discoveries of feminist critical theory and postcolonial theory. Loomba finds an affinity between the female skin / male mask predicament of the transgressive woman and the black skin / white mask oscillation identified by Fanon as defining the psyche of the colonised. The 'division of experience' Loomba refers to is a series of fissures between male and female, public and private, goddess and whore. In the course of the extracted chapter, she refers to the work of Alan Sinfield, Catherine Belsey and Jonathan Dollimore, all of whom have interrogated the nature of dramatic 'character', and emphasised the ways in which the discontinuities and inconsistencies of the subjectivities of individual *dramatis personae* reveal what Sinfield would identify as ideological 'faultlines'. Loomba also reflects on the significance of Elizabeth I in debates about female authority and subjugation, and concludes with a reflection on their relevance to an understanding of the experience of Indian women in the patriarchal social structures in which they find themselves. What Loomba is uncovering here is not the traditional liberal humanist notion of the universality of great literature; rather, she draws provocative parallels between certain features of the social and ideological landscapes of two very different historical and cultural contexts. In this way, the texts can be made to open up new perspectives on both those contexts.

This long and important chapter has, unfortunately, had to be cut, omitting, in particular, a number of passages discussing Middleton's *Women Beware Women*, which is not one of the plays covered by this volume. The extract covers a range of texts, including *The Changeling* and *The Duchess of Malfi*, but it is placed near the beginning of the collection because the issues it raises are fundamental to many of the essays that follow, to which it serves as an important introduction, given its radical perspective. Ed.]

1. Jane Anger, *Jane Anger her Protection for Women* (1589), in *The Women's Sharp Revenge: Five Pamphlets from the Renaissance*, ed. Simon Shepherd (London, 1985), p. 35.

2. Catherine Belsey, 'Constructing the subject: deconstructing the text', in Judith Newton and Debroah Rosenfelt (eds), *Feminist Criticism and Social Change: Sex, Class and Race in Literature and Culture* (New York and London, 1985), p. 45.

3. Christine de Pisan, *The Book of the City of Ladies*, trans. Earl Jeffrey Richards (London, 1983), p. 5.

4. Catherine Belsey, *The Subject of Tragedy* (London and New York, 1985), p. 183.

5. See, for example, Jonathan Goldberg, *James I and the Politics of Literature: Jonson, Shakespeare, Donne and their Contemporaries* (Baltimore and London, 1983) and Paul Brown, ' "This thing of darkness I acknowledge mine": *The Tempest* and the discourse of colonialism', in Jonathan Dollimore and Alan Sinfield (eds), *Political Shakespeare: New Essays in Cultural Materialism* (Manchester, 1985), pp. 48–71.

6. See Homi K. Bhabha, 'Signs taken for wonders: questions of ambivalence and authority under a tree outside Delhi, May 1917', *Critical Inquiry*, 12 (Autumn 1985).

7. [The chapter that follows this extract, ' "Travelling thoughts": theatre and the space of the other', challenges the hegemony of linear and teleological structures in the interpretation of early modern drama. It considers the usefulness of a Brechtian approach (drawing on the technique of montage in particular) in subverting the dominant Western aesthetics of catharsis and moral order – Ed.]

8. Alan Sinfield, '*Othello* and the politics of character' (paper given at the University of Santiago de Compostella, Nov. 1987), pp. 14–26. [See also two chapters in particular in Alan Sinfield, *Faultlines: Cultural Materialism and the Politics of Dissident Reading* (Oxford, 1992): 'Cultural Materialism, *Othello*, and the Politics of Plausibility' (pp. 29–51) and 'When is a Character Not a Character? Desdemona, Olivia, Lady Macbeth and Subjectivity' (pp. 52–79) – Ed.]

9. Sinfield, ibid., p. 24.

10. See Irving Ribner, *Jacobean Tragedy: The Quest for Moral Order* (London, 1962) and Robert Ornstein, *The Moral Vision of Jacobean Tragedy* (Madison and Milwaukee, 1965).

11. T. S. Eliot, 'Thomas Middleton', in *Selected Essays* (London, 1932), p. 169.

12. François Truffaut, *Hitchcock* (London, 1978), p. 210.

13. See Juliet Dusinberre, *Shakespeare and the Nature of Women* (London, 1975), p. 92; Lisa Jardine, *Still Harping on Daughters: Women in Seventeenth Century Drama* (Brighton, 1983), p. 69.

14. Frank Whigham, 'Sexual and Social Mobility in *The Duchess of Malfi*', PMLA, 100 (March 1985), 172.

15. See Sudhir Kakar, *The Inner World: a Psychoanalytic Study of Childhood and Society in India* (New Delhi, 1978) and Fatima Mernissi, *Beyond the Veil: Male–Female Dynamics in Muslim Society* (London, 1985, revd edn).

16. See Whigham, 'Sexual and Social Mobility', for the Duchess's relation to Cariola.

17. Belsey, *The Subject of Tragedy*, p. 160.

18. Una Ellis-Fermor, *The Jacobean Drama: An Interpretation* (1936), p. 142.

19. See Thomas Middleton, *Women Beware Women*, in Roma Gill (ed.), *Elizabethan and Jacobean Tragedies* (Kent, 1984), p. 379; emphasis added.

20. Dale B. J. Randall, 'Some observations on the theme of chastity in *The Changeling*', *English Literary Renaissance*, 14:3 (Autumn 1984), 348–9.

21. See Jonathan Dollimore, *Radical Tragedy: Religion, Ideology and Power in the Drama of Shakespeare and his Contemporaries* (Brighton, 1984) and Belsey, *The Subject of Tragedy*.

22. Sigrid Weigel, 'Double focus: on the history of women's writing', in Gisela Ecker (ed.), *Feminist Aesthetics* (London, 1985), p. 80.

23. Martha Andreson-Thom, 'Thinking about Women and their prosperous art: a reply to Juliet Dusinberre's *Shakespeare and the Nature of Women*', in *Shakespeare Studies*, 11 (Columbia, 1978), p. 276.

24. Citing the pronouncements of Vives, Cornelius Agrippa, Stephen Guazzo and William Heale in favour of remarriage, Frank Wadsworth argues that 'the evidence suggests that when Webster decided to dramatise the story of the Duchess of Malfi, he would not have had to assume that his audience would immediately and automatically condemn the Duchess for remarrying' ('Webster's *Duchess of Malfi* in the light of some contemporary ideas on marriage', *Philological Quarterly*, 35 [1956], 398). While there is evidence to suggest that widow remarriage is technically permissible in the eyes of religion and law, I think Wadsworth is wrong to assume that remarriage was tolerated because the widow of substance was a desirable economic proposition. In fact he himself notes that the King's widows (i.e. those women who inherited property held by him) were allowed to remarry

as long as they did not claim this property or paid the necessary fee for it. Wadsworth concludes that the attitude towards widow remarriage was economic instead of moral. However a crude separation of the two is not possible: hence while it may be suggested that the richer the widow the more the disapproval, it is also true that the disapproval would bolster itself by the moral tones of religion and misogynist prejudice and filter downwards to all widows. On the other hand this suggests a debate over the question of remarriage, a tension rather than a confirmed and unequivocal indictment from all sections of society.

25. Linda Woodbridge, *Women and the English Renaissance: Literature and the Nature of Womankind 1540–1620* (Brighton, 1984), p. 260.

26. Lisa Jardine, 'The Duchess of Malfi', in *Still Harping on Daughters: Women in Seventeenth Century Drama* (Brighton, 1983).

27. Simon Shepherd, *Amazons and Warrior Women: Varieties of Feminism in Seventeenth Century Drama* (Brighton, 1983), p. 117.

28. Belsey, *The Subject of Tragedy*.

29. Ibid., pp. 197–200.

30. William Painter, *The Palace of Pleasure* (1567), in J. R. Brown (ed.), *The Duchess of Malfi* (London, 1964), p. 184.

31. Simon Shepherd, *Amazons and Warrior Women*, p. 119.

32. The term is J. R. Brown's: see J. R. Brown (ed.), *The Duchess of Malfi* (London, 1964), p. xxxi.

33. [In chapter 3 of *Gender, Race, Renaissance Drama*, Loomba notes how 'Patriarchal thought incorporates the possibility of female movement in order to control it, investing women's stability with moral values. Thus the wandering woman is evil ... The good woman is still. But every woman is a devil within, so all women's capacity for movement must be anticipated and curtailed' (p. 74) – Ed.]

34. Belsey, *The Subject of Tragedy*, pp. 149–91.

35. I am deeply indebted to Judith Blair's brilliant essay 'Private parts in public places' for my analysis of duplicity. This article and others in Ardener's collection, *Women and Space*, provide an introduction to spatial analysis generally and directed my attention to the social and sexual *placement* of women. [See Shirley Ardener (ed.), *Women and Space: Ground Rules and Social Maps* (London, 1981) – Ed.]

36. Anne Thorne, 'Women's Creativity: Architectural Space and Literature' (unpublished DipArch thesis, Polytechnic of Central London, 1979).

37. See Madhu Kishwar and Ruth Vanita (eds), *In Search of Answers: Indian Women's Voices from Manushi* (London, 1984), p. 254.

38. Alison Heisch, 'Queen Elizabeth I: parliamentary rhetoric and the exercise of power', *Signs*, 1:1 (1975), 34.

39. John Berger et al., *Ways of Seeing* (London, 1972), p. 47.

40. Shirley Ardener (ed.), *Women and Space*, p. 206.

41. Gisela Ecker (ed.), *Feminist Aesthetics*, p. 21.

42. Jonathan Dollimore, 'Subjectivity, sexuality and transgression: the Jacobean connection' (forthcoming).

43. Joan Kelly, *Women, History, Theory* (Chicago, 1984), p. xxv.

44. See Dollimore, *Radical Tragedy*.

45. Ursula Sharma, 'Purdah and public space', in Alfred de Souza (ed.), *Women in Contemporary India and South Asia* (Delhi, 1975), p. 227.

46. Natalie Zemon Davis, 'Women on top: symbolic sexual inversion and political disorder in early modern Europe' in Barbara Babcock (ed.), *The Reversible World: Symbolic Inversion in Art and Society* (Ithaca, NY, 1978), pp. 154–5.

47. Kamladevi Chattopadhyay, *Times of India*. Chattopadhyay is a veteran freedom-fighter and author of *Indian Women's Battle for Freedom*; she typifies the postcolonial dilemma of third world women, which Mernissi talks of in *Beyond the Veil*, where an indigenous heritage and mode of struggle becomes imperative and yet leads into the pitfalls, indicated by Fanon, of asserting some of the most retrogressive elements of tradition.

48. Sudhir Kakar, *The Inner World*, p. 67.

49. See Lawrence A. Babb, 'Marriage and malevolence: the uses of sexual opposition in a Hindu pantheon', *Ethnology*, 9 (1970); Deviprasad Chattopadhyay, *Lokayata: A Study in Ancient Indian Materialism* (New Delhi, 1973); Gowrie Ponniah, 'Ideology and the status of women in Hindu Society' (unpublished MA thesis, University of Sussex, 1976).

50. Joanna Liddle and Rama Joshi, *Daughters of Independence: Gender, Caste and Class in India* (New Delhi / London, 1976), p. 55.

51. Bruce Elliott Tapper, 'Widows and goddesses: female roles in deity symbolism in a South Indian village', *Contributions to Indian Sociology* (new series), 13:1 (1979), 24.

52. Ibid., pp. 24–5.

53. Ruth Vanita, ' "Ravana shall be slain and Sita freed ...": The feminine principle in Kanthapura', in Lola Chatterji (ed.), *Woman Image Text: Feminist Readings of Literary Texts* (New Delhi, 1986), p. 189.

54. Catherine Belsey, 'Disrupting sexual difference: meaning and gender in the comedies', in John Drakakis (ed.), *Alternative Shakespeares* (London and New York, 1985), pp. 166–90.

3

The Theatre and the Scaffold: Death as Spectacle in *The Spanish Tragedy*

I

Traditional criticism regards Kyd's *Spanish Tragedy* as important primarily for its historical position at the head of the revenge tradi-tion. Its violence has frequently been attributed to Senecan models, and its dramatic deaths, including the spectacular *coup de theatre* in the closing scene, analysed primarily for their influence on Shakespeare's dramaturgy. And yet, though the Senecan influence has been well documented, critics have paid little attention to con-temporary cultural practices such as public executions and hang-ings at Tyburn to explain the play's particular fascination with the hanged man and the mutilated and dismembered corpse. No other play of the Renaissance stage dwells on the spectacle of hanging as Kyd's does, and the Senecan influence will not in itself account for the spectacular on-stage hangings and near-hangings in the play.[1]

During Elizabeth's reign, 6160 victims were hanged at Tyburn, and though this represents a somewhat smaller figure than those hanged during Henry VIII's reign, Elizabethans were certainly quite familiar with the spectacle of the hanged body and the disembow-elled and quartered corpse. In Kyd's treatment of the body as spec-tacle, we witness most vividly the earliest coalescence of the theatrical and punitive modes in Elizabethan England. Kyd also

71

heightens the ambivalence inherent in the public hanging as spectacle and deliberately weakens the frames that separated spectators
from the spectacle.

Kyd's merger of the spectacles of punishment and enacted
tragedy was perhaps inevitable in light of the remarkable similarities in the format and ends of these popular events in early modern
England. Indeed, the stage and the scaffold seem to have been
closely related historically.[2] The famous Triple Tree, the first permanent structure for hangings in London, was erected at Tyburn in
1571, during the same decade which saw the construction of the
first public theatre.[3] At Tyburn, seats were available for those who
could pay, and rooms could be hired in houses overlooking the
scene; the majority of spectators, however, stood in a semi-circle
around the event, while hawkers sold fruits and pies, and ballads
and pamphlets detailing the various crimes committed by the man
being hanged. Other kinds of peripheral entertainment also occurred simultaneously. In short, hangings functioned as spectacles
not unlike tragedies staged in the public theatres.[4] The organisation
of spectators around hangings and executions and in the theatres,
and the simultaneous localisation of these entertainments through
the construction of permanent structures, suggest the close alliance
between these communal worlds in early modern England. Evidence
also suggests that theatre and public punishment provided entertainment to upper and lower classes and that both events were generally well attended. Contemporary letters abound in accounts of
executions and hangings, details of which are interspersed among
court gossip and descriptions of Parliament sessions. In a letter to
Dudley Carleton, for example, John Chamberlain describes the
hanging of four priests on Whitsun eve in 1612, noting with mild
surprise the large number of people, among them 'divers ladies and
gentlemen', who had gathered to witness the event which took
place early in the morning between six and seven.[5]

I am not alone in suggesting links between these modes of
popular public spectacle in Renaissance England. Stephen
Greenblatt argues for the implicit presence of the scaffold in certain
kinds of theatre when he writes:

> the ratio between the theatre and the world, even at its most stable
> and unchallenged moments, was never *perfectly* taken for granted,
> that is, experienced as something wholly natural and self-evident ...
> Similarly, the playwrights themselves frequently called attention in the
> midst of their plays to alternative theatrical practices. Thus, for

example, the denouement of Massinger's *Roman Actor* (like that of
Kyd's *Spanish Tragedy*) turns upon the staging of a mode of theatre in
which princes and nobles take part in plays and in which the killing
turns out to be real. It required no major act of imagination for a
Renaissance audience to conceive of either of these alternatives to the
conventions of the public playhouse: both were fully operative in the
period itself, in the form of masques and courtly entertainments, on
the one hand, and public maimings and executions on the other.[6]

Presumably, the relationship between theatre and the scaffold
worked both ways: if dramatic deaths could suggest public maimings and executions, the latter could as easily and as vividly evoke
its theatrical counterparts.

Indeed, contemporary narratives about public hangings and executions frequently insist on the theatrical analogy. Carleton, for
example, in a letter to Chamberlain, details in vividly theatrical
terms the trial and executions of several conspirators, including two
priests, implicated in the plot to harm King James I shortly after his
ascension to the throne in 1603. The letter moves from a casual
narrative to a concentrated exposition of the drama as it unfolded.
Carleton begins his account with the hangings of two papist priests:
'The two priests that led the way to the execution were very blood-
ily handled; for they were cut down alive; and Clark to whom more
favour was intended, had the worse luck; for he both strove to help
himself, and spake after he was cut down ... Their quarters were set
on Winchester gates, and their heads on the first tower of the
castle.' This was followed by the execution of George Brooke,
whose death, Carleton notes wryly, was 'witnessed by no greater an
assembly than at ordinary executions', the only men of quality
present being the Lord of Arundel and Lord Somerset.[7] Three
others, Markham, Grey, and Cobham, were scheduled to be executed on Friday; Carleton narrates the sequence of events as it
occurred, retaining information about their narrow escape from the
gallows until the very end:

> A fouler day could hardly have been picked out, or fitter for such a
> tragedy. Markham being brought to the scaffold, was much dis-
> mayed, and complained much of his hard hap, to be deluded with
> hopes, and brought to that place unprepared ... The sheriff in the
> mean time was secretly withdrawn by one John Gill, Scotch groom of
> the bedchamber ... The sheriff, at his return, told him [Markham]
> that since he was so ill prepared, he should have two hours respite,
> so led him from the scaffold, without giving him any more comfort.[8]

Lord Grey's turn followed, and he spent considerable time repent-
ing for his crimes and praying to be forgiven, all of which, Carleton
points out, 'held us in the rain more than half an hour'. As in the
case of Markham, however, the execution was halted, the prisoner
being told only that the sequence of executions had been altered by
express orders from the King, and that Cobham would die before
him. Grey was also led to Prince Arthur's Hall and asked to await
his turn with Markham. Lord Cobham then arrived on the scaffold,
but unlike the other two, came 'with good assurance and contempt
of death'. The sheriff halted this execution as well, telling Cobham
only that he had to first face a few other prisoners. Carleton then
describes the arrival of Grey and Markham on the scaffold, and the
bewildered looks on the three prisoners who 'nothing acquainted
with what had passed, no more than the lookers on with what
should follow looked strange one upon another, like men beheaded,
and met again in the other world'. 'Now', Carleton continues, 'all
the actors being together on the stage, as use is at the end of the
play', the sheriff announced that the King had pardoned all three.
Carleton concludes his account by noting that this happy play had
very nearly been marred 'for John Gill could not go so near the
scaffold that he could speak to the sherrif, ... but was fain to call
out to Sir James Hayes, or else Markham might have lost his neck'.[9]

The metaphoric alliance between theatre and public punishment,
which permeates Carleton's narrative, might be regarded as fundamental in Renaissance England. The theatre and the scaffold provided occasions for communal festivities whose format and ends
emerge as remarkably similar; early plays such as Kyd's *Spanish
Tragedy* register the close alliance between these popular activities
especially vividly. But the influence of the scaffold may also account
for a general dramatic fascination with the spectacle of death
evident throughout the late sixteenth and early seventeenth cen-
turies. In fact, the close alliance between theatre and public punishment frames the great age of drama in England; after all, the period
culminates with the greatest theatrical spectacle of all, the public
execution of King Charles I.

Despite my collapse of the theatrical and punitive modes,
however, an important distinction needs to be made between the
festivity of theatre and the spectacle of the scaffold. Theatre estab-
lishes distance between spectacle and spectators, and festivity implicitly or explicitly invokes the frame to separate itself from
everyday living. Indeed, distance in the theatre and framing in festivity perform similar functions. However, the authenticity in the

enactment of public punishment makes its distance considerably more nebulous. In fact, participants in public executions and hangings remained acutely aware of their profound relevance both to the authorities who orchestrated the performance and to the spectators who viewed it. Such awareness frequently resulted in conscious attempts by victims to manipulate and modify the distance that separated criminals from onlookers. In such circumstances, the formal efficacy of the execution diminished considerably and events could easily transform into celebration of the condemned victim's role as a defier of repressive authority. As Michel Foucault illustrates:

> the public execution allowed the luxury of these momentary saturnalia, when nothing remained to prohibit or punish. Under the protection of imminent death, the criminal could say everything and the crowd cheered ... In these executions, which ought to show only the terrorising power of the prince, there was the whole aspect of the carnival, in which the rules were inverted, authority mocked and criminals transformed into heroes.[10]

Executions where the margins remained tenuous and where festivity merged so fully with the enactment of terror may be especially important to an understanding of the drama of death on the Renaissance stage. In early plays such as Kyd's, in the concluding representation of theatre within theatre, for example, we witness a conscious manipulation of distance and framing, dramatic exposition of the precarious nature of public spectacle itself as an illustration of royal and state power. The inner play's exposition of the shallowness of state authority gains added potency from the composition of its audience, the royal houses of Spain and Portugal. Hieronimo, the author of the inner play, even taunts his audience's reliance on the framed nature of theatrical tragedy:

> Haply, you think, but bootless are your thoughts,
> That this is fabulously counterfeit,
> And that we do as all tragedians do:
> To die today, for fashioning our scene,
> The death of Ajax or some Roman peer
> And in a minute, starting up again,
> Revive to please tommorow's audience.
>
> (IV.iv.76–82)

At this, its most clearly self-reflexive moment, Kyd's tragedy simultaneously indulges and exposes its reliance on the drama of terror, and, through the mixed reactions of its stage audience who at first applaud the tragedy for its realistic enactment and then condemn it for its gory authenticity, invites a re-evaluation of the spectacle of terror itself.

II

The Spanish Tragedy was staged within a decade after the construction of both the Triple Tree and the Theatre, and this perhaps accounts for the hangings, murders, and near deaths which abound in the play.[11] Lorenzo and Balthazar hang Horatio in the arbour in a spectacularly gruesome scene, Pedringano's death by hanging occurs on stage, Alexandro narrowly escapes being burnt at the stake, Villuppo exits the play presumably to be tortured and hanged, and Hieronimo tries unsuccessfully to hang himself in the last scene, though he duplicates the effects of a hanging by biting his tongue out. Of all these, however, Horatio's gruesome murder in the arbour remains the centrepiece; we come back to it again and again through Hieronimo's recounting of it, and as if to reiterate its centrality, the playwright exploits the value of the mutilated body as spectacle by holding Horatio's body up to view either literally or metaphorically several times in the course of the play.

Kyd thus exploits thoroughly the audience's voyeuristic interest in the hanged and mutilated corpse, but he prepares us for his centrepiece, Horatio's murder in the arbour, even from the opening scene through promises of torture, mutilation, and death. Repeated promises of more blood and gore, in fact, distinguish Kyd's version of the revenge play from Shakespeare's later rendering in *Hamlet*. While in the later play, Hamlet Senior insists that the torments of the netherworld are too horrible to be recounted (he is also forbidden to reveal its secrets), in the opening scene of Kyd's tragedy, Don Andrea's ghost provides with relish a vivid and detailed account of his sojourn through the underworld:

> Through dreadful shades of ever glooming night,
> I saw more sights than a thousand tongues can tell,
> Or pens can write, or mortal hearts can think.
> Three ways there were: ...
> ....
> The left-hand path, declining fearfully,
> Was ready downfall to the deepest hell,
> Where bloody Furies shake their whips of steel,
> And poor Ixion turns an endless wheel;

Where usurers are choked with melting gold,
And wantons are embraced with ugly snakes,
And murderers groan with never killing wounds,
And perjured weights scalded in boiling lead,
And all foul sins with torments overwhelmed.

(I.i.56–70)

The underworld, not constrained by economic considerations, retains ancient methods of public deaths such as boiling and drowning, punishments long abandoned in England as too costly and troublesome; indeed, at the end of the play, Don Andrea's ghost envisions similar elaborate deaths for his murdered enemies in the afterworld. The opening and concluding accounts of the underworld which frame the play emphasise the tragedy's links with the spectacle of public punishment, the primary purpose of which was to replicate torments awaiting the victim after death. The opening scene even concludes with Revenge promising us better entertainment than that detailed by Don Andrea, more blood and gore through the murder of the princely Balthazar by Don Andrea's 'sweet' Bel-imperia.

Indeed, the very next scene provides more elaborate fare; the king's request for a 'brief discourse' concerning the battle between Spain and Portugal elicits from his general a detailed description complete with similes and accounts of mutilated and dismembered bodies:

On every side drop captains to the ground,
And soldiers, some ill maimed, some slain outright:
Here falls a body sundered from his head,
There legs and arms lie bleeding on the grass,
Mingled with weapons and unbowelled steeds,
That scattering overspread the purple plain.

(I.ii.57–62)

The king's satisfied response to this narrative, which ultimately details Spain's success in battle, captures the value of death as entertainment, an idea emphasised throughout the play in a variety of ways.

The audience hears four different versions of the battle in succession in these opening scenes – by Don Andrea, the Spanish general, Horatio, and Villuppo in the Portuguese court – and each account either elicits pleasure from the listener as in the scene just described or reveals the delight and ingenuity of the speaker.[12]

The latter seems true of Villuppo's account of Balthazar's death to the viceroy in the scene which follows. Jealous of Alexandro's success at court, Villuppo fabricates a tale about Balthazar's treacherous betrayal by Alexandro in the midst of battle. The temperamental and fickle viceroy responds to the tale of his son's death with 'Ay, ay, my nightly dreams have told me this' (I.iii.76) and immediately has Alexandro imprisoned. Villuppo closes this scene with an aside in which he revels in the ingenuity of his 'forged tale'. However, Villuppo's fantastic narrative must remind the audience of the uncanny way in which art mirrors life, for we have already been promised Balthazar's death by Revenge; when his murder occurs later in the play, its sequence mimics Villuppo's account, for the unsuspecting Balthazar is killed by his supposed wife-to-be, Bel-imperia, at what appears to be the height of his success. Even the viceroy's claim about his prophetic dreams gains ironic accuracy as the scene provides a narrative account of events yet to occur.

We arrive thus, via numerous accounts of death and mutilation, to the scene in the arbour where Bel-imperia and Horatio meet. Already aware of Pedringano's betrayal, however, the audience would view the images of war and love in the opening section of this scene as ominous. Interestingly, Pedringano, like the hangman who sometimes remained masked and hooded, conducts the ceremony of the hanging in disguise with the aid of his assistant Serebrine, while Lorenzo gives orders and joins in the stabbing after Horatio has been hanged. Though stage directions remain unclear, we can assume that Balthazar and Bel-imperia witness the stabbing, for Bel-imperia responds immediately to the horrible crime. Their function as spectators parallels our own and underscores Kyd's exploitation of the event as public spectacle. Foucault's argument that in early modern Europe, 'in the ceremonies of the public execution, the main character was the people, whose real presence was required for the performance' proves especially appropriate to this hanging performed on a raised stage for an audience whose arrangement in 'the pit' and the balconies above recalls the scaffold, and which certainly indulges the spectators' voyeuristic interest in death as spectacle.[13] The double framing of this event – the audience as spectators watching an already framed event – also anticipates the play within the play in Act IV which more explicitly raises questions about the value of death as entertainment.

A few scenes later, we are treated to a review of this event and later to another hanging (Pedringano's), whose format, however, remains remarkably different from the one we have just witnessed. Before turning to the later hanging, I would like to consider briefly the play's uncanny reliance hereafter on the spectacle of Horatio's mutilated body.

We are never allowed to forget this spectacle, and characters keep reminding us of this event in various ways. In fact, after the staging of this gory death, the earlier revenge plot associated with Don Andrea is all but forgotten; Horatio's murder and the collusive revenge orchestrated by Bel-imperia and Hieronimo on his behalf take centre stage. Horatio's body, hanged and multilated before a full house, thus takes precedence over Don Andrea, whose death has been narrated rather than witnessed. Interestingly, Don Andrea's funeral rites were conducted by Horatio in a private cere-mony, and all that remains of him is a bloody scarf; it might even be argued that the complete obliteration of Don Andrea's corpse and the repeated emphasis on Horatio's symbolically reiterates the precedence of the second revenge plot over the first. Even Don Andrea's bloody scarf is duplicated through the rest of the play by Horatio's handkerchief which Hieronimo dips in his son's blood and presents on stage several times as a reminder of his unavenged death. This token of death also recalls a conventional practice at hangings and executions; onlookers frequently dipped their hand-kerchiefs in the blood of the victim which was believed to carry curative and divine powers.[14]

Unlike in *Hamlet* where murdered corpses remain hidden behind curtains or stuffed under the stairwell, Kyd's play thus presents death in vivid detail and follows this up with an elaborate scene of discovery in which both Hieronimo and Isabella identify Horatio's corpse. The ghost, perhaps echoing the audience's reaction to these events, expresses dismay at witnessing Horatio's murder rather than Balthazar's as promised, but Revenge, relishing the bloody detour, insists on the relevance of these events as preambles to more cunning deaths yet to occur: 'The end is crown of every work well done; / The sickle comes not till the corn be ripe' (II.v.8–9).

After this murder, the focus of the play shifts to the psychological dilemma faced by Hieronimo as he plans revenge. The most inter-esting aspect of his character hereafter becomes his mental absorp-tion with duplicating his son's murder. At first, he tries to duplicate bodies by re-enacting the event with himself as victim; in a vividly dramatic scene which takes place at court, he enters with a poniard in one hand and a rope in the other and debates his route to death:

> Turn down this path – thou shalt be with him [Horatio] straight –
> Or this, and then thou need'st not take thy breath.
> This way or that way?
>
> (III.xii.14–16)

Tormented by his inability to accomplish revenge, he spends most of his time wandering in the arbour looking for his son; here, near the very tree on which Horatio was hanged, the painter Bazulto, seeking justice for his own son's murder, visits him. In a psychologically revealing moment explored in one of the 'additions', Hieronimo requests Bazulto to paint the scene of Horatio's murder, complete with the victim's doleful cry and his own emotional frenzy at discovering his son's body. In language, Hieronimo re-creates the event for us yet again: 'Well sir, paint me a youth run through and through with villains' swords hanging upon this tree'; and later, describing his discovery of the body, he wishes to 'behold a man hanging: and tottering and tottering, as you know the wind will weave a man' (Addition, III.xiii.131–2, 151–3). His desire to re-create events through painting at first and later through the drama at court contrasts sharply with Isabella's desire a few scenes later to destroy the arbour and the tree on which her son was murdered. Both scenes, however, serve to keep the gruesome murder firmly in our minds.

The play even provides a semi-comic version of this murder in another hanging a few scenes later. Pedringano's hanging also takes place on stage and provides a semi-comic and officially authorised spectacle, a direct contrast to Horatio's base and treacherous murder committed in secret and under cover of night. Through the attitudes of Pedringano who reaches his death with a merry jest, and the clown who cannot resist the event despite his sympathy for the deluded victim, the scene simultaneously exploits and satirises the value of the public hanging as a reiteration of justice.

Commenting on the propensity for travesty inherent in the format of the public execution, Foucault illustrates that because the ritual of torture was sustained 'by a policy of terror' which made everyone aware 'through the body of the criminal of the unrestrained presence of the sovereign', it was especially susceptible to manipulation by its participants.[15] As I suggested earlier, the public execution's social relevance depended so fully on its proper enactment through the collusion of all participants, including the hangman as an instrument of the law, the criminal as a defier of divine and sovereign authority, and spectators as witnesses to the efficacy of royal power and justice, and the slightest deviation could lead to redefinitions and reinterpretations of power relations between subjects and the sovereign. Indeed, this happened frequently enough to cause some concern to the authorities.[16] The speech delivered on the scaffold by the victim provided an especially suitable opportunity for such manipulation; intended to reinforce the power of justice, it frequently questioned rather than emphasised legal efficacy. Chamberlain, for example, bemoans the custom of allowing the condemned to address the audience and cautions about the inherent danger of this practice; describing the bravely rendered speech by a priest who was hanged at Tyburn, he notes that 'the matter is not well handled in mine opinion, to suffer them [condemned prisoners] to brave and talk so liberally at their execution'.[17]

Pedringano's defiant attitude when faced with death reiterates the carnivalesque possibilities of the public execution. Duped by Lorenzo into thinking that he will be pardoned, Pedringano insists on mocking the authorities who sentence him. Even the hangman expresses shock at his callous indifference to death: 'Well, thou art even the merriest piece of man's flesh that e'er groaned at my office door' (III.vi.81–2). Indeed, it might even be argued that despite his role as victim, Pedringano has the final say on this travesty of justice, for he exposes Lorenzo's crimes in a letter, and thus forces Hieronimo to confront the inadequacy of the judicial system. In his mockery from beyond the grave, Pedringano becomes a version of the grinning skeleton in the *danse macabre* as he exposes the futility of human endeavour. The clown's attitude also reiterates the inherent irony of this grotesque enactment of state justice. Having opened the empty box which supposedly contains a pardon sent by Lorenzo, the clown reacts to the trick with infinite glee; his reaction parodies similar responses towards death voiced throughout the play by many characters, among them Balthazar, Lorenzo, Villuppo, and Pedringano himself:

> I cannot choose but smile to think how the villain will flout the gallows, scorn the audience, and descant on the hangman, and all presuming of his pardon from hence. Will't not be an odd jest for me

to stand and grace every jest he makes, pointing my finger at this box, as who would say, 'Mock on; here's thy warrant'. Is't not a scurvy jest that a man should jest himself to death?

(III.v.10–18)

Indeed, he expedites Pedringano's death by playing his part to perfection.

In effect, the clown's attitude in this scene parallels the court's applause for the 'Tragedy of Soliman and Perseda' staged as part of Bel-imperia's nuptial ceremony. After the tragedy, Hieronimo holds up his son's body to the bewildered court as justification for the multiple deaths that have occurred: 'See here my show; look on this spectacle' (IV.iv.89). The court's reaction as the truth unfolds changes from applause to anger and condemnation. Implicitly, Kyd invites the audience to re-evaluate its response to the tragedy of evil so cunningly staged, for Hieronimo's theatrical production necessarily draws attention to the nebulous nature of the boundary that separates spectators from the spectacle.

Kyd's conscious exposition of this fragile distance may be best understood perhaps through Gregory Bateson's theory about frames in 'play' and 'fantasy' activities.[18] Bateson argues that in metacommunicative statements such as 'This is play', 'the subject of discourse is the relationship between speakers', and participants recognise the paradox generated by the statement which is 'a negative statement containing an implicit negative metastatement'. As he insists, 'Expanded, the statement ... looks something like this: "These actions in which we now engage do not denote what those actions *for which they stand* would denote".'[19] The idea holds also for specific forms of play such as the theatre. Communication such as the above 'This is play', in which participants recognise the metacommunicative implications of the statement, involves a complex set of rules, as Bateson notes, and 'language bears to the objects which it denotes a relationship comparable to that which a map bears to territory'.[20] But as Bateson insists, 'the discrimination between map and territory is always liable to break down', and we frequently encounter situations which involve a more complex form of play where the game is constructed 'not upon the premise "This is play" but rather around the question "Is this play?" '[21] Certainly, *The Spanish Tragedy* concludes by posing this question. Indeed, in problematising boundaries, Kyd's tragedy imitates the scaffold most vividly; it also begins a trend in theatrical experimentation with framing that culminates in radical realignments considerably later, in the tragedies of Middleton, Ford, and Shirley.

Kyd's tragedy, in fact, closes by reminding us of yet another frame, that provided by Don Andrea and the ghost who have witnessed events with the theatrical audience, and whose pleased reactions underscore the value of death as entertainment. The ghost, in fact, catalogues the list of deaths with obvious relish:

> Aye, now my hopes have end in their effects,
> When blood and sorrow finish my desires:
> Horatio murdered in his father's bower,
> Vild Serebrine by Pedringano slain,
> False Pedringano hanged by quaint device,
> Fair Isabella by herself misdone,
> Prince Balthazar by Bel-imperia stabbed,
> The Duke of Castille and his wicked son
> Both done to death by old Hieronimo,
> My Bel-imperia fall'n as Dido fell,
> And good Hieronimo slain by himself.
> Ay, these were spectacles to please my soul.
>
> (IV.v.1–12)

His response reminds us of several such reactions to death in the course of the play: the court witnessing the 'Tragedy of Soliman and Perseda' had commended the actors; Villuppo had revelled in anticipation as he plotted the death of Alexandro; the clown had marvelled at the plot to send Pedringano to his 'merry' death. Revenge even concludes the play with promises of further torments for the villains in the underworld. Thus, the play blatantly presents its multiple deaths as dramatic entertainment, but through Hieronimo's taunting condemnation of his audience's expectations, it also raises questions about theatre's very status as a framed spectacle and about the value of death as public entertainment.

In short, the spectacular success of Kyd's play might be attributed in part to the author's ingenious transference of the spectacle of public execution with all its ambiguities from the socio-political to the cultural worlds. Greenblatt has suggested that traces of similar transference and appropriation are evident throughout the early modern period; 'the textual traces that have survived from the Renaissance,' he writes, 'are products of extended borrowings. They were made by moving certain things – principally ordinary language, but also metaphors, ceremonies, dances, emblems, items of clothing, well-worn stories, and so forth – from one culturally demarcated zone to another.' He goes on to insist that 'we need to understand not only the construction of these zones but also the process of movement across the shifting boundaries between them'.[22] In Kyd's early revenge tragedy, we witness the process of movement between social and cultural boundaries perhaps more vividly than in plays by his contemporaries. Like Greenblatt, Michel de Certeau in his arguments concerning the practice of daily living focuses on infinite borrowings among socio-cultural practices, the 'tactics' of consumption and appropriation that 'lend a political dimension to everyday practices'.[23] 'Everyday life,' he insists, 'invents itself by *poaching* in countless ways on the property of others.'[24] The same might be said about the dramatic mode in particular in early modern England as it transferred, questioned, and modified elements from popular public institutions; certainly, Kyd's tragedy of death and evil bears testimony to this ingenious transference of the spectacle of death from the punitive to the dramatic modes.[25]

From *Studies in English Literature*, 32 (1992), 217–230.

NOTES

[Molly Smith's essay is a good demonstration of one of the ways in which contemporary critical approaches have shifted the focus of enquiry in literary studies. In the past, Kyd's *The Spanish Tragedy* was studied primarily in terms of its significance as a prototype of the revenge tragedy genre, analysed for its debt to Seneca and its influence on later work, especially Shakespeare's. Smith's aim is to approach the play from a fresh angle, paying attention to 'contemporary cultural practices' (specifically executions) in order to increase our understanding of it. She begins by relating the on-stage hangings of Horatio and Pedringano in the play to public executions in Elizabethan England. She considers how the spectacle of public punishment is a crucial weapon of the state, a manifest display of its power. Smith's essay collapses the theatrical and the punitive modes, but at the same time remains aware of their fundamental difference: the purpose of the punitive mode was intended as a forceful reminder to audiences of the relevance and immediacy of execution. Theatre audiences were held at a distance from the on-stage action via devices designed to draw attention to them as spectators, observers of something non-mimetic.

The second part of the essay considers in more detail Kyd's exploitation of his audience's taste for violence and spectacular deaths. Like Katharine Maus (essay 4), Smith devotes attention to the execution of Pedringano. While Maus reads the incident in terms of the play's interrogation of providential belief, Smith sees it as an ironic reflection on the workings of state justice. The essay ends with further reflections on the play's use of metatheatre; its self-reflexivity offers the spectators the opportunity to critique the boundary that separates performer and audience. Though it acknowledges a debt both to Foucault and to Stephen Greenblatt, both closely associated in their different ways with new historicism, the essay's evocation of the carnivalesque (particularly in relation to Pedringano) finally aligns the essay more closely with cultural materialist approaches. All quotations are taken from Philip Edwards (ed.), *The Spanish Tragedy* (Cambridge, MA, 1959). Ed.]

1. Frank Adolino has recently argued for a more specific connection between the play's depictions of death and the St Bartholomew's Day Massacre in Paris in 1572; see ' "In Paris? Mass, and Well Remembered!": Kyd's *The Spanish Tragedy* and the English Reaction to the St Bartholomew's Day Massacre', *The Sixteenth Century Journal*, 21:3 (Fall 1990), 401–9. For a discussion of relationships between public executions and Marlowe's dramaturgy, see Karen Cunningham, 'Renaissance Execution and Marlovian Elocution: The Drama of Death', *PMLA*, 105:2 (March 1990), 209–22.

2. I include both executions and hangings under the term scaffold, but the distinction between these two forms of punishment is important. Executions were reserved for the upper classes and important criminals, while criminals of the lower classes were hanged. When William Laud appealed his death sentence, for example, the only concession made was to revise the sentence from hanging to execution in recognition of the prisoner's social stature.

3. Whether James Burbage's Theatre in Shoreditch was the first public playhouse is a matter of some dispute. See for example Herbert Berry's 'The First Public Playhouses, especially the Red Lion', *Shakespeare Quarterly*, 40:2 (Summer 1989), 133–48, where he argues that the Red Lion (which critics such as Chambers have regarded as an inn) was an earlier playhouse deliberately ignored by Cuthbert Burbage because of a falling out between his father, James Burbage, and Brayne, the owner of the Red Lion. But as Berry himself acknowledges, the Red Lion 'must have been a very play shadow of the Theatre ... So far as one can see, it had no walls or roofs, and the turret was to rest on the plates on the ground rather than on secure footings, along with, one might guess, the stage and galleries' (p. 145). The 'secure footing' at least was provided only with the erection of the Theatre in 1576.

4. For descriptions of public executions and hangings in early modern England, especially at Tyburn, see Alfred Marks, *Tyburn Tree* (London, no date), and John Laurence, *A History of Capital Punishment* (Port Washington, 1932). See also Douglas Hay, Peter Linebaugh et al. (eds), *Albion's Fatal Tree* (New York, 1967), though it deals primarily with the eighteenth century.

5. Thomas Birch (ed. R. F. Williams), *The Court and Times of James the First*, 2 vols (London, 1849), vol. 1, p. 173.

6. Stephen Greenblatt, *Shakespearean Negotiations: The Circulation of Social Energy in Renaissance England* (Berkeley and Los Angeles, 1988), p. 15.

7. Birch, *Court and Times*, vol. 1, p. 27.

8. Ibid., p. 29.

9. Ibid., pp. 31–2.

10. Michel Foucault, *Discipline and Punish: The Birth of the Prison*, trans. Alan Sheridan (New York, 1977), p. 61.

11. The earliest and last possible dates for the play are 1582 and 1592, respectively. I have gone by the generally accepted date of 1586–87. For a discussion of the problems in dating the play accurately, see Philip Edwards's introduction to his edition, pp. xxi–xxvii.

12. The exception to this might be Horatio's account of Don Andrea's death to Bel-imperia, though it also raises questions of authenticity by modifying two earlier accounts we have heard, the first by Don Andrea's ghost and the other by the Spanish general. Discrepancies among the earlier narratives should caution us, however, that the scene provides yet another tale glossed by the teller to satisfy Bel-imperia, a listener with different allegiances from the king and viceroy.

13. Foucault, *Discipline and Punish*, p. 57.

14. Peter Linebaugh, 'The Tyburn Riot Against the Surgeons', in Hay, Linebaugh et al. (eds), *Albion's Fatal Tree*, pp. 65–118, 109–10.

15. Foucault, *Discipline and Punish*, p. 49.

16. In the eighteenth century, official concern about the efficacy of public executions and hangings in reinforcing royal and social authority became especially acute as these occasions increasingly provided excuses for rioting and general merrymaking (Foucault, *Discipline and Punish*, p. 68).

17. Birch, *Court and Times*, vol. 1, p. 215.

18. Gregory Bateson, 'A Theory of Play and Fantasy', in Robert E. Innis (ed.), *Semiotics: An Introductory Anthology* (Bloomington, IN, 1985), pp. 129–44.

19. Bateson, 'A Theory of Play', p. 133.

20. Ibid., p. 134.

21. Ibid., p. 135.

22. Greenblatt, *Shakespearean Negotiations*, p. 7.

23. Michel de Certeau, *The Practice of Everyday Life*, trans. Steven Rendall (Berkeley, Los Angeles and London, 1984), p. xvii.

24. Ibid., p. xii.

25. Research for this essay began during an NEH summer seminar at Berkeley in 1989 directed by Stephen Greenblatt. I am grateful to Professor Greenblatt for useful comments on the chapter from which this essay is taken. I am also grateful to the Cornell University Humanities Center for a fellowship in the summer of 1990 which enabled me to revise and prepare my manuscript for publication.

4

The Spanish Tragedy, or, The Machiavel's Revenge

KATHARINE EISAMAN MAUS

The ends of machiavellian inwardness are emphatically not contemplative: we have already seen how Gygean invisibility repudiates divine authority, and it manifestly defies secular masters as well.[1] The machiavel exploits his self-awareness by undertaking a *coup d'état*. What, then, is the relationship between inwardness and rebellion?

The significance of the machiavel's disruptiveness depends, of course, upon what he is disrupting: upon the context in which he acts. By the end of the War of the Roses in *Richard III*, every claimant to the throne is a kind of usurper, even Richmond, who must miraculously revive a sense of legitimate entitlement almost hopelessly compromised by preceding events. While radical social breakdown makes Richmond's task more difficult in some ways, it also preserves him from the taint of treason, a crime which can only occur in a world where there are allegiances to violate. Richard's 'illegitimacy' – his personal defectiveness and his faulty title to the throne – both helps justify Richmond's action and strongly implies that English institutions may be rescued simply by installing a more deserving person as England's king. Although there is indeed something the matter with Richard, there is nothing the matter with the monarchy that a personnel change will not repair.

Like the usurper, the hero of English Renaissance revenge tragedy comes to self-consciousness by first experiencing, and then effecting, a profound alteration in his relationship to authority. Revengers are driven to their bloody task because a ruler has failed to punish injustice properly, usually because he himself or members of his family are implicated in the wrongdoing. Most conspicuously, revengers assault the body of the sovereign or the bodies of his close kin. Less obviously, the revenger's outlaw legalism commandeers the monarch's exclusive prerogative over the prosecution of felonies, which were defined as crimes to which the crown was always supposedly a party. The grounds for the revenger's aggression, however, differ from Richard's or Richmond's. Although rulers in revenge plays are incompetent or wicked, no one denies their title to their offices: that the King in *The Spanish Tragedy* is the rightful monarch, that Lussurioso is heir to the dukedom in *The Revenger's Tragedy* – or even that Claudius is really King of Denmark, having been, as Hamlet tells us late in the play, *elected* to his throne. Thus revengers, despite their corrosive attack on royal power, are not primarily concerned with establishing their own claims to the throne. Most are too obsessed with retaliation to concern themselves with their personal prospects afterwards, and at any rate their own deaths follow so quickly upon the wreaking of vengeance that they have no time to install themselves in place of their enemies. In consequence the relative optimism of *Richard III* rarely seems plausible in the revenge play, where the institutions of government, not merely the persons who happen to inhabit those institutions, seem irremediably defective. A revenger can exterminate a particular criminal ruler, but the general difficulty posed by hierarchical social organisation – the vulnerability of inferiors to irresponsible superiors – seems endemic and intractable.

These differences in the way sovereignty is conceived translate into differences in the way 'machiavellianism' is structured and motivated in the revenge play. In Kyd's *Spanish Tragedy* these differences are already fully apparent. The few scenes devoted to the court of Portugal contain the play's simplest episode of lethal insincerity. When Villuppo maliciously accuses Alexandro of murdering Prince Balthazar, Alexandro has no alibi with which to counter his confident account. The unexpectedness of the accusation hardly constitutes evidence for Alexandro's innocence: just the opposite, in fact. For a noble bystander, the occasion brings to mind the familiar distinction between inward truth and external manifestation:

> I had not thought that Alexandro's heart
> Had been envenomed with such extreme hate;

> But now I see that words have several works,
> And there's no credit in the countenance.
> (III.i.15–18)

Since the signs of Alexandro's integrity speak equally plausibly to his guilt, Villuppo replies to the nobleman by cleverly drawing attention to, rather than minimising, Alexandro's apparent forthrightness and loyalty:

> No; for, my lord, had you beheld the train
> That feignéd love had coloured in his looks,
> When he in camp consorted Balthazar,
> Far more inconstant had you thought the sun,
> That hourly coasts the centre of the earth,
> Than Alexandro's purpose to the prince.
> (III.i.8–23)

When a seemingly loyal and straightforward subordinate commits treason, he subverts not only an individual superior, but more fundamentally, the publicly shared perceptions upon which any social structure relies. The traitor clever enough to erase the evidence of his crime in the very act of committing it is – like the 'incarnate devils' of Lodge's *Wit's Misery* – both supremely dangerous and indistinguishable from an innocent man.

In fact, Villuppo's tactics develop out of and exacerbate a paranoia identical to that simultaneously paraded and assuaged by the authors of 'discovery' literature, who claim to possess knowledge of cunningly concealed vice. The only way to defend oneself against such an accusation is to turn it back upon the accuser. Like the mutual recriminations of Catholics and Protestants, or like Richard's reproach of Hastings, Villuppo's indictment is curiously transitive: his treason consists in accusing another of betrayal. (In chapters 4 and 5 [not included here – Ed.] we shall deal at more length with this multiplication of inwardnesses, and their confusing displacement and substitutability: one person's traitorous intentions for another's loyal 'conscience'; one person's guilty dreams for another's supposed secrets.) The Viceroy has no criterion for deciding between Villuppo's avowal and Alexandro's defence, but his 'nightly dreams' support Villuppo, and he sentences Alexandro to death. The fortuitous arrival of the Ambassador with news of Balthazar's prospects in Spain saves Alexandro at the last minute. But the troubling issues raised by Villuppo's accusation hardly vanish so easily.

Indeed, they are echoed and immensely amplified in the main plot of *The Spanish Tragedy*, which concerns a violent struggle between male members of the aristocratic and professional classes over the competing claims of birth and merit. Strength and beauty of mind and body are, of course, the traditional markers of aristocratic status, but in *The Spanish Tragedy*, they are better exemplified by persons of unremarkable lineage. Don Andrea and Horatio's valour in battle surpasses that of their superiors, and their reward is Bel-imperia, who contemptuously ignores the obligation of highborn women to await arranged marriages to suitable patricians. The moments of escape into meritocratic utopia are brief, however; class distinctions are oppressively reinforced almost as soon as they are overthrown. Andrea excels in battle until Prince Balthazar's hench-men bayonet his horse's belly, and Balthazar unchivalrously presses his advantage and kills him. Horatio defeats Balthazar, but partial credit goes to Lorenzo. Bel-imperia dallies with her lowborn lovers, but both are slaughtered, and she eventually is forced into a dynas-tically advantageous wedding to a man she abhors.

It is easy to imagine the heavy investment of a man like Thomas Kyd – a gifted, bankrupt scrivener's son – both in Hieronimo's nightmare of injustice and in his retaliatory triumph. It is also easy to see allegorised in the struggle between Lorenzo and Hieronimo the conflict between an old-fashioned aristocratic esteem for inher-ited status and a new emphasis on the intellectual and practical ac-complishments demanded by the recently centralised Tudor bureaucracy.[2] The relationship of *Spanish Tragedy* to a historically momentous, personally experienced class conflict means that Kyd's conception of machiavellian inwardness differs from Shakespeare's in *Richard III*.

As we have seen, Richard commences his career as a machiavel when loyalty to people or causes outside himself no longer seems possible. He forthwith announces his isolation and uniqueness, and fortifies the boundary between himself and others. *The Spanish Tragedy* similarly chronicles the disintegration of social ties, but the dynamic which produces machiavellian inwardness is considerably more complex. Early in the play, matters are neither so bleak nor so clearly delineated as they later become. The fathers and uncles – the King, Castile, Hieronimo – provide hints of a bygone order in which inherited and acquired entitlements were not imagined to be at odds. Even when, in the first act, Lorenzo and Horatio both lay claim to the capture of Balthazar, an equitable settlement seems possible. The King's meticulous division of the spoils, although it appears to give more credit to Lorenzo than he deserves, seems to content all parties. By the same token, Hieronimo's pride in his son, and his faith that Horatio will be rewarded and advanced, do not mean that he expects Horatio to take Lorenzo's place at court. Rather he hopes that his son's 'merit' will earn him a position of respect much like Hieronimo's own. Hieronimo is proud, not mortified, when the King holds a banquet for Prince Balthazar, Horatio's prisoner of war, and asks Horatio to wait upon their cups.

The safety of the competent professional class is, however, a function not only of its own restricted aspirations but of the self-confidence of the aristocrats who employ professionals. Once Horatio begins to seem a rival to people like Lorenzo and Balthazar, his very excellences make him vulnerable. Horatio's courage on the battlefield diminishes Lorenzo's triumph, his erotic success displaces Balthazar. As his lynched body dangles in the arbour, Lorenzo quips:

> Although his life were still ambitious-proud,
> Yet is he at the highest now that he is dead.
> (II.iv.60–1)

Since Balthazar, Lorenzo, and their henchmen stab Horatio to death, the hanging itself is technically superfluous, but symbolically satisfying for the aggressors, who thereby assign an ignominious death to a perceived transgressor of social hierarchy.

Thus although Lorenzo is quite as ruthless and manipulative as Shakespeare's Richard, his 'machiavellianism' contrasts markedly from Richard's in its motivation and its goals. Lorenzo curiously combines the revolutionary possibilities of amoral individualism with intense class pride. Far from attacking wholesale the structure of the aristocratic order, Lorenzo attempts to preserve it for those born into it, against the pretensions of those who practise its ancestral virtues. To effect this preservation he actually disregards his individual interests, narrowly conceived.[3] For if his sister remains unmarried, or marries a commoner, or irremediably disgraces herself, he may well inherit the Spanish throne; but one of the provisions of the nuptial treaty between Balthazar and Bel-imperia provides for the passage of the kingdom directly to their male issue. Therefore Lorenzo's father, trying to puzzle out Lorenzo's hostility to Hieronimo, supposes that it obscurely reflects Lorenzo's desire to 'intercept' Bel-imperia's marriage – whereas in fact Lorenzo is its principal contriver.

Lorenzo's rigorous enforcement of class boundaries, however, decisively redefines class relationships. With Balthazar's collaboration, Lorenzo estranges traditional aristocratic privilege – the licence to behave as one pleases – from the traditional aristocratic obligation to support loyal or talented subordinates. Hieronimo, who has not previously conceived the possibility of separating duties from entitlements, is hurled over the brink of madness by this moral innovation. The Knight Marshal mourns the loss not only of his son, but of an implicit contract between social classes so basic to his life and work that it seems to underlie rationality itself.

Hieronimo's own birth into machiavellian cunning thus represents – as it does in Haggard or Shakespeare – an adaptation to a drastic crisis of authority, a crisis that seems both to necessitate and to enable circuitous illegalities. As in *Richard III*, the immediate formal consequence of Hieronimo's transformation is a new preference for soliloquy: for speech too conspiratorial, too intimate, or too unbalanced for another's ear. Alone onstage in Act III, scene xiii, he lays his devious plans:

> I will revenge his death.
> But how? Not as the vulgar wits of men,
> With open, but inevitable ills,
> As by a secret, yet a certain mean,
> Which under kindship will be cloaked best.
> (III.xiii.20–5)

'Kindship' – both 'benevolence' and 'blood-relatedness' in Renaissance English – once wholly determined Hieronimo's sense of identity. Now, however, 'kindship' is hollowed out, a mask behind which the alienated subject works his treachery. In this respect Hieronimo differs little from the monsters imagined by religious polemicists. Moreover Hieronimo's estrangement and duplicity, like Richard III's, proceeds from a perception of defectiveness. As Richard must contend with his deformity, Hieronimo must accommodate his tactics to his relatively low status:

> Nor aught avails it me to menace them,
> Who, as a wintry storm upon a plain,
> Will bear me down with their nobility.

No, no, Hieronimo, thou must enjoin
Thine eyes to observation, and thy tongue
To milder speeches than thy spirit affords.
(III.xiii.39–44)

Like Gyges, Hieronimo makes himself unseen – or at least unno-
ticed – but whets his own perspicacity, a strategy that allows him
an access to power he would otherwise not possess.

At the same time, just as Lorenzo's 'machiavellianism' is founded
upon a primary allegiance not to 'himself alone' but to a particular
social order, Hieronimo's 'machiavellianism' redeploys rather than
repudiates family and class ties. His task, after all, originates in a paternal responsibility to find and punish his son's murderers, and more
generally 'his anguished need for vengeance', as C. L. Barber
remarks, 'is a function of the violation of an original investment of
social piety'.[4] Not surprisingly, then, the Knight Marshal resorts to
procedures that reflect the values and competences of his caste.
Whereas Lorenzo derives his claim to power over others from his
noble rank, Hieronimo grounds his on the intellectual superiority of
the court professional. Eager to differentiate himself from 'vulgar
wits' who cannot settle important legal cases, write court masques,
or effect clever reprisals, he cultivates an intellectually elitist connois-
seurship of violence, privileging secret ingenuity over open brutality.

In fact, the key to Hieronimo's triumph lies in class-bound differences in the way *The Spanish Tragedy's* battling machiavels develop
their fantasies of masterful secret knowledge. Lorenzo thinks of
power in old-fashioned aristocratic terms, as emanating from an
immediate physical presence. He refuses to trust secondhand
reports. When Pedringano informs him that Horatio is Bel-
imperia's lover, he does not simply accept the account as true, but
confirms it by eavesdropping upon the couple in person.
Conversely, he assumes that other people's power will be neu-
tralised by their bodily absence. His matter-of-fact advice to the
lovelorn Balthazar sounds like the solution to a problem in elementary engineering:

Some cause there is that lets you not be loved;
First that must needs be known, and then removed.
(II.i.31–2)

Once Horatio and Pedringano are dead, once Bel-imperia is hustled
out of the way, Lotenzo assumes they need no longer be feared.

And he is right that in the Spanish court, where authority is highly personalised, out of sight seems to be out of mind: Castile does not inquire after his missing daughter, nor the King after his young war hero.

Lorenzo's manipulation of the conditions of visibility and invisibility, however, turns out to be too simple in its premises. He ignores incentives and effects that do not require physical presence: specifically, the ghostly mechanisms of memory, which insistently bring the dead or absent before the minds of the living, and the equally ghostly art of writing, which permits the dead or absent a voice. It fails to occur to Lorenzo that Bel-imperia's loyalty to Don Andrea may make Balthazar a target for her hatred even before Horatio's murder. Nor does he anticipate Hieronimo's refusal to forget his son. His only concern for a document is a pretence: the non-existent pardon he promises Pedringano in order to buy his silence.

Hieronimo, by bureaucratic training and by bitter experience, is more sophisticated. His literary productions – the masque he produces for the Portuguese ambassador and the play he directs at Bel-imperia's wedding – both purport to derive from the history of the Iberian peninsula, reanimating the past in the present.[5] This revivalism and concern for precedent, the Renaissance-humanist proclivities of a poet and a lawyer, likewise sustain Hieronimo's desire for a revenge that protests against equating the past with the forgotten, that returns obsolete calamities to a traumatised present. Specific connections between revenge and literacy are made throughout the play not only in imagery insistently linking blood and ink, but in the practical details of Hieronimo's eventually successful criminal investigation. Hieronimo depends heavily upon the written testimony of Bel-imperia and Pedringano for his enlightenment. No more than Lorenzo is he willing to trust unsupported rumour and conjecture: Bel-imperia's letter does not verify its own claims, but puts him on his guard.

> I therefore will by circumstances try
> What I can gather to confirm this writ.
> (III.ii.48–9)

But Hieronimo's conception of what can count as relevant 'circumstances', and his procedures for acquiring crucial information, are more extensive and flexible than Lorenzo's. Likewise he exploits his own familiarity with textual possibility, and the corresponding naïveté of his opponents, to effect his revenge in the final act.

Kyd's versions of the machiavel thus significantly redelineate the distinction I made earlier between a subjectivity of inwardness and a subjectivity defined by kinship and social place. Whereas in religious polemic personal inwardness, whether subversive or centred upon God, is contrasted with an identity centred upon social relationships of all kinds, in *The Spanish Tragedy* the characters constitute their interiors by selectively introjecting socially available materials and attitudes. Even Bel-imperia's defiance of patriarchal mandates is not invented out of whole cloth. Both her boldness and her calculating use of inferiors are thoroughly aristocratic qualities; she bears a strong family resemblance, in fact, to the brother she so violently resents.

> Yes, second love shall further my revenge.
> I'll love Horatio, my Andrea's friend,
> The more to spite the prince that wrought his end.
> (I.iv.66–8)

Likewise Hieronimo's apparently unexceptionable demand for 'justice' seems a product of his particular social positioning, a professional advocate's idealisation of a law that promises to compensate individuals on the basis of behaviour rather than on the basis of rank. The meticulous contextualisation of Kyd's characters makes it difficult to associate his intriguers with the unfettered, presocial morality-play Vice to whom some stage machiavels, like Richard III, are arguably indebted.[6] The implications of Kyd's characterology are close, in fact, to the claims of recent critics like Stephen Greenblatt, Jonathan Goldberg, Jonathan Dollimore, and Catherine Belsey, who maintain that the structure of personality is a 'cultural artifact' that derives from social structures, rather than anteceding or escaping them.[7]

It is, I would argue, no accident that the contemporary critics whose views most resemble Kyd's should treat traditional religious claims with frank incredulity. One consequence of Kyd's distinctive construal of machiavellian inwardness is that the characters of *Spanish Tragedy* occupy a very different relationship to transcendental truths than do the martyrs and hypocrites of Renaissance religious polemic. Orthodox Renaissance doctrine imagines earthly justice as a pale, flawed derivative of a perfect divine pattern. In this arrangement, God presides over the ultimate court of appeal, definitively punishing criminal secrecy and vindicating obscure righteousness. This attractive conception is not entirely absent from *Spanish Tragedy*. Shortly after his son is murdered, Hieronimo's conviction that the world is a 'mass of public wrongs' naturally leads him to reflect upon another world in which those wrongs might be corrected. The griefstricken Isabella envisages her slaughtered boy singing hymns among the cherubim. Alexandro, too, puts his hopes in heaven, confident at the point of death that a divine overseer will confirm his undisplayable innocence:

> As heavens have known my secret thoughts,
> So am I free from this suggestion.
> (III.i.45–6)

All the virtuous characters, in fact, console themselves in adversity with the thought of a vaguely Christian otherworld presided over by a just, all-knowing God.

The induction and entr'actes, however, give us not the fair, clear-sighted heavenly jurisdiction that Alexandro, Isabella, and Hieronimo in some moods piously anticipate, but a pagan underworld, capriciously administered. In the courts of Spain and Portugal, categories of class, gender, and merit become blurred as male aristocrats degenerate, and females and underlings aspire to heroic status. It seems unlikely that remedies for the resulting inequities will be forthcoming from the bumbling divine bureaucrats of the induction, gravelled as they are by the elementary challenge Don Andrea's case presents to the infernal classification scheme. More vigorous, and more providentially supervisory, is the ominous figure of Revenge.[8] Revenge, however, sleeps through much of the action: allegorically expressing the occult workings of vengeance, but also, surely, its blindness to the details of its victims' offences. The rough, partisan justice that concludes the play condemns Castile, an innocent bystander, as harshly as the true villains, and assigns inapposite penalties even to the real offenders: punishing Lorenzo, for instance, as an aspiring erotomaniac. In *The Spanish Tragedy* 'the absorption of the human into the divine justice machine', G. K. Hunter writes, 'is the destruction of the human'.[9] Hunter is correct in the sense that Kyd's otherworld fails to exemplify humane ideals of justice, and in that Hieronimo is brutalised by being made an instrument of vengeance. In another sense, however, Kyd's 'divine justice machine' is all too human. Kyd seems to share with his more orthodox contemporaries a conviction that the otherworld has an especially intimate relationship to the personal interior. But just as the inwardness that might conceivably provide an escape from an oppressive social formation in *Spanish Tragedy* turns out merely to duplicate its flaws, so Kyd's otherworld reproduces in grander form the favouritism, irrationality, and sheer carelessness of earthly rule.

As Hieronimo increasingly loses faith in procedures of justice he has always taken for granted, the supervenient authority that had seemed to guarantee just outcomes early in the play simply evaporates. The King, alert and responsive to his subjects in the first Act, becomes strangely distracted and unreachable. At the same time it occurs to Hieronimo that the cosmic order from which the King has supposedly derived his legitimacy suffers the same defects:

> Yet still tormented is my tortured soul
> With broken sighs and restless passions,
> That, winged, mount, and, hovering in the air,
> Beat at the windows of the brightest heavens,
> Soliciting for justice and revenge:
> But they are placed in those empyreal heights,
> Where, countermured with walls of diamond,
> I find the place impregnable; and they
> Resist my woes, and give my words no way.
>   (III.vii.10–18)

In place of the orthodox scheme, in which justice cascades downward from god to king to commoner, Hieronimo imagines the demand for equity, and an intuition about what justice means, erupting from below. The action of the play bears him out: the relatively powerless, violently silenced Bel-imperia and Pedringano provide evidence against Lorenzo and Balthazar, and the disregarded Hieronimo exacts the penalty. The weak *need* justice, Kyd seems to suggest, whereas the strong can obtain what they want by any number of means.

The Renaissance conception of machiavellian hypocrisy, as we have already noted, closely associates power with spectatorial prowess. Even as Kyd calls the nature and efficacy of such power into question, he populates his play with supervisory figures, constructing, again and again, scenarios in which voyeurs suppose themselves unseen, but prove actually visible in ways they do not suspect. Thus the courtship of Bel-imperia and Horatio is watched by Lorenzo and Balthazar, who are observed by Revenge and Andrea, who are themselves displayed for the theatre spectators. The spectatorial dynamic in which persons are imagined to achieve their reality is not eradicated – if anything, it is all the more oppressively enforced – but the reassuring connections *Richard III* implies between that dynamic and an ultimately beneficent universe are ruptured. For unless omniscience is linked with the effective administration of transcendental justice, it threatens rather than fortifies human hopes for personal vindication. To keep Pedringano from informing upon him, Lorenzo cynically sends him a boy with a pardon supposedly enclosed in a black box. But the boy surreptitiously opens the box and finds it empty. The box that pretends to contain an authoritative, salvific text may be understood as a figure for the opaque, perjured subjectivity of the machiavel, but also, perhaps, as a comment upon the hollow promises of a Christianity *The Spanish Tragedy* both evokes and renounces.

The scepticism, even nihilism, of *The Spanish Tragedy* makes the machiavellian adaptation to hostile circumstances seem more justified than it does in *Richard III*. In a Christian universe, in which virtue imitates a divine pattern, the machiavel is a scandalous aberration. His blindness to supervising power must be elaborately accounted for: as an innate depravity commensurate with physical deformity, as a punishment for the sins of a whole society, as the perverse logic of an individual traumatically alienated from normal affiliations and affections. In the world of *The Spanish Tragedy*, riddled from the top down by hypocrisy and manipulation, Hieronimo's behaviour seems the comprehensibly desperate adaptation of a decent man to a bad world. What replaces the missing omniscience is a struggle among competing, incommensurable perspectives, all demonstrably limited, all conditioned by habit, bias, and self-interest. Without any transcendental guarantee of absolute equity, without any hope of an all-knowing supervisor in whom justice and mercy are miraculously combined, intuitions about just treatment become not imperfect human reflections of the divine perfection, but fallible forms of myopic and narcissistic special pleading that may or may not happen to be rewarded. The mystery in *Spanish Tragedy*, then, is not where 'machiavellianism' originates, but rather where convictions about order, virtue, and justice derive.

For the weird persistence of those convictions, despite their apparent groundlessness, help determine Hieronimo's calamitous course of action in the final act of the play. It is worth looking carefully at his final, extravagantly brutal display to see what it suggests both about his own vengeful endeavour, and about Kyd's conception of his theatrical project. The nuptials between Balthazar and Bel-imperia are supposed harmoniously to combine affection with expediency, passion with dynastic ambition. As such they are no different from most court spectacles, which ordinarily depict a seamless convergence between the subject's desires and the sovereign's interests. Everything that resists this complacent vision must be rigorously suppressed: in *The Spanish Tragedy*, the deserving subordinate's unaddressed demand for justice, and the bride's abiding hatred of her criminal bridegroom. Hieronimo's 'Tragedy of Soliman', then, voices what has been silenced, releases what has been thwarted. A form traditionally designed to depict the world as seen from the perspective of the rulers is turned upside-down to express the perspective of the ruled. The effect is to deny the comprehensiveness of the sovereign's vision, and to insist upon the significance of the subject's occluded point of view. The playwright's hidden plot begs to be set against the ideologically motivated concealments of court spectacle, his ferocity against the violence with which the two victim-conspirators have been stifled and overridden. Just as Kyd's machiavels do not disavow their social positioning, but rather create their interiors by a process of introjection, Hieronimo does not simply renounce court spectacle, but *infiltrates* it in order to turn it against itself.

To their betters, Hieronimo and Bel-imperia do not count; that is, they do not constitute independent centres of consciousness that need to be taken seriously. Thus Hieronimo's revenge consists not merely of killing Horatio's murderers, but of enlightening his oppressors in the significance of their mistake. In order to convey such a lesson, Hieronimo must establish some common ground with them – must attempt to make them see him as like themselves. In an earlier scene, Hieronimo had discovered a capacity to cross class boundaries and commiserate with Bazulto, a powerless and impoverished old man whose son had, like his own, been slaughtered.

> Here, take my handkercher and wipe thine eyes,
> Whiles wretched I, in thy mishaps, may see
> The lively portrait of my dying self.
> (III.xiii.83–5)

The force of empathy seems to propel the confrontation into the register of the aesthetic: the Old Man is Hieronimo's 'portrait'. The ambiguous word 'lively', which could mean either 'living' or 'life-like', suggests that mimetic representation heightens rather than diminishes real-life pertinence. The uncanny interview with the Old Man conflates the diverse intensities of actual suffering and fictional contrivance.

In the last act, in a fable that turns out to be true, Hieronimo attempts to enforce upon the rulers of Spain and Portugal the acknowledgement of likeness that had overcome him spontaneously in his encounter with Bazulto – as if sharing his affliction will make them comprehend his plight.

> As dear to me was my Horatio,
> As yours, or yours, or yours, my lord, to you.
> (IV.iv.168–9)

Ranging the corpse of his socially inferior son alongside the bodies of the heirs apparent, Hieronimo stages and voices a radically levelling sentiment: that one dead child is very like another, that paternal love feels essentially the same for noble and commoner, that his suffering is worth as much as the suffering of princes.

> With soonest speed I hasted to the noise,
> Where hanging on a tree I found my son,
> Through-girt with wounds, and slaughtered as you see.
> And grieved I, think you, at this spectacle?
> Speak, Portuguese, whose loss resembles mine:
> If thou canst weep upon thy Balthazar,
> 'Tis like I wailed for my Horatio.
> And you, my lord, whose reconciléd son
> Marched in a net, and thought himself unseen …
> How can you brook our play's catastrophe?
> (IV.iv.110–16)

Hieronimo's strict talion – son for son, spectacle for spectacle, wail for wail – ignores disparities between one person and another, insisting upon equivalence and substitutability. Balthazar and Lorenzo are higher in rank than Horatio, but just as dead by the end of Hieronimo's play. The climax of his stagecraft is the sudden and surprising revelation of Horatio's corpse – not a verbal recollection, but an actual corporeal presence. His stubborn emphasis on the body and its vicissitudes in the final scene of *Spanish Tragedy* relies upon an intuition which, as we shall see, Shakespeare will find attractive in later plays: that human beings despite their differences share an experience of embodiment, a 'common human lot' that can provide a basis both for social cohesion and for theatrical pedagogy.

One effect of Hieronimo's seditious infiltration of court spectacle, then, is to suggest an alternative to what has become, in the course of the play, the radically atomised individualism of the Spanish court. In this respect his theatricality differs fundamentally from Richard's: whereas Richard's theatre, revelling in trickery, insists upon the distance between himself and others, Hieronimo's obliterates, in a sumptuously bloody catastrophe, the ideological gap between royal and subjected flesh. Kyd apparently recognises that such drama of fellow feeling, although it may seem to rely upon a communal impulse, hardly conduces to the maintenance of social stability: just the opposite, in fact, insofar as granting the full humanity of one's inferiors tends to call into question the naturalness and propriety of disproportionate entitlements. English theatre in the decades after Kyd seizes enthusiastically upon this conundrum, cultivating empathy in a large, diverse group of spectators with unprecedentedly naturalistic characters across boundaries of class, sex, and nationality. This theatrical tradition is continually drawn to plots of usurpation and revenge, plots which insist upon the capacity of the marginalised and the alien for independent agency. Its formal indecorousness, its mingling of kings and clowns, thus often seems almost *per se* levelling or subversive, even when the overt lessons of such mingling seem to reinforce authoritarian hierarchies.

In *Spanish Tragedy*, however, Hieronimo's theatre fails to educate its audience in the way he claims he has intended it to do. 'Soliman and Perseda' is, in fact, virtually guaranteed to miscarry. Hieronimo arranges for each of the characters to speak a different language: unintelligible to one another and to the audience, sundered, as in the Babel legend Hieronimo himself invokes, from originary or conclusive sources of meaning. Even while 'Soliman and Perseda' urges the parallel between Horatio's vulnerability and the vulnerability of his superiors, between Hieronimo's grief and the grief of kings and princes, it simultaneously emphasises the irreducible separateness of revenger and victim, between one who punishes and one who endures castigation. To show the King and Castile what the death of a son feels like, Hieronimo has to harden himself to the prospect of their suffering, to refuse to acknowledge a pain his own experience has uniquely qualified him to anticipate. Likewise, and unsurprisingly, his onstage audience resists his invitation to see his grievances duplicated in their own. 'Why hast thou done this undeserving deed?' ask the King and the Viceroy, after Hieronimo has spent seventy-five lines explaining his reasons, and Lorenzo's and Balthazar's deserts. The apparent obtuseness of the royal audience at this moment has led some editors to suspect textual corruption;[10] but perhaps Kyd is merely dramatising a hopeless inability to grasp Hieronimo's theatrical point. The King, Castile, and the Viceroy imagine that an erstwhile loyal servant has shown himself to be radically alien. They cannot conceive of him as a suffering father like themselves but only as a 'traitor', a 'damnéd, bloody murderer', a 'wretch'.

As pedagogy, then, Hieronimo's playlet is a failure; but as insurrection it is eminently successful. The denouement of *Spanish Tragedy* suggests that for Kyd, the connection between a challenge to authority and a highly developed sense of personal inwardness is not accidental but absolutely intrinsic. Recognising what one does not share with one's superiors – the significance of experiences that are irreducibly one's own – upsets the deference to others' interests that is the essence of subordination. Understanding, at the same time, what one *does* share with one's superiors – a common bodily vulnerability – provides the basis of an effective defiance. Pressed to reveal more than he wishes to, Hieronimo first bites out his tongue and then uses a penknife to kill himself: violently repudiating first verbal and then written means of expression. Hieronimo's suicide 'ruptures', in his word, the transfer of inside to outside, protecting his hard-won privacy. A creature that seems wholly realised through forms of theatrical and rhetorical display finally declares the insufficiency of those forms. It is a twist in Kyd's conception of his art that Shakespeare may recall when he eventually bases his own revenge play on a Kydian prototype and creates a character who repudiates 'trappings and suits' in favour of 'that within'.

There is despair in *The Spanish Tragedy*, as there is in *Richard III*, but there is also, strangely, a kind of triumph. If a beneficent providence does not exist, there is little hope for the redress of injustice in this world or the next; at the same time, divine punishment for self-assertion is less automatic and thus perhaps less fearsome. Instead of reassuring his audience with a theologico-theatrical fiction of beneficent omniscience, Kyd acquaints it with the disquieting possibility that it is caught in the same ironies that doom his characters, victims of powers that are not necessarily either just or merciful, and whom they are incapable of understanding. If *Richard III* more faithfully reproduces the spectatorial economy of late sixteenth-century religious polemic, *The Spanish Tragedy* more effectively stages its deepest fears.

From Katharine Eisaman Maus, *Inwardness and Theater in the English Renaissance* (Chicago and London, 1995), pp. 55–70.

NOTES

[This essay is taken from Katherine Eiasaman Maus's monograph *Inwardness and Theater in the English Renaissance*. Maus studies works by Kyd, Shakespeare, Marlowe, Jonson and Milton alongside early modern pamphlets and medical and legal treatises and documents with a specific focus: the dialectic of exterior display and interior authenticity. In so doing, Maus places her analysis at the heart of current preoccupations of literary critics working in the field of early modern studies. In particular, the issues of subjectivity and identity preoccupy key works of criticism that are touchstones for many of the contributors to this volume – Catherine Belsey's *The Subject of Tragedy* (1985), Jonathan Dollimore's *Radical Tragedy* (1984) and Francis Barker's *The Tremulous Private Body* (1984). Maus disputes the claims made by some cultural materialists and new historicists that the rhetoric of inwardness, of an essential self, is to be discounted, and that an early modern consciousness could only conceive of itself as a social being. For Maus, the stage 'machiavel' provides a powerful counter-argument, personifying as he does 'a radical, unprincipled estrangement of internal truth from external manifestation', Maus, *Inwardness and Theater*, p. 35.

As well as intervening in debates about subjectivity, Maus's essay provides acute insights into other aspects of Kyd's remarkable play. She deals with its class politics, and also touches on its religious dimensions, presenting the play as a work of dark pessimism, sceptical of orthodox beliefs about a providential God: the whole play, she reminds us, is presided over by the ghost of the slaughtered Andrea, and the figure of Revenge (who sleeps through much of the performance). For some readers, the departure from Christian orthodoxy may bring to mind Kyd's sometime room-mate, the reputed atheist Christopher Marlowe (perhaps those heretical papers found in their shared lodgings, which Kyd disowned and pinned on Marlowe, were Kyd's after all). Finally, Maus alerts us to the subversive potential of the revenger figure, since the hero of the revenge tragedy 'comes to self-consciousness by first experiencing, and then effecting, a profound alteration in his relationship to authority'. Quotations from *The Spanish Tragedy* are taken from Katharine Eisaman Maus (ed.), *Four Revenge Tragedies* (Oxford, 1995), and citations from *Richard III* refer to David Bevington (ed.), *Complete Works of Shakespeare*. Ed.]

1. [The term 'Gygean' is explained by reference to an earlier chapter in Maus's book. She cites the Catholic Myles Haggard, writing during

Mary Tudor's reign, who refers to Plato's account of Gyges. Falling into a crack in the earth, Gyges came upon a brazen horse. When he opened the side of the animal, he found a huge human corpse, and from a finger of this body he drew a ring which he found gave him the power to make himself invisible. Gyges used this magic ring to sleep with the wife of the king of Lydia. For Haggard, Gyges represented the hypocrisy of the Protestants. In the pages preceding this extract, Maus has studied Shakespeare's Richard III as a kind of Gyges, noting his ability to 'circumvent the ordinary social restraints upon his behaviour' and remarking how his 'subsequent career rehearses Gyges's almost exactly: the seduction of a predecessor's wife, regicide, usurpation' (Maus, *Inwardness and Theater in the English Renaissance* [Chicago and London, 1995], p. 50 – Ed.]

2. For this change in attitude during the sixteenth century, see Mark H. Curtis, *Oxford and Cambridge in Transition* (Oxford, 1959), esp. pp. 265–81; Joan Simon, *Education and Society in Tudor England* (Cambridge, 1961), pp. 333–68; and Laurence Stone, *The Crisis of the Aristocracy* (Oxford, 1965), pp. 672–724.

3. In a paper written in 1976 but not published until 1994, William Empson finds this point so curious that to account for it he proposes that the printed text of *The Spanish Tragedy* is a version massively cut by the censor. See John Haffenden (ed.), *Essays on Renaissance Literature, Vol. Two: The Drama* (Cambridge, 1994), pp. 41–65.

4. C. L. Barber, *Creating Elizabethan Tragedy: The Theatre of Marlowe and Kyd* (Chicago, 1988), p. 143.

5. For an alternative view *contrasting* Hieronimo's activities as a court entertainer with his activities as a lawyer, see Kay Stockholder, ' "Yet Can He Write": Reading the Silences in *The Spanish Tragedy*', *American Imago*, 47 (1990), 93–124. Despite Stockholder's strange and logically superfluous insistence that the whole play constitutes Hieronimo's dream, her analysis of class relationships in *The Spanish Tragedy* is very acute.

6. See, for instance, Bernard Spivack, *Shakespeare and the Analogy of Evil* (New York, 1958).

7. See Stephen Greenblatt, *Renaissance Self-Fashioning* (Chicago, 1981); Jonathan Dollimore, *Radical Tragedy: Religion, Ideology and Power in the Drama of Shakespeare and his Contemporaries* (Chicago, 1984); Catherine Belsey, *The Subject of Tragedy: Identity and Difference in Renaissance Drama* (New York, 1985). The phrase 'cultural artefact' is Clifford Geertz's in *The Interpretation of Cultures* (New York, 1973).

8. For another view of this issue, see Geoffrey Aggeler, 'The Eschatological Crux in *The Spanish Tragedy*', *JEGP*, 86 (1987), 319–31.

9. G. K. Hunter, 'Ironies of Justice in *The Spanish Tragedy*', *Renaissance Drama*, 8 (1965), 101.

10. See, for instance, Philip Edwards (ed.), *The Spanish Tragedy* (London, 1959) and Anrew Cairncross (ed.), *the First Part of Hieronimo and The Spanish Tragedy* (Lincoln, 1967).

5

The Revenger's Tragedy: Providence, Parody and Black Camp

JONATHAN DOLLIMORE

Many critics have felt that if *The Revenger's Tragedy*[1] cannot be shown to be fundamentally orthodox then it cannot help but be hopelessly decadent. If, for example, it can be shown to affirm morality-play didacticism and its corresponding metaphysical categories (and hence idealist mimesis), an otherwise very disturbing play is rendered respectable. Moreover, the embarrassing accusation of a critic like Archer – that the play is 'the product either of sheer barbarism, or of some pitiable psychopathic perversion' – can be countered with the alternative view that it is a 'late morality' where 'the moral scheme is everything'.[2]

Numerous critics have tried to substantiate the morality interpretation by pointing to (i) the orthodox moral perspective which is, allegedly, implicit in characters' responses to heaven, hell, sin and damnation, and (ii) the extensive use of ironic peripeteias which allegedly destroy evil according to a principle of poetic justice. I want to challenge in turn each of these arguments.[3]

PROVIDENCE AND PARODY

In Vindice's rhetorical invocations to heaven there is a distinctive sense of mockery:

> Why does not heaven turn black, or with a frown
> Undo the world? – why does not earth start up,
> And strike the sins that tread upon't?
> (II.i.254–6)

The implied parody of the providential viewpoint, the *caricature* of the vengeful god, becomes stronger as the play progresses:

> **Vindice**   O, thou almighty patience! 'Tis my wonder
>   That such a fellow, impudent and wicked,
>   Should not be cloven as he stood, or with
>   A secret wind burst open.
>   Is there no thunder left, or is't kept up
>   In stock for heavier vengeance? [*Thunder sounds*] There it goes!
> (IV.ii.194–9)

Here the traditional invocation to heaven becomes a kind of public stage-prompt ('Is there no thunder left …') and God's wrath an undisguised excuse for ostentatious effect. In performance such lines beg for a facetious Vindice, half turned towards the audience and deliberately directing its attention to the crudity of the stage convention involved.[4] In effect, the conception of a heavenly, retributive justice is being reduced to a parody of stage effects. In the following pun on 'claps' heaven is brought down to the level of a passive audience applauding the melodrama: 'When thunder claps, heaven likes the tragedy' (V.iii.47). Vindice becomes the agent of the parody and is invested with a theatrical sense resembling the dramatist's own: 'Mark, thunder! Dost know thy *cue*, thou big-voic'd cryer? / Duke's groans are thunder's *watchwords*' (V.iii.42–3, my italics; cf. Vindice's earlier line: 'When the bad bleeds, then is the tragedy good' [III.v.205]).

It gives an intriguing flexibility to Vindice's role, with the actor momentarily stepping through the part and taking on – without abandoning the part – a playwright's identity. This identity shift is instrumental to the parody: at precisely the moments when, if the providential references are to convince, the dramatic illusion needs to be strongest, Vindice (as 'playwright') shatters it. He does so by prompting for thunder from the stage, by representing thunder as a participant in a melodrama waiting for its 'cue', and by re-casting the traditionally 'frowning' heaven as a spectator clapping the action. The convention linking 'heaven', 'thunder' and 'tragedy' is, together with its related stage effects, rendered facile; providentialism is obliquely but conclusively discredited.[5] The letter of providentialist orthodoxy and, perhaps, of censorship, is respected but in performance their spirit is subverted through a form of parody akin to 'the privy mark of irony' described in the Dedication to Beaumont's *The Knight of the Burning Pestle*.

Peter Lisca, in seeing the references to thunder and heaven as eliminating any doubt as to the play's 'sincere moral framework',[6] seems to miss an irony in tone and delivery which, in performance, would actually contradict the kind of moral conclusions he draws. Discussions of the extent to which a play is indebted to older dramatic forms are often marred in this way by an inadequate discrimination between the dramatic use of a convention and wholesale acceptance of the world view that goes (or *went*) with it. Obviously, the distinction becomes more than usually crucial when, as is the case here, the convention is being subjected to parody.

This play also exposes the hypocritical moral appeals which characters make to the providential order. An audience will, for example, simply *hear* the sermonising rhetoric of the Duchess' attack on illegitimacy:

> O what a grief 'tis, that a man should live
> But once i' th' world, and then to live a bastard,
> The curse o' the womb, the thief of nature,
> Begot against the seventh commandment,
> Half-dammn'd in the conception, by the justice
> Of that unbribed everlasting law.
>
> (I.ii.159–64)

The hollowness of this rhetoric is, of course, compounded by the sheer hypocrisy of its delivery: the Duchess is seen speaking not from the pulpit, but in the act of seducing her stepson and inciting him to murder his own father.

Still in Act I there is a moral posturing more revealing even than that of the Duchess. Antonio, celebrating publicly his wife's 'virtue' (she has committed suicide after being raped) is seen to value it even more than her life. 'Chastity' and 'honour' emerge in fact as the ideological imposition and self-representation of the male ego in a male dominated world. What compels us to consider the episode

thus is not the simple facts themselves but the fact of their caricature; thrown into exaggerated relief 'honour' and 'chastity' are
turned inside out and held up for inspection. As with the interroga-
tive representation of providence, parody here invites distrust,
ironic distance and refusal. Thus, discovering his wife's dead body
to 'certain lords' Antonio exclaims:

> be sad witnesses
> Of a fair, comely building newly fall'n ...
> Piero   That virtuous lady!
> Antonio   Precedent for wives!
> (I.iv.1–7)

A language of artificial grandeur reeking of affected grief tells us
that what is being celebrated is not her innate virtue but her dutiful
suicide, her obedience to male-imposed terms of sexual honour:

> Antonio   I joy
> In this one happiness above the rest ...
> That, being an old man, I'd a wife so chaste.
> (I.iv.74–7)

Chastity in this court involves a life-denying insularity dictated by
male vanity, not disinterested virtue. Again, it involves a hypocrisy
masked by an appeal to the providential order: 'Virginity is par-
adise, lock'd up. / You cannot come by yourselves without
fee, / And 'twas *decreed* that man should keep the key' (II.i.157–9).
Male relations of power and possession are sanctioned in terms of
female virtue and providential design, while the death of Antonio's
wife, though presented as the cause of ensuing conflict, is in fact the
excuse for its continuation. In effect she is the instrument of a
power struggle quite independent of her.

Peripeteias allegedly constitute the structural evidence for the
providential interpretation of the play. Lisca for example has
argued that its moral attitude 'proceeds from a Christian point of
view (the Puritan)' and that the peripeteias indicate 'the intestinal
division of evil itself, a division which while seeming to lead to multiplication ironically ends in cross cancellation'.[7] Often the assumption behind this approach is that peripeteia possessed an inherently
providential meaning. This was not the case with Aristotle's
definition of it and nor, at this time, with its use in the Italian
novelle and the plays influenced by them.[8] In *The Revenger's*

Tragedy the ironic reversal is manifestly bound up with Vindice's (and the theatre's) sense of artistry and 'jest' (V.i.64) and what Nicholas Brooke characterises as a humour 'in marvellously bad taste'.[9] In particular the art of revenge is seen to aim at a vicious blend of the appropriate and the unexpected. Vindice's advice to Lussurioso on how to kill the Duchess and Spurio (whom they expect to find in bed together) is an extreme case in point: 'Take 'em finely, finely now ... Softly, my lord, and you may take 'em twisted ... O 'twill be glorious / To kill 'em doubled, when they're heap'd. Be soft, / My Lord' (II.ii.169 – II.iii.4). Here both peripeteia and poetic justice are construed in terms of a villainous aesthetic delight. It is a mode of appropriation which makes for a kind of double subversion: the play not only refuses two principles of moralistic drama, it presses them ignominiously into the service *of* play. Likewise with its own formal closure: 'Just is the law above!' cries Antonio with orthodox solemnity in relation to the series of murders in the final scene; ' 'twas somewhat witty carried, though we say it' replies Vindice coyly, referring to one of the same. In that reply, as elsewhere, the play's mocking intelligence and acute sense of parody – the kind that 'hits / Past the apprehension of indifferent wits' (V.i.134) – converge in a 'witty' subversion of Antonio's crude, providential rationalisation.

DESIRE AND DEATH

Inseparable from this play's subversion of some of the conventions of idealist mimesis is an alternative representation of the relations which bind sexuality, power and death. It centres on the frenetic activity of an introverted society encompassed by shadows and ultimately darkness – the 'heedless fury' and 'Wildfire at midnight' which Hippolito describes (II.ii.172). The Court, 'this luxurious circle', is a closed world where energy feeds back on itself perpetuating the 'unnatural' act in unnatural surroundings: the location of the Duke's death is an 'unsunned lodge', 'Wherein 'tis night at noon'. Decay and impermanence stress the futility of each person's obsessive struggle for power. Yet there is no anticipation of otherworldly compensation, Junior's cynical rejection of the relevance of heaven to his impending death (III.iv.70–4) being typical. The play's view of mortality is reminiscent of Schopenhauer; I quote briefly from his *Parerga and Paralipomena* simply to emphasise that it is

not necessarily a view which entails a conception of man as inherently sinful or governed by divine law. The experience
Schopenhauer describes is a contingent one with secular
boundaries:

> The vanity of existence is revealed in the whole form existence
> assumes ... in the fleeting present as the sole form in which actuality
> exists, in the contingency and relativity of all things ... in continual
> desire without satisfaction; in the continual frustration of striving of
> which life consists ... Thus its form is essentially unceasing *motion*
> without any possibility of that repose which we continually strive
> after ... existence is typified by unrest ... Yet what a difference there
> is between our beginning and our end! We begin in the madness of
> carnal desire and the transport of voluptuousness, we end in the dis-
> solution of all our parts and the musty stench of corpses.[10]

One is reminded too of the more restrained, yet somehow almost as
pessimistic, account of London by Tourneur (or whoever that 'C.T.'
was)[11] at the opening of 'Laugh and Lie Downe: Or, the Worldes
Folly':

> Now in this Towne were many sundrie sorts of people of all ages; as
> Old, and young, and middle age: men, women and children: which
> did eate, and drinke, and make a noyse, and die ... they were
> Creatures that serued the time, followed Shaddowes, fitted humours,
> hoped of Fortune, and found, what? I cannot tell you.[12]

In *The Revenger's Tragedy* this sense of court life as futile striv-
ing is intensified by the dramatist's insistence that here there is no
alternative: activity occupying the immediate dramatic focus – 'this
present minute' – is made, through graphic 'off-stage' description,
to appear as just a bolder representation of that which pervades the
rest of life:

> My lord, after long search, wary inquiries,
> And politic siftings, I made choice of yon fellow,
> Whom I guess rare for many deep employments;
> This our age swims within him ...
> He is so near kin to this present minute.
>
>   (I.iii.21–6)

Moreover, characters move into the line of vision already 'charged'
with a common motivating energy – sexual, aggressive or otherwise
– which varies in intensity only depending on whether it is the dra-

matic foreground or background that they occupy. It is, consequently, a world whose sense ends with its activity – a world, that
is, whose senselessness becomes instantly apparent when activity
culminates in death. Vindice highlights this through a detached
awareness which Tourneur exploits to full effect as part of a structural interplay between movement and stasis.

Movement illustrates repeatedly the forces that impel, but simultaneously constrain and destroy people; the most extreme is the
sexual – the 'riot' of the blood (I.i.11). 'I am past my depth in lust, /
And I must swim or drown' says Lussurioso (I.iii.88–9), testifying
to the destructive yet compulsive force of desire. Social forces are
powerfully realised as either grinding poverty or thwarted ambition
– both of which render the individual vulnerable to court exploitation. Thus we see Hippolito being sent from court –

> To seek some strange-digested fellow forth,
> Of ill-contented nature, either disgrac'd
> In former times, or by new grooms displac'd –
> (I.i.76–8)

while for Lussurioso 'slaves are but nails, to drive out one another'.
For his second slave he demands one who,

> being of black condition, suitable
> To want and ill content, hope of preferment
> Will grind him to an edge.
> (IV.i.69–71)

Both Machiavellian intrigue and lust are depicted as inherent
aspects of the frenetic movement and become inextricably linked
with it in imagination:

> **Vindice**   my brain
> Shall swell with strange invention; I will move it
> Till I expire with speaking, and drop down
> Without a word to save me; but I'll work –
> **Lussurioso**   We thank thee, and will raise thee.
> (I.iii.119–23)

The point is stressed throughout with the recurrence of that word
'swell' in imagery of tumescence: 'drunken adultery / I feel it swell
me' (I.ii.190–1); 'I would embrace thee for a near employment, / And thou shouldst swell in money' (I.iii.76–7); 'Thy veins

are swell'd with lust, this shall unfill 'em' (II.ii.94); see also Act, I, scene ii, line 113 and Act IV, scene i, line 63.

Movement involves an incessant drive for self-fulfilment through domination of others.[13] It is also represented as a process of inevitable disintegration; dissolution and death seem not in opposition to life's most frantic expression but inherent within it: 'O, she was able to ha' made a usurer's son / *Melt* all his patrimony in a kiss' (I.i.26–7, my italics); 'I have seen patrimonies washed a-pieces, fruit fields turned into bastards, and, in a world of acres, not so much dust due to the heir 'twas left to, as would well gravel a petition' (I.ii.50–3). The assertion of life energy does not stand in simple contrast to the process of disintegration but rather seems to feed – to become – the very process itself.[14]

Vindice's silk-worm image makes for the same kind of emphasis at a point immediately prior to the height of the dramatic action (the bizarre murder of the Duke with a skull, poisoned and disguised as a 'country lady'): 'Does the silk worm expend her yellow labours / For thee? For thee does she undo herself?' (III.v.72–3).[15] Dissolution, the sense of helpless movement and lack of purpose are all concentrated in this image. The sense of uncontrollable movement towards dissolution also recalls Vindice's earlier lines where drunkenness releases barely conscious desire: 'Some father dreads not (gone to bed in wine) / To slide from the mother, and cling the daughter-in-law' (I.iii.58–9). Here, in lines whose meaning is reinforced by the stress falling on 'slide' and 'cling', the involuntary action of a human being is reduced (casually yet startlingly) to the reflex action typical of an insentient being. In all these ways the futility and destructiveness of social life seem to have their source in some deeper condition of existence; at the very heart of life itself there moves a principle of self-stultification.

Contrary to this use of movement, the stasis with which it contrasts involves a form of detachment, the medium of insight and a limited foresight. Whereas to be caught up in the temporal process is to be blindly preoccupied with the present 'minute' (a recurring expression – see especially Act I, scene ii, line 168; Act I, scene iii, line 26; Act I, scene iv, line 39; Act III, scene v, line 75), the brief moments of inaction allow for a full realisation of just how self-stultifying is this world's expenditure of energy, of just how poor is the benefit of the 'bewitching minute'. It is reflected, initially, in the way Vindice's opening commentary is delivered from a point of detached awareness – a detachment represented spatially with him withdrawn into the shadowed region of the stage and directing attention at the procession. And at Act III, scene v, lines 50 ff., just before the (by now) anticipated climax, his own contemplative state directs attention to the lifelessness of the skull, a wholly static but tangible representation of death and a striking visual contrast to the frenetic activity of life in this court. Insight of this kind is limited to Vindice; by others it is actually evaded. Thus whereas Vindice realises that 'man's happiest when he forgets himself' (IV.iv.84) but cannot in fact forget himself for very long, Ambitioso checks his realisation that 'there is nothing sure in mortality, but mortality' with a resolve to action: 'Come, throw off clouds now, brother, think of vengeance, / And deeper settled hate' (III.vi.89–90; 92–3).

There is one view of the characters in this play which sees them as morality type abstractions – 'simply monstrous embodiments of Lust, Pride and Greed'.[16] But their subhumanity indicates more: displaying considerable desire, some intelligence but little self-awareness, they fit this play's depiction of life lived obsessively and destructively within the dislocated social 'minute'. Moreover such awareness as does exist is turned inward, brought to bear on immediate desire, but always in a way that fails to discover a unified, autonomous self. Instead their soliloquies indicate the forces which in-form and dislocate them. The Duchess, for example, is first seen as a voice of 'natural' mercy pleading for her 'youngest, dearest son' (I.ii.103). But in her first soliloquy, while presumably retaining this affection, she becomes the ruthless schemer intent on having her husband killed by his bastard son and herself having an illicit – in the terms of the play, 'incestuous' (I.ii.175) – sexual relationship with the latter. Moments later, the bastard, Spurio, accedes to both proposals only to then repudiate the Duchess just as she repudiated her Duke: 'Stepmother, I consent to thy desires, / I love thy mischief well, but I hate thee' (I.ii.193–4). Thus Spurio casts himself as the avenger, making the appropriate alliance, but in so doing makes a distinction in commitment that stalls all possibility of empathy. In the same soliloquy, brilliant, imaginative compression of mood and image suggests a dissolving of Spurio's present consciousness into the very circumstances of his conception: '... some stirring dish / Was my first father ... / ... drunken adultery / I feel it swell me' (ll.181–2; 190–1). 'Impudent wine and lust' now infuse his veins such that 'Adultery is my nature' (l.179), while alliteration and stressed single-syllable words give a rhythmic insistence blending into the 'withdrawing hour' to insinuate exactly the concealed activity in which he was 'stol'n softly':

> In such a whisp'ring and withdrawing hour,
> When base male-bawds kept sentinel at stair-head,
> Was I stol'n softly
>
> (I.ii.187–9)

Imagery of sexuality becomes this play's most powerful signifier of a society deriving initial impetus from, yet finally stultified by, the contradictions within it. Thus the old Duke is sexually 'parch'd and juiceless' – one with 'scarce blood enough to live upon' (I.i.9, 10) – yet his very impotence is paradoxically though not untypically the source of a sterile and destructive life force.

Given a world of dislocated energy as its dramatic subject, what kind of formal unity is such a play likely to possess? The answer is suggested in Vindice. Disguise, intelligence and the capacity to see the futility of others' endeavour, give him a kind of freedom. Yet it is at best partial and probably illusory, being, in effect, a knowledge of the fate of the society to which he is inescapably confined. It is as such that, at the play's close, he surrenders his life with comparative indifference, a surrender recalling his earlier expression of estrangement: 'My life's unnatural to me, e'en compelled / As if I lived now when I should be dead' (I.i.120–1). Unemployed and with his family in poverty he articulates the tensions and contradictions of his world, becoming the focal point for those dimensions of the play which, though inextricably linked will not – indeed, cannot – be finally resolved into a single coherent 'vision'. Even when he is most apparently an agent – as for example in the famous fifth scene of Act III – he is really a victim and he knows it; hence his sharply alternating moods: detached, exhilarated, despairing, sadistic. Vindice as malcontented satirist is corrupted by the society he condemns because inescapably a part of that society; to put it another way, he condemns it because he is corrupted – inevitably corrupted by it. In this respect satirist figures like Vindice and Flamineo (*The White Devil*) share much in common with other malcontented rebels like, for example, Antonio (*Antonio's Revenge*), Bussy d'Ambois, and Edmund (*King Lear*): estrangement from society, whether because of poverty, dispossession, unemployment, injustice or thwarted ambition, provokes in them an aggressive reaction; heroic or criminal it adds up to the same thing: a desperate bid for reintegration. In its vindictiveness this bid becomes the contradictory attempt to destroy that which they are within and which they cannot survive without. The experience of estrangement reveals on the one hand the futility and worthlessness of the existing social order, on the other the estranged subject's dependence upon it; most extremely, to be reintegrated is to embrace destruction. Yet the alternative – estrangement itself pushed to an extreme – leads to poverty, mental collapse or suicide.

In *The Revenger's Tragedy* a vital irony and a deep pessimism exist in disjunction; if they are held together dramatically they are not in any sense aesthetically integrated, either in tone or character. And if there is an attitude yoking them by violence together it is not that of the unified sensibility once thought to characterise the period, but rather that of a subversive black camp. It is sophisticated and self-conscious, at once mannered and chameleon; it celebrates the artificial and the delinquent; it delights in a play full of innuendo, perversity and subversion; by mimicking and misappropriating their glibness it exposes the hypocrisy and deception of the pious; through parody it declares itself radically sceptical of ideological policing though not independent of the social reality which such scepticism simultaneously discloses. Vindice, living that reality in terms of social displacement and exploitation, lives also the extreme instability of his society and is led thereby to meditate on mutability and death. Even the meditation takes on a subversive edge because transferred from the study to that place to which Vindice's displacement has led him: the domain of sexuality and power, the 'accursed palace' where his brother finds him 'Still sighing o'er death's vizard' (I.i.30,50). Just as displacement compels action so the meditation is, as it were, enacted. Yet no one in the process is allowed the role of heroic despair; in relation to no one is human suffering made to vindicate human existence. To that extent *The Revenger's Tragedy* is beyond – or before – 'tragedy'.

From Jonathan Dollimore, *Radical Tragedy* (1984; Brighton and Chicago, 1989), pp. 139–150.

NOTES

[Jonathan Dollimore's discussion of *The Revenger's Tragedy* is taken from his book *Radical Tragedy*, which stands alongside *Political Shakespeare* as a key foundation text in the development of the movement known as cultural materialism. *Political Shakespeare*, co-edited by Dollimore and Alan

Sinfield, was published in 1985, a year after *Radical Tragedy*. Both books can be read as responses to the political climate of their time. Deeply and vociferously committed to left-wing politics at the height of Thatcherism, Dollimore and Sinfield challenged the essentialist principles of traditional criticism, revealing the extent to which those principles, in their conservatism, could be understood to be complicit with the political hegemony.

Adopting a familiar cultural materialist strategy, Dollimore locates a fissure in the legacy of criticism of this play, as critics line up either to dismiss it as decadent, or else praise it for its orthodox moral *schema*. Drawing attention to the text's frequent forays into self-parody, Dollimore describes the play's arch self-consciousness as 'subversive black camp' which celebrates 'the artificial and the delinquent' (p. 117), a description anticipating the development of queer theory in the early 1990s. When Vindice talks of heaven applauding the tragedy, he is acknowledging the artifice of the play and inviting the audience to share the joke. He may also, Dollimore suggests, be engaging in a more radical critique that questions not just the nature of theatre, but the validity of providential belief. A similar technique – challenge via parody – may also inform the approach to gender ideology in the play, with terms like 'honour' and 'chastity' being cast into ironic relief.

The extent to which a text like *The Revenger's Tragedy* is truly radical has to remain an open question, but in one sense this is precisely the point that cultural materialism reinforces at every turn. Dollimore chooses to challenge traditional criticism of these plays, and its inherently conservative foundations, and in its place he posits provocative, subversive readings that just as readily reveal his own political agenda. The ways in which texts like *The Revenger's Tragedy* intervened in their cultural milieux at the time they were first produced and consumed is a question which remains largely unanswerable. What the texts can be made to reveal now, as we watch and read them again, is another matter altogether. All quotations from *The Revenger's Tragedy* are taken from the Revels Plays version edited by R. A. Foakes (London, 1966). Ed.]

1. I am assuming nothing, nor contributing to the debate, about the authorship of this play.

2. William Archer, *The Old Drama and the New* (London, 1923), p. 74; John Peter, *Complaint and Satire in Early English Literature* (Oxford, 1956), p. 268. Instead of Archer's indignation, or Peter's rendering of the play respectable, another tradition of critics showed a deep fascination with 'Tourneur's' psychopathology. Thus J. Churton Collins writes that 'Sin and misery, lust and cynicism, fixed their fangs deep in his splendid genius, marring and defacing his art, poisoning and paralysing the artist' (Cyril Tourneur, *The Plays and Poems*, ed. J. Churton Collins [London, 1978], p. lvi), while T. S. Eliot described the motive of *The Revenger's Tragedy* as 'truly the death motive, for it is the loathing of horror and of life itself' (*Selected Essays*, 3rd edn [London, 1951], p. 190).

3. These arguments are more fully outlined, and contested, in Jonathan Dollimore, 'Two Concepts of Mimesis: Renaissance Literary Theory and *The Revenger's Tragedy*', *Themes in Drama*, 2, *Drama and Mimesis*, ed. James Redmond (Cambridge, 1980), pp. 38–43.

4. This is, perhaps, the 'pose of indignant morality' that Archer detected (*The Old Drama and the New*, p. 74) but misunderstood. But even Archer had misgivings: 'One cannot, indeed, quite repress a suspicion that Tourneur wrote with his tongue in his cheek' (ibid., p. 75). Indeed one cannot!

5. If, as seems probable, *The Revenger's Tragedy* was written after May 1606, such obliquity may, apart from anything else, have been an effective way of avoiding a tangle with the statute of that month to restrain 'Abuses of Players'. This act not only forbade the player to 'jestingly or profanely speak or use the holy name of God or of Jesus Christ, or of the Holy Ghost or of the Trinity', but also commanded that the same were not to be spoken of at all 'but with *fear and reverence*' (my italics). It is precisely this kind of 'fear and reverence' which is being parodied. The statute is reprinted in W. C. Hazlitt, *The English Drama and the Stage* (London, 1869), p. 42.

6. Peter Lisca, '*The Revenger's Tragedy*: A Study in Irony', *Philological Quarterly*, 38 (1959), 250.

7. Ibid., pp. 242, 245.

8. See also J. M. R. Margerson, *The Origins of English Tragedy* (Oxford, 1967), p. 136; G. Boklund has demonstrated how Webster uses repeated ironic reversals for an entirely different purpose – namely to demonstrate that it is 'chance, independent of good and evil' which governs events in *The Duchess of Malfi (The Duchess of Malfi: Sources, Themes, Characters* [Cambridge, MA, 1962], pp. 129–30). Webster's *The Devil's Law-Case* offers an overt parody of peripeteias and providentialist intervention not dissimilar to that found in *The Revenger's Tragedy* (see especially Act III, scene ii, lines 147–58).

9. Nicholas Brooke, *Horrid Laughter in Jacobean Tragedy* (London, 1979), p. 14.

10. From R. J. Hollingdale's selection, *Essays and Aphorisms* (Harmondsworth, 1970), pp. 51–4; for a complete edition of *Parerga and Paralipomena*, see E. F. J. Payne's two-volume translation (Oxford, 1974).

11. See A. Nicoll (ed.), *The Works of Cyril Tourneur* (London, 1929), pp. 16–18.

12. Ibid., p. 275.

13. Compare Hobbes: 'I put for a general inclination of all mankind, a perpetual and restless desire of power after power, that ceaseth only in death' (*Leviathan*, ch. 11).

14. Compare Shakespeare's *Timon of Athens*: 'thou wouldst have plunged thyself / In general riot, *melted* down thy youth / In different beds of lust' (IV.iii.256–8) [author's emphasis – Ed.]; and Spenser's Redcrosse, with 'The false Duessa', 'Pour'd out in looseness on the grassy ground, / Both careless of his health, and of his fame' (*The Faerie Queene*, 1.7.7).

15. Compare Montaigne: 'Men misacknowledge the natural infirmity of their mind. She doth but quest and ferret, and incessantly goeth turning, winding, building and entangling herself in her own work; as do our silk-worms, and therein stiffleth herself' (*Essays*, III.325). This image was a popular one, and the Montaigne passage was twice borrowed by Webster (see R. W. Dent, *John Webster's Borrowings* [Berkeley, CA, 1960], p. 85).

16. L. G. Salingar, '*The Revenger's Tragedy* and the Morality Tradition', *Scrutiny*, 6:4 (1938), 404.

6

'For Show or Useless Property': Necrophilia and *The Revenger's Tragedy*

KARIN S. CODDON

> Kiss me, kiss me, kiss me,
> Your tongue's like poison
> (The Cure)

The intersection of death and the erotic throughout Elizabethan and Jacobean tragedy is a virtual commonplace of the genre; from Hamlet's leap into Ophelia's grave to the perversities of Tourneur and Middleton, the body of death is at least symbolically conflated with the body of desire. Indeed, while granting that theatrical personae as yet do not 'go so far as making love to the corpse', Philippe Aries notes 'an almost imperceptible shift [in early modern England and France] from familiarity with the dead to macabre eroticism'.[1] Yet in Cyril Tourneur's *The Revenger's Tragedy* (1607), the eroticised body of death is more than a symbolic presence or moody memento mori: Gloriana's skull is a prop endowed with remarkable spectacular and material efficacy. Peter Stallybrass's argument that death removes Gloriana from the corrupting realm of sexual desire is doubly belied by Vindice's notably prurient obsession with the skull of his nine-years-dead betrothed and by his all but literal prostitution of the skull in pursuit of revenge against the lecherous Duke.[2] I suggest that this latter machination constitutes the play's emblematic moment: a savage literalisation of the conventional love / death conjunction as the Duke kisses – and 'like a slobbering Dutchman', at that – the skull's poisoned maw.

Without denying the rather obvious connotations of patriarchal anxiety about female sexuality – or falling into the tempting though anachronistic trap of having Tourneur 'have read' Freud or Bataille (to paraphrase Baudrillard), I would like to claim that necrophilia in *The Revenger's Tragedy* serves at once to parody and to interrogate contemporary, increasingly scientistic notions of the body. The constitution of the body as the object of scientific enquiry – perhaps most strikingly though not exclusively demonstrated in the relatively recent phenomenon of public dissection – is brutally travestied in Tourneur's insistent displacement of an 'objective' knowledge of the body by spectacular, defiantly perverse desire. Necrophilia yokes together science and seduction; discipline does not replace the unruly erotic but instead precariously displaces it in the elision of the body by the cold medium of the scientific gaze.[3] Tourneur's play does not simply eroticise 'the idea of death' – it does not disembody death by rendering it into a discourse as does that paradigm of proto-modern subjectivity, Hamlet; rather, the play theatricalises death in the specific, material dead body. Gloriana's skull becomes perversely seductive, in Baudrillard's sense of the term, playing alternately at being pure referent and pure signifier, the revenger's 'form and cause' at once conjoined and confounded: '*Every interpretative discourse ... wants to get beyond appearances*: this is its illusion and fraud. But getting beyond appearances is an impossible task: inevitably every discourse is revealed in its appearance, and is hence subject to the stakes imposed by seduction, and consequently to *its own failure as discourse*.[4] The Jacobean spectacle, situated as it is in a liminal position between the emblematic and mimetic – between theatricality and interpretation – undermines its own ostensible truth value by foregrounding the instability yet opacity of appearances. Confounded as well in the play's erotics of death is the distinction between an emergent scientism and the repressed, residual otherness of the transgressive corporeality identified with madness, witchcraft, and necromancy.

Even among the grotesqueries of Jacobean theatre, *The Revenger's Tragedy* is notably macabre; it is small wonder that Eliot singled it out for its' cynicism ... loathing and disgust of humanity'.[5] Yet the morbid interest in the corporeality of death and decomposition that so distinguishes Jacobean tragedy is at least as residual as emergent, given what Lynn White has called a pervasive 'socially manifested necrophilia' of the fifteenth century.[6] As Foucault, Aries, and others have remarked upon, the Cimetière des Innocents, Danse Macabre, and *artes moriendi* are cultural productions of late fourteenth- and early fifteenth-century Europe, phenomena that have been attributed, alternately though not exclusively, to a burgeoning humanism, the lingering psychic, social, and economic effects of the Black Death, and an ecclesiastical interest in promoting anxiety about death and hence the economic and political well-being of church bureaucrats.[7] Literary treatments of Eros / Thanatos tend to be more decorous in the Middle Ages than in Jacobean tragedy, if not terribly less frequent; the intertwining of love and death figures prominently in the *Tristan* tales, and Mallory's *Morte d'Arthur* features a number of implicit and explicit necrophiliac episodes.[8] In fact, in the fifteenth century occurred the most notorious documented case of necrophilia in early modern Europe, that of Gilles de Rais, a French nobleman who had fought alongside Jeanne d'Arc, and who was to become the inspiration for the fictive Bluebeard. After Jeanne's capture and execution, Gilles evidently retired to his castle, where he proceeded to seduce, murder and mutilate scores of young boys, not only copulating with the corpses but preserving various body parts for posterity. Upon his arrest, Gilles confessed to his crimes, his pre-execution repentance likely of greater edification to the Church than to the soul of the necrophile himself, for '[Gilles's] confession, repentance, and resignation were acclaimed as an elaborate example of Christian penance'.[9]

Yet despite these fifteenth-century analogues, death, and dead bodies, seemed to retain a kind of quotidian respect due to the inexplicable if not the magical; it was seldom the focus of derisive parody such as one finds in Tourneur, Webster, and Middleton. Compared to post-Reformation Europe, a relative tolerance for the magical seems at least partly responsible for the 'familiarity' with death that Aries notes about the late Middle Ages. Unlike the lofty ritual of public anatomy, in which an audience of cowed, reverent observers watched an expert dissector anatomise, analyse, and label the dead body, popular practices well into the seventeenth century treated of the corpse in every-day, efficacious terms; various parts and fluids of the corpse were commonly assumed to have medicinal value – 'the perspiration of corpses is good for haemorrhoids and tumours, and the hand of a cadaver applied to a diseased area can heal, as in the case of a woman suffering from dropsy who rubbed her abdomen with the still-warm hand of a corpse'.[10] As late as the Restoration, so lofty a personage as the ailing Charles I of England 'drank a potion ... containing forty-two drops of extract of human skull'.[11]

One is tempted, perhaps, to concur with Giovanna Ferrari's claim that the practice of anatomy descends from traditional, popular pharmaceuticals of the dead body.[12] Yet the relation between popular practice and science in the early modern period is less one of integration than of co-optation. By 1604 in England, it was a felony 'to take up a dead body in whole or part for magical purposes'.[13] Anatomy and dissection were the territory of the specialist; for the non-specialist, traffic with the dead body constituted necromancy, witchcraft. Although in France, desecration of the corpse could serve as an act, however unsanctioned, of religious sedition, for the most part in early modern Europe, contact with the dead body was expressly limited to men of science.[14]

I agree with Francis Barker that the rise of the 'science' of anatomy in early modern Europe is very much bound up in an ideological reformation of the subject that entailed an elision of the body.[15] For Foucault, these strategies focus 'on the body as a machine: its disciplining, the optimisation of its capabilities, the extortion of its foes, the parallel increase of its usefulness and its docility, its integration into systems of efficient and economic controls ... ensured by the procedures of power that characterised the *disciplines*.'[16] Strikingly, these 'anatomo-politics of the body' were applied to the dead as well as the living.[17] That artists like Leonardo, Rembrandt, and Vesalius partook in the discipline of anatomy along with physicians, humanists, and even noble amateurs suggests slippages between object and representation, ostensible referent and simulacrum.[18] It seems no cultural accident that the popularity of the *trompe l'oeil* in early modern Europe roughly coincides with the radical anti-mimesis of Jacobean tragedy.[19] For while the *trompe l'oeil* seems at first to be simulation at its most diabolical, it 'does not attempt to confuse itself with the real. Fully aware of play and artifice, it produces a simulacrum by mimicking the third dimension, and by mimicking and surpassing the effect of the real, radically questioning the principle of reality'.[20] On a certain level, then, the *trompe l'oeil*, like Jacobean tragedy, parodies and even resists the emergent proto-empirical discourses that are predicated on the assumption of access to knowledge via the 'objectivity' of bodies and equally stable subjectivity of the humanist subject. Spectacular representation becomes the site of radical contradiction, in which the unstable play of signifier and referent foregrounds its attempts – almost literally – to *deceive the eye*, the objectifying, diagnostic eye of discipline as well as the 'I' that discipline homologously constitutes.

'The king is a thing – of nothing', Hamlet utters paradoxically; as I have argued elsewhere, this intersection of madness with the paradox of the dead body disrupts the ideological conflation of the sovereign's mystic corpus and the subject's docile and obedient inwardness.[21] For the corpse is at once a *thing*, materially present yet marked by the absolute absence of subjectivity – and *no*-thing, a signifier severed from its referent, its 'owner'. According to emergent scientism, to be a 'thing' and a 'thing of nothing' is redundant. Hence the hegemonic co-optation of the body is as mystified as the colonisation of 'savages' in the New World, both imperative and necessary for the primacy and sustenance of European rationality. And, as with the violence of imperialistic conquest, the more obnoxious aspects of conquest of the body were often viewed as the unpleasant but unavoidable 'dirty work' justified by the rationality, even the nobility, of the end. Leonardo, though an experienced dissector, granted that 'though you have a love of such things you will perhaps be hindered by your stomach; and if that does not impede you, you will perhaps be impeded by the fear of living through the night hours in the company of quartered and flayed corpses fearful to behold'.[22] Alissandro Benedetti, a learned Italian Renaissance doctor and author of a 1502 treatise on anatomy, refers to dissection in a tellingly oxymoronic phrase as 'a horrifying task, an object worthy of a special theatrical presentation'.[23] In his treatise on urn excavations, Sir Thomas Browne seems to justify his own scientific necromancy on grounds that cremated remains, unlike buried corpses, cannot be desecrated: 'To be gnaw'd out of our graves, to have our souls made drinking bowls, and our bones turned into Pipes, to delight and sport our Enemies, are Tragicall abominations, escaped in burning Burials.'[24]

Interestingly, the category of gender was pointedly not elided in anatomy; rather, dissection of the female corpse offered the possibility of an ultimate, literal penetration, surveillance, and disciplining of female sexuality. Leonardo urged that 'three [anatomies] need to be made of a woman, in whom there is great mystery on account of her uterus and its fetus' (in fact, he did dissect the body of a pregnant woman).[25] Contemporary illustrations of dissection are likewise, and tellingly, gendered. The frontispiece for Vesalius's *Fabrica* (1543) and *Epitome* (1543) features a woodcut depicting the public anatomy of a female: surrounded by a crowd of avid observers, the anatomist has opened up the corpse's abdominal cavity, toward which he gestures. But the woman's body is, significantly, facing the viewer of the illustration, legs slightly spread, bare breasts evident above the huge gaping hole that is the rest of her torso.[26] Similarly, a woodcut from Jacob Rueff's *De conceptu et generations hominus* (1554) shows a (presumably) living, naked woman with her abdomen – from her vaginal lips to just beneath her breasts – completely opened up, her reproductive organs once again directly facing the reader's eye.[27] Illustrations of the dissection of male corpses typically present the body laid in horizontal (that is, left to right) position; even Rembrandt's *Anatomy of Dr. Joan Deyman*, in which the male body is facing the spectator of the painting, depicts the corpse with his groin area discreetly covered. The convergence of science with a means of absolute, violent control and containment of female sexuality is hardly arbitrary; for with the emergence of rationalist, empirical discourse comes an explicit irrationalisation of the female body.[28] The scientistic paradigm aspires to universalise the Other as object; hence the female corpse is doubly objectified, the disciplinary intervention serving to expose the biological, 'natural' bases for gender.

While the skull of Gloriana in Tourneur's play literally lacks a body, it does not, as I have already suggested, lack a sexuality. Her mutilated state certainly evokes contemporary depictions of anatomised female corpses, and while her sexual organs have presumably long turned to dust, the fact that the skull kills with its 'lips' suggests the *vagina dentata*, even without an actual vagina. Yet Gloriana's skull, and its function in the play, is not so easily reduced to simple imagings of misogyny. For the skull is gendered only because we are told so; it obviously bears no visible mark of its sex. Indeed, when Vindice, in Act III, scene v enters '*with the skull of his love dressed up in tires*', the skull's gendering is clearly a contrivance. The dead body, far from fixing gender categories (as it does in anatomy), here emblematises the material contingency of gender. The play's relentless confusion of identity with disguise and thus of the referent with radically unstable signifiers, in which not even the skull, a 'thing of nothing', can be identified outside of the duplicity of theatricality, overturns the very epistemological and ideological bases for power / knowledge.

In fact, Vindice's characteristic, quasi-prurient misogyny subverts itself throughout the play by its association of vile female sexuality with artifice and disguise – de/vices that wholly construct (and deconstruct) this most decentred of Jacobean revengers. By his own admission, 'My life's unnatural to me, e'en compelled, / As if I lived now when I should be dead' (I.i.119–20). The conflation of the 'unnatural' or artificial with life is striking; if a corpse is a body without subjectivity, then Vindice is on a certain level 'dead'. Indeed, his assumption of the role of Revenger, of Piato the bawd, and even of his 'actual self' after the Duke's murder is not fundamentally different from Gloriana's skull dressed up in tires. To an extent, then, the profound sexual nausea of the play may be seen to derive not only from the destabilised discourse of misogyny, but also from the fact that in this 'unnatural' realm, all the players are vampires and necrophiles. In his opening speech, Vindice remarks of the Duke, 'Oh that marrowless age / Would stuff the hollow bones with damned desires, / And 'stead of heat kindle infernal fires of a dry duke, / A parched and juiceless luxor' (I.i.5–9). The Duke is characterised not only as impotent, but as having 'hollow bones' – a figuring of death that prepares for the transition to Vindice's address to Gloriana:

> Thou shallow picture of my poisoned love,
> My study's ornament, thou shell of Death
> Once the bright face of my betrothed lady,
> When life and beauty naturally filled out
> Those ragged imperfections;
> When two heaven-pointed diamonds were set
> In those unsightly rings – then 'twas a face
> So far beyond the artificial shine
> Of any woman's bought complexion
> That the uprightest man – if such there be,
> That sin but seven times a day – broke custom
> And made up eight with looking after her.
> (I.i.14–25)

The address to Gloriana, like the spectacle itself, is marked by semiotic instability. The skull is initially described as a 'picture', an 'ornament', a 'shell' of the dead woman. Yet the living Gloriana can be characterised only in terms of the artifice and ornamentation employed by other ladies as a substitute for 'natural' beauty; her eyes were like 'two heaven-pointed diamonds', and a few lines later, Vindice remarks 'Thee when thou were *apparelled in thy flesh*, the old duke poisoned' (I.i.31–2; emphasis added). If living flesh is but the 'apparel' for dead bones, then the skull must be the referent, not merely the relic; yet its referentiality is problematised by the visual absence of anything distinctively 'Gloriana' about it. The body thus evades discipline by resisting a stable semiotic character: the will to knowledge can occupy the status only of a perverse and displaced voyeurism. It is interesting to consider Tourneur's own 'anatomo-politics' in light of Derrida's commentary on Artaud's 'theatre of cruelty':

> Evil, pollution, resides in the *critical* or the *clinical*: it is to have one's speech and body become works, objects which can be offered up to the furtive haste of the commentator because they are supine. For, by definition, the only thing that is not subject to commentary is the life of the body, the living flesh whose integrity, opposed to evil and death, is maintained by the theatre.[29]

In the theatre of Tourneur if not that of Artaud, the matter is complicated further by a parodic confusion – both discursive and spectacular – of the semiotics of the dead body.

Thus, too, the play's immediate and persistent, morbid foregrounding of the skull – and of Vindice's eroticised attachment to it – displaces the 'disinterested', disciplinary gaze of anatomy with a transgressive voyeurism – displaces the scientist with the necrophile, so to speak. The repulsiveness explained away in the name of science by Leonardo, Bennedetti, and even Browne becomes itself the object of desire. Moreover, the play's subversive slippages between the body of death and the body of desire are perhaps better historicised than psychoanalysed. The humanistic valorisation of the body (a valorisation that in many ways enabled the co-optation of the corpse in the pursuit of higher knowledge), as well as the post-Reformation sanction of conjugal life, cannot be taken to suggest simply a cultural shift away from medieval *contemptus mundi* and toward an enlightened and affirmative embracing of the sexual body. In her discussion of Holbein's harrowingly realistic *The Body of Dead Christ in the Tomb*, Julia Kristeva provocatively poses the question: 'Did the Reformation influence such a concept of death [as Holbein's], and more specifically, such an emphasis on Christ's death at the expense of any allusion to the Redemption and Resurrection?'[30] The Reformation's simultaneous privilege of inwardness and denial of individual agency *vis-à-vis* salvation may well have provoked greater anxiety about death; the prominence of the 'food for worms' topos, emphasising the decomposition and putrefaction of the corpse, is scarcely less morbid than the medieval Dance of Death.[31] As for the living, sexual body, Lawrence Stone suggests that for most early modern English women and men, intercourse likely exposed them to flesh that must have appeared well on the way to putrefaction:

> Both sexes suffered long periods of crippling illness which incapacitated them for months or years. Even when relatively well, they often suffered from disorders which made sex painful to them or unpleasant to their partners. Women suffered from a whole series of gynaecological disorders, particularly leucherrhoea, but also vaginal ulcers, tumours, inflammations and haemorrhages which often made sexual intercourse disagreeable, painful, or impossible. Both sexes must very often have had bad breath from the rotting teeth and constant stomach disorders which can be documented from many sources, while suppurating ulcers, exzema, scabs, running sores and other nauseating skin disorders were extremely common, and often lasted for years.[32]

Stone's catalogue of 'nauseating' physical ailments comes dangerously close to absolutising cultural norms, but it is equally misguided to assume that because of the commonness of such complaints, the average Elizabethan or Jacobean paid them no heed. Most important to attend to, I believe, is that for many sixteenth- and seventeenth-century women and men, sexual intercourse was accompanied by pointedly un-romanticised assumptions about the body of desire that would likely strike the twentieth-century Western sensibility as revolting.

This is not to suggest, however, that Vindice's obsession with Gloriana's skull might have been taken by a Jacobean audience as naturalistic, much less normative. When Hippolito enters after the opening soliloquy, and asks his brother rhetorically, 'Still sighing o'er Death's vizard?' (I.i.49), the effect is to underscore Vindice's perversity. 'Sighing', of course, has sexual connotations; and 'Death's vizard' is yet another startlingly ambiguous phrase, seeming to contradict Vindice's prior characterisation of Gloriana's flesh as the mask. For the skull marks not the limit or antithesis of corporeal desire but is rather its object. Hippolito has sought out Vindice to play the role of 'base-coined pandar' (I.i.80), spurring Vindice's remark, 'I wonder how ill-featured, vile proportioned / That one should be, if she were made for woman, / Whom at the insurrection of his lust / He would refuse for once: heart, I think none; / Next to a skull, though more unsound than one, / Each face he meets he strongly dotes upon' (I.i.86–9). The syntax is peculiar: does 'Next to a skull' refer to the precedent 'He' or following 'Each face'? The ambiguity is intriguing, for the skull may be seen as simultaneously the boundary and the culmination of desire, the site where licit and illicit desires become mutually indistinguishable. Lust does not 'disguise itself' as necrophilia so much as necrophilia disguises itself as lust, Vindice seems to imply, both in the aforementioned lines and in his contradictory expressions of derision of lechery and erotic attachment to Gloriana in 'her' present state. But as I have already suggested, Vindice no less than the skull functions more as prop, as a 'thing of nothing', than as an agent. He agrees to 'put on that knave' (the role of bawd; I.i.92), right away, the elision of '*the role of*', or '*the disguise of*' 'that knave' justified by his ensuing remark, 'For to be honest is not to be i' the world' (I.i.94). Charles and Elaine Hallett have observed that 'Vindice's journey is a journey into madness in the sense that he creates an alter-ego and loses all grip on himself. Eventually, there is no longer a real Vindice; he has entered so far into deceit that he is the man he pretends to be. To put on the role of Vindice again is to put on a new disguise.'[33] But I would question the Halletts' assumption that 'a real Vindice', an originally centred subject, is available anywhere in the play.[34] By his own definition, 'to be honest is not to be i' the world' – 'the world' being the realm of Jacobean theatrical representation, which in its radical anti-mimesis anticipates Artaud (or, at least, Derrida's reading of Artaud) in 'announc[ing] the limit of representation'.[35] For no 'real Vindice' is possible in the play, not only in the banal sense that theatrical personae are by definition roles and not 'subjectivities', but also, and more provocatively, because the absence of *honesty* (a claim to authentic subjectivity) in the play's world parodically reduces the dramatis personae to the level of props, deconstructing the precarious distinction between the 'dead' body as object and the animate one, with illusions of its own autonomous subjectivity, as agent or even actor.[36] The opening scene closes with Vindice's aside, 'I'll quickly turn into another' (I.i.134) but the collapse of boundaries between subject and object has already been put forth as a given of the play. The subsequent theatricalisation of disguise is a savage self-parody that seems to acknowledge that the dismantling of the illusion of 'honesty' – or *mimesis* – makes representation a metaphysical impossibility. And in the absence of metaphysics this theatre can proffer only the arbitrary materiality of bodies stripped even of the ostensibly stable semiotic distinctions between living and dead.

Thus, when Vindice appears in his disguise, his question to Hippolito – 'What brother, am I far enough from myself?' (I.iii.1) – underscores not only the infinite substitutability of 'subjectivity', but on a practical, spectacular level, functions to inform the audience that this disguised figure is indeed the same 'character' introduced in scene i, Act I, given that the actor obviously has been physically 'translated'. Yet if Vindice's 'life is unnatural to [him]', the 'self' to which he refers is no less an artifice than this late guise of Piato the bawd. Similarly, Vindice's invocation of 'Impudence, / Thou goddess of the palace' (I.iii.5–6) to 'Strike thou mine forehead into dauntless marble, / Mine eyes steady sapphires' (I.iii.8–9), seems to echo his opening meditation on Gloriana's skull – 'When two heaven-pointed diamonds were set / In those unsightly rings – then 'twas a face / So far beyond the artificial shine / Of any woman's bought complexion' (I.i.19–22). The mask that Vindice has put on is strikingly similar to that which 'apparelled [Gloriana] in [her] flesh'. With no stable semiotic to mark off natural from unnatural, life from death, the ontological status of playing is itself thrown into question in a far more radical way than one finds in the typical 'world-as-stage' topos. Again, the characters function as virtual props; thus the spectators, situated in the position of viewing the prurient machinations less of mimetic characters than of objects, are themselves inscribed as voyeuristic necrophiles.

When Vindice announces himself to Lussurioso as 'A bone setter ... A bawd, my lord, / One that sets bones together' (I.iii.42–4), he foreshadows the sexual assignation he will arrange between the Duke and Gloriana's skull: the 'setting together' of 'hollow bones' with the 'the bony lady'. Yet as go-between, the bawd is doubly implicated – indeed, is situated between the dead bones. Vindice's proclamation upon Lussurioso's exit – 'Now let me burst, I've eaten noble poison!' (I.iii.170) – aligns him (as has the sapphire-eyed figure) not only with the poisoned Gloriana, but also with the lecherous Duke, who will literally eat poison in the upshot of Vindice's revenge. The wholesale instability of Vindice's identity accounts for the play's somewhat solipsistic quality; on a symbolic level, he is both Gloriana and her ravisher, for on a semiotic and hence epistemological level the play makes it impossible to distinguish him, whose 'life's unnatural', from the 'hollow bones' and 'bony lady'. If the construction of subjectivity functions to establish boundaries between identity and difference, Self and Other, then the refusal of subjectivity and parodic embrace of objectification and disguise produce an anarchy in which identity is radically interchangeable. Hence the following scene's perverse disclosure of the rape and suicide (by poison) of Antonio's wife not only mirrors the 'main plot', but rehearses and duplicates it. Once again, the effect is that of the *trompe l'oeil*, wherein the seeming exactitude of mimesis actually serves to render imitation itself static and artificial: the parodic precision of the duplication of the Vindice–Gloriana–Duke triad is in fact the very antithesis of verisimilitude. To use Baudrillard's terminology, the scene is a simulacrum of the third order, in that it mimics a prior model that has no epistemological foundation itself – they are signs referring to and interacting only with other signs, all of them *'variables'*.[37] Antonio displays the dead body of his raped wife: 'Behold my lords / A sight that strikes man out of me' (I.iv.4–5). In turn, the lords praise the object set forth for their perusal: Piero cries, 'That virtuous lady!' while Hippolito extols 'The blush of many women, whose chaste presence / Would e'en call shame up to their cheeks / And make pale wanton sinners have good colours' (ii.6–9). The paeans to the woman's corpse – 'Precedent for wives' (I.iv.6) – seem to imply that the emblematic desirable female body is a dead one, spectacularly displayed to appraising, evaluating male gazes.[38] Antonio's narration of the events leading to his wife's suicide significantly confuses the objectified but living female body with the object that is the eroticised body of death: 'The duchess's younger son ... / Singled out that dear form, who ever lived / As cold in lust as she is now in death' (I.iv.32–36). That the woman's death makes her all the more 'wondrous', an 'empress', even (ll.49–50), is not to say that she is removed from the realm of sexuality; for the spectacular display of her dead body rather undercuts the conventional and disembodying tributes to her chastity.[39] Antonio's claim that 'this is my comfort gentlemen, and I joy / In this one happiness above the rest, / Which will be called a miracle at last, / That being an old man I'd a wife so chaste' (I.iv.75–8) is one of the play's more incongruous speeches, for the conventional misogyny of the sentiment is ironised not only by the voyeurism incited by her corpse's display, but by the erotic investment of Vindice's lust for revenge that frames the Antonio subplot.

Similarly, the disguised Vindice's attempt to procure his sister for Lussurioso, and seduction of his mother to consent to the pandering, is on the level of signification no less perverse and even incestuous than Spurio's liaison with his stepmother. For despite Vindice's declared intention merely to test the ladies' virtue, disguise and dissimulation so subsume any essential referentiality that there is only signification; the play precludes any stable spectacular or semiotic criteria by which to distinguish unnaturally-disguised (and -minded) 'Piato' from Vindice, whose 'life is unnatural'. 'Piato's' mastery of the very discourses of sensuality that Vindice ostensibly loathes, and the persistence with which he employs it to Gratiana and Castiza, indicts language itself as but a habit that aptly is put on. The boundaries by which kinship bonds are constructed (*and* incest forbidden) are disclosed as contingent, dependent on a stable semiosis that exists nowhere in the world of the play – just as distinctions between necromancy (with its evocations of necrophilia) and science, madness and sanity, are debunked as binarisms themselves violently imposed in the process of constructing early modern subjectivity. For, as Foucault has compellingly shown, the incitements of distinct categories of sexuality were bound up in the development of the disciplines (not the least of which is *self*-discipline).[40] The play's semiotic anarchy effects and virtually promotes the proliferation of illicit sexualities in excess of any subject's 'intentions'.

So, too, Vindice's exhortation to Lussurioso to murder the Duke and Duchess in bed 'doubled, when they're heaped' (II.iii.4) conflates the spectacle of voyeurism with evocations of incestuous oedipal desire and necrophilia. For Vindice has urged Lussurioso (who expects to find Spurio with the Duchess) to 'take 'em twisted' (II.iii.2), in a bitterly, literal pun on the conventional Elizabethan/Jacobean 'orgasm as death' metaphor, literal not the least because such a murder would provide a grotesque spectacle of sex and death intertwined. That Vindice is not particularly concerned that the Duke and not Spurio was discovered 'heaped' with the Duchess (II.iii.32–4) underscores the mad semiosis of necrophilic desire in excess of the object or referent (ostensibly, revenge against the Duke). Vindice shrugs off the missed opportunity: 'Would he [Lussurioso] had killed him, 'twould have eased our swords' (II.iii.34). What is constantly being provoked and incited in the play is not justice or even spectacle *per se*: it is the desire to present spectacularly the coupling of the quick and the dead, a desire that implicates not only Vindice but the audience as well.[41]

Thus the play's pivotal scene, Act III, scene v, is remarkable both for its relative prematurity, given revenge tragedy conventions, and for the vehemence with which it parodies the genre's, and the culture's, own governing symbolics of death. Romeo and Juliet's final moments in Capulet's tomb, Hamlet and Laertes' fight in Ophelia's grave, these staged conjunctions of Eros and Thanatos are decorous because desire remains in the realm of the symbolic and metaphorical. That is, it was for the audiences to accept the premise that these scenes take place in tombs and graveyards, given the relative austerity of Elizabethan and Jacobean scenic design. Vindice bounds onstage with the exclamation 'Oh sweet, delectable, rare, happy, ravishing!' (III.v.1), directly following the prurient remarks of the Duke's Younger Son condemned to die for the rape of Antonio's wife: 'My fault was sweet sport which the world approves; I die for that which every woman loves' (III.iv.78). The slippage between lust and the ecstasy of violence is parodically foregrounded; when Hippolito asks his brother the cause of his ecstatic mood, Vindice replies, 'Oh 'tis able / To make a man spring up and knock his forehead / Against yon silver ceiling' (III.v.2–4), an idiom with overt erotic connotations. Indeed, Vindice is almost too overcome to share with Hippolito the cause for 'the violence of my joy' (III.v.27) – a phrase that mockingly recalls the throes of Petrarchan love such as one finds in *Romeo and Juliet*. When Hippolito persists in asking about the identity of the lady Vindice has procured for the Duke, Vindice responds, 'Oh at that word I'm lost again, you cannot find me yet, I'm in a throng of happy apprehensions' (III.v.28–30), as though it is Vindice and not the Duke who anticipates a tryst. He runs off-stage to fetch the 'lady', returning shortly with '*the skull of his love dressed up in tires*'. Even the generally amenable Hippolito seems shocked: 'Why brother, brother' (III.v.49). But Vindice persists in his lascivious panderer's discourse: 'Art thou beguiled now? Tut a lady can / At such, all hid, beguile a wiser man. / Have I not fitted the old surfeiter / With a quaint piece of beauty?' (III.v.50–4). The bawdy pun on 'quaint,' like Vindice's simultaneous sexual revulsion and sexual fascination with Gloriana's remains, once again yokes together the ostensibly disembodied skull with the sexual body of desire. Even the play's most celebrated set speech, which seems to begin as a somewhat conventional, if eloquent, meditation on mortality and corporeality, concludes with an acknowledgement of semiotic confusion in place of any concrete point of reference.

> And now methinks I could e'en chide myself
> For doting on her beauty, though her death
> Shall be revenged after no common action.
> Does the silkworm expend her yellow labours
> For thee? For thee does she undo herself?
> Are lordships sold to maintain ladyships
> For the poor benefit of a bewitching minute?
> Why does yon fellow falsify highways
> And put his life between the judge's lips
> To refine such a thing, keeps horses and men
> To beat their valours for her?
> Surely we're all mad people and they,
> Whom we think are, are not; we mistake those.
> 'Tis we are mad in sense, they but in clothes.
>   (III.v.68–81)

Alas, poor Gloriana; yet Vindice's reflections on the decomposition of his lost love and the treacherous, because transitory, nature of female desirability are problematised by the conclusion that semiosis is irrational, and the 'sane' man madder than the lunatic, a distinction that Hippolito reminds him is moot anyway, given that they 'in clothes too' (their disguises) are mad, their identities effaced. Moreover, the temporal ambiguity of the speech's opening lines – for it is most unclear how long Vindice has ceased to 'dote … on her beauty' or if he has ceased to dote at all – further compounds the confusion.

Just as confused is the ensuing apostrophe to Gloriana: Vindice no sooner bids 'Thou may'st lie chaste now' (III.v.89) than he pictures the skull's presence 'at revels, forgetful feasts and unclean brothels' (III.v.89), a peculiar imagined situation of the virtuous lady's skull in the very spaces of lechery. Readdressing Hippolito, Vindice turns to his 'tragic business':

> I have not fashioned this only for show
> Or useless property, no – it shall bear a part
> E'en in its own revenge. This very skull,
> Whose mistress the duke poisoned with this drug,
> The mortal curse of the earth, shall be revenged
> In the like strain and kiss his lips to death.
>   (III.v.99–104)

The sexual puns continue, with Hippolito 'applaud[ing] ... The quaintness of the malice' (III.v.107–8), and Vindice replying, 'So 'tis laid on' (III.v.109). But what is interesting as well is Vindice's justification of the ruse in the name of theatrical efficacy – 'I have not fashioned this only for show / Or useless property' (III.v.99–100) – a theatrical efficacy the play itself has resoundingly deconstructed, replacing it with a prurient spectacle that traffics chiefly in the titillation of its spectators via representation of overtly decentred, semiotically unreadable objects of transgressive desire. Indeed, on a certain level, the whole of *The Revenger's Tragedy* is given over to 'show and useless property' – props, things of nothing, theatrically manipulable but inherently meaningless. What if, the play seems to be brutally suggesting, the body itself were no more than a prop? Bodies of desire, bodies of death, the bodies of actual actors playing roles that have no ultimate reference to subjectivity – the enabling distinctions that divide mind from corporeality, licit from illicit desires, subjects from objects, are disintegrated.

Hence the brutality of the Duke's murder must be viewed from the perspective not of the 'ethics of revenge', but rather of the excesses of spectacular desire that cannot but convert law into licence, discipline into a violent affirmation of the transgressiveness of body-politics. The Duke's teeth and tongue are eaten away after his kiss with Gloriana – ' 'Twill teach you to kiss closer, / Not like a slobbering Dutchman', scoffs Vindice (III.v.161–2). Vindice's simplistic comment, 'When the bad bleeds, then is the tragedy good' (III.v.198), is patently ironic, for both the sadistic spectacle and the Revenger's obvious lust in torturing the Duke belie any generic notion of Old Testament-style vengeful justice. Vindice's ostensible *raison d'être* – vengeance for Gloriana's death – has been served, and yet his conclusion of the scene by urging his brother, 'As fast as they peep up let's cut 'em down' (III.v.210), marks not an ethical critique of revenge so much as the radical estrangement of signifier from referent. Gloriana has been avenged, Vindice has fulfilled his dramatic and ethical 'purpose', and yet the play's own inexorable, even tyrannical, logic subsumes its supposed premises. Though two full acts follow the Duke's murder, their narrative purpose is radically superfluous. In Act IV, scene ii, Vindice 'becomes himself' again, only to be commissioned by Lussurioso to kill 'Piato'; that he 'accomplishes' this deed by disguising the Duke's corpse in 'Piato's' garb is less ironic than brutally parodic, identity being as unstable and contingent for the dead as for the living. Likewise, Vindice's ostensible hubris in blurting out to Antonio his and Hippolito's murderous deeds signifies not tragic pride so much as the impossibility of subjectivity: "'Tis time to die when we are ourselves our foes', Vindice proclaims (V.iii.110), adding shortly thereafter that the 'dead' Piato 'was a witch' (V.iii.119). Any criteria – ethical, semiotic, or spectacular – by which subjects can be named, distinguished not only from one another but from the materiality of objects, of props, have been exploded.

What's Hecuba to him, or he to Hecuba? The play profoundly travesties the illusion of actors embodying agents, or theatre holding up a (rational) mirror to nature, or spectacular experience as possible locus of knowledge. Against the body of death as the site of stable referentiality, the desexualised object of disciplinary inquiry and the Other of the disembodied proto-humanist subject, *The Revenger's Tragedy* subversively proffers the dead body as a fetishised prop on which not reason but madness inscribes itself, the transgressive limit of desire that cannot itself be limited, neither a body of pain nor of pleasure, but one of infinite utility. In its savage parody of the scientised body, the play spectacularly confounds the transgressive and the legitimised body, desire and discipline – the very boundaries that would construct and define subject and object for early modern European epistemology.

In postmodern America, when one hears 1992 Los Angeles likened to 1991 Kuwait or Iraq, when the *political* inscription of 'anarchy', 'lawlessness', and violence is questioned, when violence against bodies of colour is justified in the name of 'due process' and 'law' – that is, 'the biological existence of a [white] population', small wonder that many of us, within and without the academy, prefer to speak abstractly about the 'ethical anarchy' of Jacobean tragedy, conveniently invoking the trope of 'historical difference' to sidestep an active engagement of readings of the past with lived experience in the present.[42] As historically situated readers, we dare not constitute *history*, either overtly or tacitly, as merely part of the body of knowledge – pun intended – that designates a discipline and a profession. Where was your body the night Rodney King's was being beaten? Where was mine? What does either question have to do with Cyril Tourneur's play? I would hope that these are questions those of us who grapple with history will continue to consider.[43]

From *English Literary History*, 61 (1994), 71–88.

NOTES

[Karin Coddon's essay works as a companion piece to Jonathan Dollimore's analysis of *The Revenger's Tragedy* (essay 5), developing further the investigation of the death and sexuality nexus that exists at the heart of this extraordinary play. However, while Dollimore reads the meta-theatrical aspect of the play as self-parody, Coddon draws a parallel between Jacobean antimimesis and the *simulacrum* of the postmodern aesthetic – the *simulacrum* being the notion of a copy that has no original.

Coddon's poststructuralist scepticism interprets the play as one that destabilises conventional distinctions between subject and object, natural and unnatural, living and dead. In one sense, this serves to push further Dollimore's claim that the play may be read as a text that subverts patriarchal discourse, for Coddon argues that Gloriana's skull and its functions in the play are more than 'simple imagings of misogyny' (p. 126). In keeping with the postmodern coordinates of the essay (Coddon draws on Derrida as well as Baudrillard), the skull becomes a slippery signifier in what Coddon evocatively terms the play's 'erotics of death' (p. 122). The principles of Eros (desire) and Thanatos (death) are inseparable in the play, and epitomised in the moment that the Duke kisses the poisoned skull of Gloriana. This spectacular evocation of necrophilia and its implications is examined in some detail in the essay, but it is also worth noting that the overtones of necrophilia in *The Revenger's Tragedy* foreshadow the more explicit couplings of sex and death that we find in Middleton's *The Maiden's Tragedy* – a connection particularly noteworthy, since current scholarship favours Middleton as the true author of *The Revenger's Tragedy*. At the climax of *The Maiden's Tragedy*, The Tyrant places the corpse of his beloved on a throne, and embraces and kisses the body. And just as in *The Revenger's Tragedy* the Duke is poisoned by the skull, so in *The Maiden's Tragedy* the Tyrant is poisoned by the painted face of the corpse.

Coddon's essay concludes with a tentative step outside of literary critical discourse, inviting us to consider what her reflections on *The Revenger's Tragedy* might mean to us in contemporary society. Criticism with a sharp deconstructive edge too often sidles away from the political. Coddon asks us to relate the play to a contemporary event, the beating of black American Rodney King by LA cops, and the cops' subsequent acquittal by a Simi Valley jury, which was the precipitating event for the LA riots. In this way, Coddon concludes the essay with a direct challenge, inviting us to relate our readings of the past with 'lived experience in the present' (p. 137). References are to the Norton edition of Cyril Tourneur, *The Revenger's Tragedy*, ed. Brain Gibbons (New York, 1989). Ed.]

1. Philippe Aries, *The Hour of Our Death*, trans. Helen Weaver (New York, 1981), p. 376.

2. Peter Stallybrass, 'Reading the Body: *The Revenger's Tragedy* and the Jacobean Theatre of Consumption', *Renaissance Drama*, 18 (1987), 129–32.

3. See Francis Barker, *The Tremulous Private Body* (London, 1984), p. 80.

4. Jean Baudrillard, *Selected Writings*, trans. Jacques Morrain and Charles Levin, ed. Mark Poster (Stanford, CA, 1989), p. 150.

5. T. S. Eliot, *Essays on Elizabethan Drama* (New York, 1932, 1960), p. 120.

6. Lynn White, Jr, 'Death and the Devil', in Robert Kinsman (ed.), *The Darker Vision of the Renaissance* (Berkeley, CA, 1974), p. 31.

7. For discussion of humanism, see Donald Howard, 'Renaissance World-Alienation', in Kinsman (ed.), *Darker Vision*, pp. 47–76; for black death see White, 'Death and the Devil', pp. 30–2; and for church bureaucracy see Aries, *Hour of Our Death*, p. 298.

8. See, for example, Book 6, ch. 17 of *Morte d'Arthur*. I am grateful to Elizabeth Bryan for this reference, as well as for pointing out the frequent intersection of spectacles of torture and death with the erotic in medieval 'virgin martyrs' accounts.

9. Vern L. Bullough, *Sexual Variance in Society and History* (New York, 1976), p. 401.

10. Aries, *Hour of Our Death*, p. 357.

11. Ibid., p. 358.

12. Giovanna Ferrari, 'Public Anatomy Lessons and the Carnival: The Anatomy Theatre of Bologna', *Past and Present*, 117 (Nov. 1987), 100–1.

13. Keith Thomas, *Religion and the Decline of Magic* (New York, 1971), p. 443.

14. Natalie Zemon Davis, *Society and Culture in Early Modern France* (Stanford, CA, 1975), p. 179.

15. Barker, *Tremulous Private Body*, pp. 73–80.

16. Michel Foucault, *The History of Sexuality*, vol. 1, trans. Robert Hurley (New York, 1978), p. 139.

17. Ibid.

18. Aries, *Hour of Our Death*, pp. 368–70.

19. See Baudrillard, *Selected Writings*, pp. 155–9.

20. Ibid., p. 156.

21. Karin S. Coddon, ' "Suche Strange Desygns": Madness, Subjectivity and Treason in *Hamlet* and Elizabethan Culture', *Renaissance Drama*, 20 (1989), 67–8.

22. Kenneth D. Keele, *Leonardo da Vinci's Elements of the Science of Man* (New York, 1983), p. 197.

23. Quoted in Ferrari, 'Public Anatomy Lessons', p. 57.

24. Sir Thomas Browne, *Hypdriotaphia or Urne-Burial*, in *The Works of Thomas Browne*, ed. Geoffrey Keynes (Chicago, 1964), p. 155.

25. Keele, *Leonardo*, p. 197.

26. William S. Hecksher, *Rembrandt's Anatomy of Dr. Nicholas Tulp: An Iconological Study* (New York, 1958), fig. 54.

27. Marcie Frank, 'The Camera and the Speculum: David Cronenberg's *Dead Ringers*', PMLA, 106 (1991), 459–70 (fig. 468).

28. See Foucault, *The History of Sexuality*, p. 104.

29. Jacques Derrida, 'The Theater of Cruelty and the Closure of Representation', in *Writing and Difference*, trans. Alan Bass (Chicago, 1978), p. 183.

30. Julia Kristeva, 'Holbein's Dead Christ', trans. Leon S. Roudiez, in Michel Feher with Ramona Naddaff and Nadia Tazi (eds), *Fragments for a History of the Human Body* (New York, 1989), p. 252.

31. Arnold Stein, *The House of Death* (Baltimore, MD, 1986), p. 13.

32. Lawrence Stone, *The Family, Sex and Marriage 1500–1800*, abridged edn (New York, 1979), p. 306.

33. Charles and Elaine Hallett, *The Revenger's Madness* (Lincoln, NA, 1980), p. 239.

34. See, for example, Catherine Belsey, *The Subject of Tragedy* (London, 1985), p. 31.

35. Derrida, 'The Theater of Cruelty', p. 234.

36. By 'honesty', I refer not only to the modern definition of 'truthfulness', but also, and perhaps chiefly, to the sense of *authenticity* invoked by Hamlet when he tells Horatio, 'Touching this vision here [the spectre of King Hamlet] / It is an *honest* ghost' (T. S. B. Spence [ed.], *Hamlet* [Harmondsworth, 1980], I.v.143–4; emphasis added).

37. Baudrillard, *Selected Writings*, p. 135.

38. See Barker, *Tremulous Private Body*, on Andrew Marvell's 'To His Coy Mistress': 'The text exhibits, and even in its brutal way – within the economy of violence and the *imago* of the fragmented body discloses within the conventional lyricism – celebrates the body of the beloved in public view ... It is still there to be seen, and is acknowledged openly as the object and site of desire' (p. 89).

39. Here I disagree with Stallybrass's claim that the raped body of Lady Antonio is not 'sexualised ... In the silence of death, Lady Antonio is made to speak only of religion and virtue, to speak as a "precedent for wives" ' (Stallybrass, 'Reading the Body', p. 130). Rather, I believe

that the spectacular display of her body invokes and invites desire, not unlike Marvell's 'Coy Mistress'; see Barker, *Tremulous Private Body*, p. 89.

40. Foucault, *History of Sexuality*, pp. 17–35.

41. See Aries, *Hour of Our Death*, p. 377.

42. Foucault, *History of Sexuality*, p. 137.

43. I am grateful to Elizabeth Bryan, Louis Montrose, and Don Wayne for their interest and valuable suggestions concerning this project. Renie Henchy was an attentive and scrupulous reader; finally, for his sustaining dialogue and advice, I wish to thank Tom Harshman.

7

'As Tame as the Ladies': Politics and Gender in *The Changeling*

CRISTINA MALCOLMSON

In their recent books on seventeenth-century drama, Margot
Heinemann and Jonathan Dollimore have characterised Thomas
Middleton as a Puritan writing 'opposition drama' and a playwright composing 'radical tragedy'. Heinemann sees Middleton
appealing to and encouraging ' "anti-establishment", generally
Parliamentary Puritan sympathies'. Dollimore understands
Jacobean dramatists to be engaged in the 'demystification of state
power and ideology', and a 'contemporary critique of power relations'. Both encourage critics to identify drama during this period
as potentially subversive, and to recognise the extent to which plays
by Middleton and others actively stimulated, as Dollimore puts it,
'the crisis in confidence in the integrity of those in power'.[1]

My argument will depend on these claims, but also qualify them.
I hope to demonstrate that Thomas Middleton appealed to
Parliamentary opposition to Stuart policy by objecting to James's
plans for a Spanish marriage two years before *A Game at Chesse*, in
fact in *The Changeling* in 1622.[2] But the strategy of *The
Changeling* suggests that Middleton's work is far more patriarchal
in a traditional sense than these characterisations would imply. *The
Changeling* examines hierarchical relations in terms of male control
over women and the institution of marriage, and in doing so

subverts its own potential for a truly radical critique of 'state power and ideology'.

In January 1622, King James suspended Parliament and imprisoned several members because they advised him against planning a marriage for his son Charles to a Spanish Catholic princess. In May 1622, Middleton and Rowley presented *The Changeling*, a play which represents Spanish intrigue and villainy, as well as the repressive use of autocratic government. In the play's first scene the Spanish aristocrats Vermandero and Alsemero refer to their enemies as 'those rebellious Hollanders', the Protestant Dutch who had in 1621 renewed their battle with Spain for religious and political independence (I.i.178). The phrase 'rebellious Hollanders' would remind a contemporary audience of the refusal by King James to create a strong Protestant coalition between the Netherlands, England, and Germany in order to fight Spain and the European Catholic powers, and it would also suggest that 'rebellion' in this play is not necessarily wicked – that the language of authority could be used to justify religious and political repression. *The Changeling* was put on by the players patronised by Elizabeth of Bohemia, King James's daughter and the wife of Frederick of Bohemia. To English Protestants, Elizabeth and Frederick represented the European Protestant cause, and their position in Europe was felt to be severely jeopardised by a marriage between Prince Charles and the Spanish Infanta. Heinemann has shown that Middleton's city pageants and masques during this period made veiled references to the danger of a Catholic queen to the English church.[3] Middleton and Rowley do the same in *The Changeling*, not only in the play's portrait of Spanish degeneracy, but also in its questioning of those in power, whether master, father, husband, or king.

The play is made up of a series of rebellions: Beatrice-Joanna plots against her father's plans for her marriage, and De Flores plots against his master in order to sleep with Beatrice-Joanna; in the subplot Lollio plots against his master in order to sleep with his wife Isabella, and Isabella plots against her husband and his servant in order to maintain her freedom and integrity. In almost every case we are encouraged to see the justice of such rebellion since those in authority are abusing their responsibility. The play ruthlessly examines hierarchical relations and exposes them as relations of power; individuals are socially superior to others not because of their higher intelligence or morality, but because of the arbitrary factors of birth and gender and because of the use of force. At important moments in this play, women are morally and intellectually superior to men, servants to masters, and the members of the middle classes to the aristocracy. The play appears to be dismantling the principle of hierarchy.

The implications of this mode of gender and political analysis would be disastrous for Stuart theories of government. When Parliament petitioned James to stop negotiations for the Spanish match in December 1621, James's imprisonment of members of Parliament and his published declarations enforced the difference between king and subject, the ruler and the ruled. He defined the petition as an attack on his royal prerogative and an example of insolent disrespect for 'what appertaineth to the height of a powerful Monarch'. James accused Parliament of using 'Anti-monarchical words', and invading his royal power: the petition was 'an usurpation that the Majesty of a King can by no meanes endure'. He insisted that his position of authority lifted him above the criticism or advice of those beneath him: 'We needed not to bee measured by any other rule, but our own Princely will.'[4] *The Changeling* suggests that such definitions of difference between higher and lower are often merely assertions of will, whether princely or otherwise. When the daughter Beatrice-Joanna and the servant De Flores begin their plotting at the end of the first scene of the play, they mark it by such an assertion: 'I'll have my will' (I.i.216, 233). But the conventional association of wilfulness with rebellion is undermined in this play by the fact that Vermandero, Beatrice-Joanna's father, has already expressed himself in these very words about his choice of a husband for his daughter: 'I'll want / My will else' (I.i.215–16). The difference between ruler and ruled collapses here as the play reveals all individuals to be governed by an irrational wilfulness; those in political or familial authority are simply more capable of enforcing it.

The play puts its dangerous political opinions in terms of sexual politics.[5] Instead of considering a repressive king who governs his country inadequately, *The Changeling* portrays repressive fathers and husbands who mistreat their daughters and wives. The play hides its political critique of the king's policy within the contemporary debate about the proper treatment of women by their male superiors. This controversy has recently been shown by many scholars to have been an exceptionally popular topic in pamphlets and on the stage, especially in the 1620s.[6] Middleton referred to this controversy in several of his plays, including *The Roaring Girl* and *Women Beware Women.*[7] In *The Changeling*, Middleton and Rowley use this controversy as a vehicle for the consideration of injustice and rebellion, but at a safe distance. In the analysis that follows I hope to show that by centring the play upon the debate about women, the writers not only protect themselves from political censure, they protect themselves and their audience from the implications of their own demystifications of power.

Middleton and Rowley use the contemporary debate about women to structure the play through their contrast between the main plot and the subplot, between the characters of Beatrice-Joanna and Isabella. The play considers the statement made by one of the participants in the debate, Joseph Swetnam, who wrote a pamphlet called *The Arraignment of Lewd, Idle, Froward, and Unconstant Women*, published in 1615: 'Women are all necessary evils, ... [Moses] also saith, That [women] were made of the Rib of a Man; and that their *froward nature* sheweth, for a Rib is a crooked thing, good for nothing else; and Women are crooked by Nature.'[8] The defenders of women who answered Swetnam, like Rachel Speght in *A Mouzell for Melastomus, The Cynical Baytor of, and foule mouthed Barker against Evahs Sex* (1617) and Esther Sowernam in *Esther hath hanged Haman* (1617), argued that women were not pernicious by nature, but that, as Speght put it, 'of men and women, there are two sorts, namely, good and bad'.[9] *The Changeling* presents the good and the bad, not only in the contrast between Isabella and Beatrice-Joanna, but in the ethical differences in the men in the play. *The Changeling* in fact argues that women are not innately evil, that their moral character is as complex as a man's, and that, whereas a morally weak woman like Beatrice-Joanna can become a monster, a strong woman like Isabella can fully protect her integrity.

The play sets up the issue by putting its two female characters under the press of circumstances that are strikingly similar: both are imprisoned by the institution of marriage and the authority of their patriarchal guardians. This was a central question for the defenders of women in the controversy: to what extent is marriage a form of male tyranny? 'Husbands should not consider their wives as their vassals,' says Rachel Speght, 'but as those that are heirs together of the grace of life.'[10] Also central to the debate during this period was the problem of early or forced marriages, in which parents arranged their children's matches before they had come of age, or forced them to marry against their will. In Middleton's *Women Beware Women*, when Isabella's father compels her to marry a man unknown to her, she complains:

> Oh the heart-breakings
> Of miserable maids, where love's enforced!
> The best condition is but bad enough:
> When women have their choices, commonly
> They do but buy their thralldoms, and bring great portions
> To men to keep 'em in subjection ...
> Men buy their slaves, but women buy their masters.
>   (I.ii.166–71, 176)

The evidence that many considered forced and early marriages to be unjust comes not only from the drama of the period: Thomas Overbury attributes to King James the remark that 'Parents may forbid their children an unfitt marriage, but they may not force their consciences to a fitt.'[11]

The major cause for public concern about this problem was not so much a new sympathy for the plight of women, but the recent annulment of the early marriage between the Earl of Essex and Frances Howard (in 1613) followed in 1615 by the murder trial of Frances Howard and her new husband, the Earl of Somerset, for the poisoning of Thomas Overbury. Frances had been married to Essex when she was thirteen, and had later become involved with Robert Carr, the King's favourite, soon to be Earl of Somerset. Thomas Overbury, Carr's adviser and friend, was an outspoken critic against the match between Carr and Howard, and was found poisoned in the Tower just before the annulment of the Countess' first marriage. Somerset and the Countess were both found guilty of the murder, but it was clear from the trial that Frances herself had instigated the crime.[12] Much of the controversy about women was influenced by this scandal: Frances Howard lies behind the figure of the 'masculine women' in many of these tracts, including the famous *Hic Mulier, or the Man-Woman*, which condemned the masculine dress of the female aristocrat, as well as her desire to be a 'man in action by pursuing revenge'.[13] Swetnam models his image of the beautiful but villainous female on the Countess, and critics have argued that Frances Howard provided the model for Beatrice-Joanna in *The Changeling*.[14] The similarities between Beatrice-Joanna and Frances Howard are too striking to ignore: aside from the murder, the Countess had to undergo a chastity test to obtain her annulment, the positive results of which were widely distrusted. According to rumour, the Countess sent one of her cousins, veiled, to take the test for her. But even those who condemned women in general because of the Countess' murder recognised that her crime was in part the result of the injustice of an early marriage. The notorious Swetnam himself admits: 'when Matches are made by the Parents, and the Dowery told and paid before the young Couple have any knowledge of it, and so many times are forced against their Minds, fearing the Rigour and Displeasure of their Parents, they often promise with their Mouths, and they refuse with their Hearts.'[15]

The Changeling itself is quite explicit in its depiction of this problem. In analyses of the opening scene critics have focused on Beatrice-Joanna's inconstancy of affection as she shifts her attentions from Piracquo to Alsemero, but they largely ignore her father's aggressive assertion of his control over her future. Vermandero speaks about Piracquo, his original choice for the marriage:

> I would not change him for a son-in-law
> For any he in Spain, the proudest he,
> And we have great ones, that you know ...
> He shall be bound to me
> As fast as this tie can hold him; I'll want
> My will else.
>
> (I.i.211–16)

Beatrice-Joanna disappears in this formulation, except as a 'tie', a symbol for the alliance between her father and her fiancé. The next scene makes visible the domineering wilfulness of Vermandero through the explicitly coercive control of the old doctor Alibius, who imprisons his wife Isabella within his asylum to protect her chastity and puts her under the supervision of his servant Lollio. Both scenes unmask not only the authoritarian use of power by father and husband, they define this power as the capacity of men to control the sexuality of women. In graphic phallic imagery, Alibius defines his marriage ring and the finger that wears it in terms of his sexual possession of Isabella. The ringed finger becomes an image for sexual intercourse: 'I would wear my ring on my own finger; / Whilst it is borrowed it is none of mine / But his that useth it' (I.ii.27–9).[16] For another man to have intercourse with Isabella would signal Alibius' loss of ownership of her and her capacity for generation; Alibius understands marriage as the husband's ability to determine whose finger thrusts into the ring. This pattern of imagery in the subplot echoes that presented in the main plot, when De Flores finds Beatrice's glove and fantasises that he could 'Thrust my fingers into her sockets here' (I.i.230). The brutal nature of this imagery reveals the element of force that can structure a man's relationship to a woman, and reminds us of the assertion of will that has, thus far in the play, marked the social roles of husband and father.

In an undercurrent of jokes and repeated images, the play extends this critique of male authority to all forms of hierarchical government. It suggests that those who rule are superior not because of their innate worth but because they possess the power to imprison and control. Lollio, the asylum's caretaker and Alibius' servant, hints constantly that nothing differentiates his master from himself except Alibius' greater wealth and greater foolishness, and that nothing differentiates the two of them as supervisors of the asylum from the madmen and fools they govern except their position of authority and the whip they use to control the inmates. Lollio explodes the hierarchy of authority through his comment to Tony: 'there is a knave, that's my master' (I.ii.186), and through his question: 'how many knaves make an honest man?' Lollio answers the question himself: 'There's three knaves may make an honest man: a sergeant, a jailor, and a beadle: the sergeant catches him, the jailor holds him, and the beadle lashes him; and if he be not honest then, the hangman must cure him' (I.ii.157–8, 161–4). Honesty here is simply the willingness to obey knaves in positions of authority: the process of teaching morality or healing fools is simply a matter of applying the lash. This lash becomes a visible prop in later scenes, when Lollio uses the whip to control the unruly madmen (III.iii.53,85 and IV.iii.60–1). Lollio's whip and the confining walls of the asylum make visible the structure of relations that govern the main plot. Alsemero's desire to ensure Beatrice-Joanna's virginity through his chastity test is shown to be just another strategy of control: when he thinks she has passed the test, he says: 'My Joanna, / Chaste as the breath of heaven or morning's womb / That brings the day forth, thus my love encloses thee' (IV.ii.149–51). The stage direction in the Regents edition repeats this image visually: 'He embraces her.' The embrace signals affection according to the code of love and marriage, yet is revealed here to be invested with the same assertion of will that motivates Vermandero and Alibius. This pattern of imagery has been introduced already in the subplot, not only in the imprisonment of Isabella, but through her objection to it. She speaks sarcastically to her husband: 'You were best lock me up.' He answers, 'In my arms and bosom, my sweet Isabella, / I'll lock thee up most nearly' (III.iii.244–6).

Through this imagery of enclosure, the play reveals that gender relations are constituted through the use of force symbolised by Lollio's whip. In a grotesque echo of the mechanicals' play in *A Midsummer Night's Dream*, Alibius plans a dance of his madmen for the wedding night revels of Beatrice-Joanna and Alsemero. In *A Midsummer Night's Dream*, Snout comically worries if the actor playing the lion will be so lifelike that he will terrify the ladies present; in *The Changeling*, Alibius fears that his madmen will 'Affright the ladies; they are nice things, you know' (IV.iii.59).[17] Lollio's response corrects his master's overly reverent sense of the delicate 'court lady' by making explicit the analogy between the imprisoned madmen and the women of the play, whether from the professional or aristocratic classes: 'You need not fear, sir; so long as we are there with our commanding pizzles, they'll be as tame as the ladies themselves' (IV.iii.60–1). Both inmates and women are governed by a force which is explicitly masculine and brutal: the phrase 'commanding pizzles' associates Lollio's whip with the male genitals and links leadership and authority with sexual aggression. In this comment the play's own gender analysis emerges: masculine action is marked not by superior rationality or morality, but by the exertion of force. Women obey male authorities as madmen obey menacing guards. Sexual politics is defined in terms of attack here: women fear the violence of 'commanding pizzles' whether in bed or out, and men only know themselves as 'men', sexually and politically, through the subjugation of the women associated with them.

The subplot exposes the tyranny and injustice of gender relations in the main plot and in the Renaissance institution of marriage. The analysis of sexual politics threatens continually to spill over into a generalised critique of hierarchical social relations, and brings the play remarkably close to what Jonathan Dollimore calls 'a demystification of state power and ideology'.

Nevertheless, the play evades its own subversive critique of those in authority by representing the effects of rebellion as far worse than tyranny. Indeed, the play's implied solution to the problems it dramatises is nothing like political or sexual equality, but rather a patriarchy which governs more wisely and sympathetically but far more powerfully than the government exercised by Alibius and

Vermandero. The need for a benevolent but potent ruler is signalled by the play's recurring image of an invasion that threatens both the city's castle and the female body.[18] The play's husbands and fathers are inadequate because they cannot protect their domain from such penetration.

Vermandero's insistence on choosing Beatrice-Joanna's husband stems from his fear about the safety of his castle. When Vermandero meets Alsemero at the beginning of the play, he hesitates to show him his citadel, since such knowledge can be abused by his enemies:

> I must know
> Your country. We use not to give survey
> Of our chief strengths to strangers; our citadels
> Are plac'd conspicuous to outward view
> On promonts' tops, but within are secrets.
> (I.i.157–61)

Vermandero fears invasion, and the imagery of penetration and invasion continues throughout the play: in the courtiers' penetration into Alibius' asylum, in their desire to penetrate his wife, in the 'private way' through which Diaphanta leads Alsemero to Beatrice-Joanna, and in the 'back part of the house' where Jasperino overhears the secret meeting between Beatrice-Joanna and De Flores. When Beatrice-Joanna's assassin De Flores kills Piracquo deep in the heart of the castle, the imagery of rings and fingers is given new meaning: whereas in the subplot, it suggested male possessiveness of the female body, here it represents castration (III.ii.25). As De Flores cuts off the ringed finger that symbolises Piracquo's intended marriage, he essentially castrates the father's plans for his daughter, destroys her fiancé's control over his potential wife's capacity for generation, and sets Beatrice-Joanna free to determine her own partner in marriage. When De Flores insists on Beatrice-Joanna's virginity as the reward for his services, the invasion is complete: Vermandero has fully lost control over his daughter. He understands the situation in just this way when he learns of the murder of Piracquo and the alliance between Beatrice-Joanna and De Flores: 'An host of enemies enter'd my citadel / Could not amaze like this' (V.iii.148–9). Vermandero's citadel is not only his castle, it is Beatrice-Joanna herself, and the threat of invasion figures the father's loss of control over the female body. Critics A. L. and M. K. Kistner point out the patriarchal implications of this pattern of imagery: 'Vermandero is morally responsible for the defence and protection of the castle and Beatrice, yet the latter citadel was entered, taken, and destroyed by the enemy without his knowledge.'[19]

The work of anthropologists and feminists who study the institution of marriage in pre-industrial societies can offer further insight into this association of the city's castle with the female body. In his discussion of the exchange of women, Lévi-Strauss states that the primary relationship established by marriage in these societies is that between two groups of men, not between man and woman: marriage 'provides the means of binding men together'.[20] Feminist Patricia Klindienst Joplin argues that this system of exchange lies behind the social value of chastity: 'Female chastity is not sacred out of the respect for the integrity of the woman as person ... The virgin's hymen must not be ruptured except in some manner that reflects and ensures the health of the existing political hierarchy. The father king regulates both the literal and metaphorical "gates" to the city's power: the actual gates in the city wall or the hymen as the gateway to the daughter's body.'[21] According to this analysis, a daughter's chastity preserves the father's right to determine who his allies will be, since it is through sexual intercourse with the daughter that a husband gains access to a larger intercourse with the father's family or city. Marriage creates alliances, and entrance into the female body represents entrance into the state.

In her book *Purity and Danger*, anthropologist Mary Douglas interprets the symbolic relationship between external boundaries of the body and the state: 'The body is a model which can stand for any bounded system. Its boundaries can represent any boundaries which are threatened or precarious.'[22] Douglas adds to this in her book *Natural Symbols*: 'The human body is always treated as an image of society ... Interest in its apertures depends on the preoccupation with social exits and entrances, escape routes and invasions.'[23] In an article entitled 'Patriarchal Territories', Peter Stallybrass describes how the surveillance of women during the Renaissance focused on the apertures of the body, particularly the mouth and the vagina, and how the chaste woman became not only an emblem of the perfect and impermeable container, but also 'a map of the integrity of the state. The state, like a virgin, was a *hortus conclusus*, an enclosed garden walled off from enemies.'[24] Queen Elizabeth's virginity signified not only her own purity, but the strength and impermeability of the boundaries of the nation, particularly during the attempted Spanish invasion of the country in 1588.

In the 1620s the pamphlets written against the Spanish marriage put their fears of invasion in terms of the female body and its sexual vulnerability. In the treatise called *The Foot out of the Snare*, John Gee describes Catholic attempts to proselytise English Protestants as a form of seduction: 'yet some, like Dinah the daughter of Jacob, have lost their virginity, I meane *primam et puram fidem*, their first faith, by *going abroad, and have returned home impure*.'[25] Middleton's own *A Game at Chesse* represents the Spanish corruption of the English church through the plot of the Black King to seduce the White Queen. The same play figures the Catholic attack on the individual Protestant soul through the attempted rape of the White Queen's Pawn by the Black Bishop's Pawn (II.i.15–26).[26] In these cases the vulnerable female body symbolises the weakness of the body of the state, disturbingly open to the infiltration of foreign Catholic powers who stand ready to enter England either through 'open Invaders or secret underminers'. A pamphlet called *Vox Populi* describes the Catholics in England: 'Besides, in a small time they should work so farre into the Body of the State, *by buying offices and the like*, whether by *Sea* or *Land*, of Justice Civil or Ecclesiastical, in *Church* or *state*, that with the helpe of the Jesuits, they would undermine [the state] with meere wit.'[27]

Fears about the seductive power of Catholic priests often became quite literal. Several pamphlets warned against priests and Jesuits who persuaded young English women to enter nunneries abroad. Such a process was described as being 'Nunnified', and it was often directly linked with sexual misconduct. *The Anatomy of the English Nunnery at Lisbon in Portugal* (1622) claimed that the priests had regular sexual relations with the English nuns, and called on their families to save them from 'such horrible and sacriligious rapine and spoile'.[28] John Gee's treatises are filled with stories of young women led astray by Catholic priests, one of whom impregnated his follower, and therefore, according to Gee, was 'a fitt man to be called a Father'.[29] He sums up his attack on the Jesuits as follows: 'Easily can they steale away *the hearts of the weaker sort*: and secretly do they creep into houses, *leading captive simple women loaden with sinnes and led away with divers lusts*.'[30] Invasion into the female body, like invasion into 'the house' of an Englishman, represents the permeability of the country's boundaries as well as its private spaces. Female sensuality represents that part of the country that Protestants cannot control, those consciences and households which elude state regulation.

A few treatises refer to unnamed but specific women in England who work as spies for the Catholic cause. As agents of Count Gondomar, the Spanish ambassador, these women are imagined as both vulnerable to Spanish manipulation and capable of extreme violence in carrying out Spanish plots. In *A Game at Chesse* the Black Knight is characterised as having 'wrought / Women's soft soules e'en up to masculine Malice / To persue truth to death if the cause rowzed 'em' (IV.ii.27–9). *Vox Populi* refers to an unnamed Catholic priest in England who is particularly able to 'serve himself into the closet of the heart, and to worke upon feminine levitie, who [that is, the women] in that Countrie have masculine Spirits to command and pursue their plots unto death'.[31] Such references to 'masculine malice' and 'masculine spirits' recall the figure of Hic Mulier, the proud woman who dresses like a man, and who wishes to be a 'man in action by pursuing revenge'. Like the detractors of women in the current controversy, the writers of these pamphlets against the Spanish marriage measure the need for a strong patriarchal governor through the 'unruliness' of women who move beyond the limits of conventional notions of gender. But the paradoxical association of vulnerability with aggressive and violent action in the masculine woman also suggests that the fear behind this gendered imagery is not only about the invasion of the country but about specific women as well.

It is not a coincidence that many observers at the time felt that Frances Howard's murder of Thomas Overbury was part of a complex plot initiated by her family, the Catholic Howards, to gain control over the King's favourite, Carr, and therefore, over the King. Frances's uncle, Henry Howard, the Earl of Northumberland, was known to be receiving a pension from the Spanish, and he had been actively working toward the success of the marriage between Prince Charles and the Infanta. Soon after Carr's marriage with Frances Howard, Carr made direct overtures to the Spanish ambassador on behalf of this marriage. Many Protestants felt that Overbury was sacrificed to ensure that such negotiations could go forward. During the Overbury murder trial, Sir Edward Coke made it clear that he suspected a Catholic plot.[32]

The association of women with Spanish infiltration in the literature on the subject articulates a powerful fear about another specific woman: the Spanish princess, who as queen would be the mother to the future English king, and under whose. Spanish Catholic influence the child would be reared. Like Queen Mary, the Spanish Infanta was seen as the avenue through which the Catholic Church and the Spanish empire would enter the English state and rob it of its national strength. As the pamphlet put it, 'If you can bring in the *Infanta*, doubt you not but she will usher in the Pope, and consequently hee the Catholic King.'[33] Although explicit attacks on the Infanta are rare in this literature, the overwhelming disturbance about the infidelity of women to the English cause and their vulnerability to Spanish influence suggests a powerful suspicion that the Infanta would be politically and religiously, if not sexually, unfaithful to her husband. In 1645, William Prynne explicitly articulates what this literature implies. He speaks of Spanish hostility to England: 'they fixed at last of latter times upon a more prevalent and successful meanes than any of the former; to wit, a project of *marrying us to the Whore of Rome* by matching the heire of the crowne of England to a *Romanist*.'[34] Here the association of the Catholic Church with the Infanta almost becomes literal – like the Church, she is the whore of Rome, whose infidelity to the English cause is inevitable.

The proper response to the Spanish threat, according to these writers, was for King James to act like a man. Fearing the emasculation of the English nation through a Catholic queen, these pamphlets did not call for a curtailing of the King's power, nor for an increase in the capacity of his subjects or of Parliament to govern themselves, but for a more aggressive exercise and enforcement of male patriarchal authority. This meant war with Spain, and James was called on to give up his negotiations and strike first. One pamphlet states, 'Tell [King James] that [which] Agesileus said, that words are feminine and deedes masculine, and that it is a great part of honour, discretion, and happiness for a Prince, to give the first blow to his Enemies ... King Phillip [of Spain] loves King James for his Gowne and Pen, yet no way feares his sword.'[35] These pamphlets argue that the English upper classes had become effeminate through the long period of peace and the decadence of court life with its 'Stage-Playes, Maskes, Revels and Carrowsing'.[36] As the *Vox Populi* puts it, 'Thus stands the state of that poore miserable Countrey, which had never *more people and fewer men.*'[37]

In his works on kingship James regularly described himself as a father and a husband to his country. In one of his addresses to Parliament he said, 'I am the Husband, and all the whole Isle is my lawfull Wife.'[38] The literature against the Spanish marriage warned that this royal husband was neglecting his responsibilities, responsibilities which were imagined in a fully patriarchal way: the King must protect the purity of the country just as a husband and father must protect the chastity of a virgin daughter and a wife. Such protection requires the maintenance of one's 'potency', and this included the capacity to defend the boundaries of the state: the English navy is defined in these pamphlets as the 'Bulwarkes and walls of England', but also as having become 'impotent' through the decay of its strength.[39] King James's status as a powerful and loving father is questioned because of his inability to protect his daughter, the Queen of Bohemia, and her husband, from the incursion of the European Catholic powers and from the loss of their patrimony, the Palatinate.[40] According to these Protestants, James was unaware and therefore vulnerable to the machinations of the Spanish, whose plots reached even into the private spaces of the country. The murder of Thomas Overbury, like the murder of Piracquo in *The Changeling*, took place in the city's fortified citadel, the Tower, and represented an invasion into the heart of English national strength. Many were shocked when King James pardoned the Countess and her husband, kept them in prison until January 1622, and then allowed them to retire to their country estate. Many had been shocked when King James failed to defend the Earl of Essex, Frances Howard's first husband, from the charge of impotency she levelled at him at the annulment trial. It could be argued that *The Changeling* attacks aristocratic degeneracy through its portrait of the corrupt Beatrice-Joanna, modelled on the figure of Frances Howard, especially in contrast to the virtuous, middle-class Isabella. But for the play, as for the opponents of the King's policy in Parliament, the point was not that members of the middle classes were more fit to rule than the aristocracy, but that King James, like Vermandero and Alibius, had become an ineffectual patriarch.

Through its questioning of hierarchical relations, *The Changeling* is both 'opposition drama' and 'radical tragedy'. But the limits of its subversion are measured by its commitment to patriarchy and the male-governed institution of marriage. The play undermines its own status as 'opposition' by displacing its dream of rebellion on to Isabella, who remains obedient, and Beatrice-Joanna and De Flores, who become horrifying. This dream of rebellion becomes most titillating in the relationship between Beatrice-Joanna and De Flores, because in this alliance hierarchy is temporarily disrupted, and the aristocrat finds that her servant is her true equal. As rebel-hero, De Flores enacts the political science of the subplot because he treats the traditional order as empty convention. As he insists on his sexual reward from Beatrice-Joanna, he brushes aside her resistance as superficial morality:

> Look but into your conscience, read me there;
> 'Tis a true book; you'll find me there your equal.
> Push, fly not to your birth, but settle you
> In what the act has made you
>
> (III.iv.133–6)

Jonathan Dollimore argues that this episode discloses ' "blood" and "birth" to be myths in the service of historical and social forms of power'.[41] But before we revel in this fantasy of equality, let us remember that at this, the play's most radical moment about the class hierarchy, it is also most traditional about the sexual hierarchy: the rising of the servant against his master is put in terms of the subordination of an upstart woman by her superior male counterpart. Beatrice-Joanna begins the scene by commanding, but ends by kneeling to her new master. This scene may be the most dramatic and erotic in the play, but we cannot afford to forget that it initiates a form of rape.[42] Middleton seemed to think of it as such, since immediately before De Flores carries Beatrice-Joanna off-stage, he describes her as panting like a turtle dove, an image that recurs precisely at the same moment in the explicit rape scene in Middleton's *Women Beware Women* (II.ii.320–1). De Flores' rape seals his rebellion against his master Vermandero, but it also ensures that the play's most vivid imagination of equality will not go too far: De Flores simultaneously challenges the aristocracy and punishes those unruly women who would rebel against male authority.

It is possible to argue that, through her encounter with De Flores, the morally naïve Beatrice-Joanna comes to recognise her sexual nature, and deepens her understanding of herself. But such a process demands that De Flores seize control over her plot and her sexuality. An examination of the literary and historical sources for the character of Beatrice-Joanna reveals that in *The Changeling* she is far less capable and alert than her precursors. In Reynold's *The Triumph of God's Revenge* the character Beatrice-Joanna has De Flores kill Piracquo and then takes De Flores as her lover.[43] Isdaura in *The Unfortunate Spaniard* is raped by a servant who, like De

Flores, demands her virginity as a fit reward for his service to her, but she then kills him in return.[44] Frances Howard was far more active than her lover Carr in planning the death of Overbury, and at the trial those who had served her in the murder were condemned to death, whereas she was pardoned. De Flores is the most original character in the play in part because he represents the playwrights' revenge against these masculine and deadly women, and the means by which the play reinstates the proper balance between female weakness and male rule. This reassertion of the conventional balance between male and female power occurs even on the most specific dramatic level: De Flores' lines are continually placed so as to deflect attention away from Beatrice-Joanna. In Act II, scene ii, she reveals to him her desire to control her own destiny, to become the Hic Mulier, or the man-woman; yet De Flores steals the spotlight. He hears her sigh, and asks her to explain it, thinking she will declare her love for him:

> **Beatrice** Would creation–
> **De Flores** Ay. Well said, that's it.
> **Beatrice** Had form'd me man.
> **De Flores** Nay, that's not it.
> (II.ii.107–9)

His comments deflate her potentially dramatic complaint and her following lines collapse a complex yearning to be free from the injustice of gender relations into what appears as a naïve desire simply to kill:

> Oh, 'tis the soul of freedom;
> I should not then be forc'd to marry one
> I hate beyond all depths; I should have power
> Then to oppose my loathings, nay, remove 'em
> Forever from my sight.
> (II.ii.109–13)

By deflecting attention from Beatrice-Joanna to De Flores, the play reasserts the potency of masculine action, and ensures that any consideration of the injustice of Beatrice-Joanna's marital situation will not go too far. We should wonder if the play has really offered us an alternative to the male authoritarianism that the subplot so effectively critiques. The gender issues in this relationship, like the play as a whole, circumscribe the authors' political thinking within the limits of patriarchy.

Because of its numerous references to *A Midsummer Night's Dream*, *The Changeling* should be read as rewriting Shakespeare's play, a revision which nostalgically laments a shift from what was considered the bright Elizabethan period to the disillusionment of the Stuart era. *A Midsummer Night's Dream* dramatises the injustice of gender relations, as well as the madness and metamorphosis that occur in love and sexuality, but ends with a last act which commemorates a set of aristocratic marriages and attempts, however partially, to accommodate all orders of society, male and female, aristocrats and commoners (see III.iii.48–52 and IV.iii.1–4). *The Changeling* not only revises comedy into tragedy, it comments on Middleton's own *Masque of Cupid*, presented in honour of the marriage between Frances Howard and Robert Carr in 1614, at a time when their complicity in the murder of Thomas Overbury was not known.[45] Like *The Changeling*'s anti-masque of madmen and fools, the play satirises the ability of such celebratory masques accurately to represent or prophesy the disruption and violence that these marriages can cause. It attempts to ward off the disorder that could result from such marriages as that between the Earl and Countess of Somerset, as well as between Prince Charles and the Infanta of Spain, marriages in which 'the masculine woman' could challenge the foundation of English national strength.

From *English Literary Renaissance*, 20:2 (Spring, 1990), 320–39.

NOTES

[One important difference between the two schools of critical theory known as cultural materialism and new historicism is revealed in what is sometimes referred to as the subversion and containment debate. Although there is an obvious danger of oversimplifying complex, subtle distinctions, a general rule of thumb states that new historicists tend to see subversive strategies being appropriated by the dominant ideology and incorporated into its system, so that the apparently radical is conceded only in as much as it can be co-opted by those in power. Cultural materialists, on the other hand, see genuine subversive potential in the efforts of the oppositional culture – book titles such as *Political Shakespeare* (ed. Jonathan Dollimore and Alan Sinfield, 1985) and Dollimore's *Radical Tragedy* (1984) are in themselves testament to that belief. Within this model, Malcolmson's essay walks a fine line between the faith of the cultural materialist and the pessimism of the new historicist. At the end, however, Malcolmson seems to concede to containment, arguing that *The Changeling* offers to attempt a critique of state power and ideology, but that it 'subverts its own potential' through its commitment to conventional gender hierarchies. By focusing not on court corruption, but on male control over women in various forms (not only husband and wife), the play remains fundamentally conservative. Malcolmson's pessimism, then, is of a specifically feminist kind.

While essays such as that by Deborah Burks (essay 8) situate the plays they analyse within their wider cultural context, putting them in dialogue with other texts such as legal documents, Malcolmson's essay reads *The Changeling* in the light of one particular sensational incident, and one specific political crisis. The incident was the murder of Sir Thomas Overbury and subsequent trial of Frances Howard and her new husband the Earl of Somerset; the situation was the national anxiety over King James I's plans for his son Charles to marry a Spanish (Catholic) princess. The Howard trial took place in 1615, the crisis around the royal marriage in January 1622; *The Changeling* was first performed in May of the same year.

Malcolmson's essay is instructive for the way in which it shows how deeply implicated state politics was in the culture of the playhouse. Contemporary criticism of early modern drama now tends to make a straightforward assumption that the monarch and his or her Privy Council took a great interest in the theatre; Elizabeth and James were both, we are told, well aware of the political significance of the public theatres. Malcolmson here provides us with solid and specific evidence of precisely why their concerns were well founded. References to the play are taken from the edition edited by George Walton Williams (Lincoln, NA, 1966). Citations for *A Game at Chess* refer to the Cambridge edition edited by R. C. Bald (1929). Ed.]

1. Jonathan Dollimore, *Radical Tragedy: Religion, Ideology and Power in the Drama of Shakespeare and his Contemporaries* (Chicago, 1984), pp. 4, 231; Margot Heinemann, *Puritanism and Theatre: Thomas Middleton and Opposition Drama under the Early Stuarts* (Cambridge, 1980), p. 16. I am indebted to the following colleagues who discussed these issues with me or reviewed earlier versions of this essay: Murray Biggs, Richard Burt, Jill Campbell, Richard Dutton, Patricia Klindienst Joplin, John Morrison, Peter Stallybrass, and Valerie Wayne.

2. For the circumstances surrounding *A Game at Chess*, see the edition edited by R. C. Bald (Cambridge, 1929), pp. 1–25.

3. Heinemann, *Puritanism and Theatre*, pp. 126–41.

4. James I, *His Majesty's Declaration Touching his Proceedings in the Late Assembly and Convention of Parliament* (1621 / 1622), sig. A3; James I, *A Proclamation declaring His Majesty's Pleasure Concerning the dissolving of the present Convention of Parliament* (1621), p. 18.

5. 'Open political-religious allegory similar to that in *A Game at Chess* later, would clearly have been too risky for the players in 1620–3, when Puritan preachers were being silenced and imprisoned for

commenting on the marriage plan' (Heinemann, *Puritanism and Theatre*, p. 141).

6. Sandra Clark, 'Hic Mulier, Haec Vir, and the Controversy over Masculine Women', *Studies in Philology*, 82 (1985), 157–83; Katherine Usher Henderson and Barbara F. McManus, *Half Humankind: Contexts and Texts of the Controversy about Women in England, 1540–1640* (Urbana, IL, 1985); Mary Beth Rose, 'Women in Men's Clothing: Apparel and Social Stability in *The Roaring Girl*', *English Literary Renaissance*, 14 (1984), 367–91; Linda Woodbridge, *Women and the English Renaissance: Literature and the Nature of Womankind, 1540–1620* (Urbana, IL, 1984), pp. 139–51. See also Louis B. Wright, *Middle-Class Culture in Elizabethan England* (Chapel Hill, NC, 1935), pp. 481–502.

7. See Rose, 'Women in Men's Clothing', and J. R. Mulryne (ed.), *Women Beware Women* (Manchester, 1975), pp. xxxv–xxxvi.

8. Swetnam, *The Arraignment of Lewd, Idle, Froward, and Unconstant Women* (1615), p. 1.

9. Rachel Speght, *A Mouzell for Melastomus, The Cynical Baytor of, and foul mouthed Barker against Evah's Sex* (1617), p. 18.

10. Ibid., p. 15.

11. Edward F. Rimbault (ed.), *Crumbs Fallen From King James's Table, Or His Table Talk*, in *The Miscellaneous Works ... of Sir Thomas Overbury* (1856), p. 265.

12. G. P. V. Akrigg, *Jacobean Pageant* (Cambridge, MA, 1962), pp. 180–204; William McElwee, *The Murder of Thomas Overbury* (New York, 1952); Beatrice White, *Cast of Ravens: The Strange Case of Sir Thomas Overbury* (London, 1965).

13. *Hic Mulier: Or, The Man-Woman: Being a Medicine to cure the Coltish Disease of the Staggers in the Masculine-Feminines of our Times* (1620), sig. B$_2$. The pamphlet refers directly but without name to the Countess and her accomplice, Mrs Anne Turner, sig. A$_3$. (See *Half-Humankind*, p. 267.) 'Hic Mulier' is a Latin joke, using the masculine form of the demonstrative adjective, 'this', with the feminine word 'woman' in order to satirise women who dress and act like men.

14. Swetnam, *The Arraignment*, pp. 6, 16, 21, 29. For discussions of *The Changeling* and the Overbury murder, see Heinemann, *Puritanism and Theatre*, pp. 178–9, and J. L. Simmons, 'Diabolical Realism in Middleton and Rowley's *The Changeling*', *Renaissance Drama*, new series 11 (1980), 290–306. The play refers explicitly to the Countess' chastity test in IV.i.99–100.

15. Swetnam, *The Arraignment*, p. 71.

16. For other interpretations of this sexual imagery, see Barbara Joan Baines, *The Lust Motif in the Plays of Thomas Middleton* (Salzburg, 1973), pp. 114–15; A. L. and M. K. Kistner, *Middleton's Tragic Themes* (New York, 1984), p. 161; and Christopher Ricks, 'The Moral and Poetic Structure of *The Changeling*', *Essays in Criticism*, 10 (1960), 290–306.

17. *A Midsummer Night's Dream*, ed. Wolfgang Clemen (New York, 1963), III.i.27. Further citations will refer to this edition.

18. For other interpretations of the image of the castle, see Thomas L. Berger, 'The Petrarchan Fortress of *The Changeling*', *Renaissance Papers* (1969), 37–46; and G. R. Owst, *Literature and Pulpit in Medieval England* (Cambridge, 1933), pp. 77–83.

19. Kistners, *Middleton's Tragic Themes*, p. 120. The Kistners present one of the most logical of the moral readings of the play, but they do not submit the play's patriarchal ideals to a feminist analysis.

20. Claude Lévi-Strauss, *The Elementary Structures of Kinship*, trans. James Harle Bell, John Richard von Sturmer and Rodney Needham; rev. edn (Boston, 1969), pp. 115, 480.

21. 'The Voice of the Shuttle is ours', *Stanford Literature Review*, 1 (1984), 38. This article and my discussions with Patricia Joplin alerted me to the central role that the exchange of women plays in *The Changeling*, the public reaction to Frances Howard, and the Spanish marriage. For another reading of the significance of the body in *The Changeling*, see Frank Whigham, 'Reading Social Conflict in the Alimentary Tract: More on the Body in Renaissance Drama', *English Literary History*, 55 (1988), 339–43.

22. Mary Douglas, *Purity and Danger* (1966; London, 1980), p. 115.

23. Mary Douglas, *Natural Symbols* (1970; New York, 1982), p. 70.

24. Peter Stallybrass, 'Patriarchal Territories: the Body Enclosed', in Margaret Ferguson, Maureen Quilligan and Nancy Vickers (eds), *Rewriting the Renaissance: the Discourses of Sexual Difference in Early Modern Europe* (Chicago, 1986), p. 129.

25. John Gee, *The Foot out of the Snare: With a Detection of Sundry late practices and Impostures of the Priests and Jesuits in England* (1624), p. 2. The story of Dinah is particularly appropriate, since her rape by Shechem the Hivite brings on the massacre of his tribe by the Israelites not because of the violence committed against Dinah, but because of Shechem's attempt to use the rape as an opportunity to intermarry with the Israelites and so pollute the purity of the tribe. Thus Dinah is described as 'defiled' (Genesis 34).

26. See also Bald (ed.), *A Game at Chess*, pp. 11, 13.

27. Thomas Scot, *Vox Populi* (1620), p. 12.

28. Thomas Robinson, *The Anatomy of the English Nunnery at Lisbon in Portugal* (1622), p. 30.

29. Gee, *Foot out of the Snare*, pp. 65–6. See also John Gee, *New Shreds of the Old Snare* (1624).

30. Gee, *Foot out of the Snare*, p. 2.

31. Scot, *Vox Populi*, p. 20.

32. See Andrew Amos, *The Great Oyer of Poisoning* (1846), p. 371; McElwee, *Murder of Thomas Overbury*, pp. 213–14; White, *Cast of Ravens*, pp. 137–8.

33. *Vox Coeli* (1624), p. 56.

34. William Prynne, *Hidden Works of Darkness Brought to Public Light* (1645), p. 1.

35. *Vox Coeli*, sig. B$_2$.

36. *Vox Coeli*, p. 36.

37. *Vox Populi*, p. 21.

38. Charles H. McIlwain (ed.), *The Political Works of James I* (Cambridge, MA, 1918), p. 272.

39. *Vox Coeli*, p. 36; *Vox Populi*, p. 16.

40. *Vox Coeli*, sig. B$_2$; *The Honest Informer or Tom tell-Truth's Observations upon Abuses of Government* (1642), sig. A$_2$. This pamphlet was passed around in manuscript in 1622, according to Samuel Rawson Gardiner, *Prince Charles and the Spanish Marriage* (London, 1869), vol. 2, p. 183. [...]

41. Dollimore, *Radical Tragedy*, p. 178.

42. In her article, 'Dissimulation Anatomised: *The Changeling*', *Philological Quarterly*, 56 (1977), 329–38, Paula Johnson defines this scene as 'a rape-fantasy objectified' (p. 334), and argues that part of the emotional power of the scene stems from the fact that 'the woman relinquishes her unnatural tyranny: the man escapes his unnatural servitude' (p. 336).

43. John Reynolds, *The Triumph of God's Revenge* (1621; 1640), pp. 41–56.

44. Leonard Digges, *Geraldo: The Unfortunate Spaniard* (1622), pp. 89–108.

45. Rev. Alexander Dyce (ed.), *The Works of Thomas Middleton*, 7 vols (1840), VII, p. xix. Dyce quotes from the City Records of January 1613 / 1614. The text of the masque has not survived.

8

'I'll Want My Will Else': *The Changeling* and Women's Complicity with their Rapists

DEBORAH G. BURKS

[...]

Sixteenth- and seventeenth-century English dramatists linked women's sexual continence and their submission to the authority of their fathers and husbands not only to the well-ordering of family life, but to the preservation of social order.[1] The ideal woman could be relied upon absolutely to protect these boundaries, and the age did have a model of such feminine purity, however unrealistic she must have seemed. Lucrece, wife of Collatine, victim of Tarquin's lustful covetousness, was the English Renaissance's archetypal pattern of the violated, yet virtuous woman. Her rape, available in Ovid and Livy (and in translations of their works), was versified by Shakespeare and Middleton, dramatised by Heywood, and echoed in plays throughout the Elizabethan and Jacobean periods, including *Titus Andronicus*, *Valentinian*, and *Appius and Virginia*.[2] Lucrece was the model wife who took her own life rather than allow any doubt that her loyalty and her children belonged solely to her husband.

English custom, which did not valorise suicide, also did not provide any clear, reassuring measure of women's purity as an alternative. Instead, the culture fed its misogynist anxieties on a steady diet of sensational tales of unchaste, quite un-Lucrece-like women who deceived their parents, their suitors, and their husbands to indulge their desires. Thomas Middleton and William Rowley's play, *The Changeling* (1622), is just such a tale. Its depiction of Beatrice-Joanna's acceptance of her role as De Flores' whore is symptomatic of a pervasive fear of women's desire.[3]

English law treated ravishment as a crime targeted at propertied men, through a piece of their property, women. The violation of the woman in this play is shown clearly and horribly to be an assault on a man. Alonzo de Piracquo's body first and most spectacularly bears the marks of De Flores' violence, but the play multiplies the male victims of Beatrice-Joanna's ravishment. Her father is a victim, betrayed by a trusted servant, deceived by his daughter, cheated of his heirs and of the allegiances his daughter's marriage could have provided him. Her husband, Alsemero (who marries her when her fiancé, Alonzo, disappears), is made a cuckold before he even sleeps with his bride. De Flores cheats him of his wedding night and mates with Beatrice-Joanna while the serving woman, Diaphanta, supplies her place as virgin in the bridal chamber. Two other gentlemen of Vermandero's household (Francisco and Antonio) very nearly become victims of De Flores' crime as well, when they are apprehended for Alonzo's supposed murder. In the nightmare world of the play, no man is safe from De Flores' lust and Beatrice-Joanna's corruption.

Not only do the victims of the ravishment multiply, but the ravishment itself doubles and redoubles crazily. The subplot chronicles the efforts of Isabella, wife of an unjustifiably jealous husband, to avoid the would-be ravishers in the household to which her husband has confined her. In the main plot, the actual rape remains hidden, while Tomazo de Piracquo chases after an imagined conspiracy between Vermandero and Alsemero to deprive Alonzo of his right and perhaps his life. On the day Alsemero marries Beatrice-Joanna, Tomazo accuses Alsemero with having stolen her from Alonzo. At the end of the play, Tomazo makes his claims of ravishment explicit, demanding 'a brother alive or dead: / Alive, a wife with him; if dead, for both / A recompense, for murder and adultery' (V.iii.136–8). Vermandero and Alsemero are innocent of the crime Tomazo imagines; all three are lost in the funhouse-mirror effect of the play, in which victims and ravishers and crimes swirl and distort.

In a culture like England's, which linked social status to property holding, it is unsurprising to find that women's vulnerability to seduction or sexual assault was a recurrent, even an obsessive concern.[4] It is a concern that intensified in the second half of the sixteenth century, when the Parliament set about to stiffen the rape statutes and the courts followed with a series of precedent-setting opinions defining the limits of this new legislation. This concern with the social ramifications of rape intensified following the accession of James I. With the new monarch came opportunities for new fortunes to be made and for old ones to be lost. Furthermore, by the 1620s when Middleton and Rowley's play was performed, the nation was in the midst of an economic downturn that made property issues seem even more crucial than they had in earlier years.[5]

RAPE AS SOCIAL TRANSGRESSION

In Jacobean England, rape was a capital offence, 'for the unlawfull and carnall knowledge and abuse of any woman above the age of ten years against her will'.[6] This simple definition of the crime belies a history of contestation over the nature of the offence and its appropriate punishment. Beginning with the first statutes of Westminster issued early in the reign of Edward I, English law conflated two crimes: 'stealing' women and forcing women to submit to sexual relations. The first crime might consist of taking poor women from their parents and pressing them into servitude against their wishes, but it also included kidnappings designed to extort money from wealthy families. An unmarried heiress might be kidnapped in order to force her parents to consent to a match between their child and a man they would not otherwise choose. Similarly, widows might be coerced into unfavourable matches under threat of violence or character assassination.[7]

This second kind of stealing was effective because a woman's marriageability could be compromised by any doubt cast on her chastity. Her parents were forced to consider whether they could make any match for their daughter other than the match proposed by the extortioner / kidnapper once the daughter's reputation had been tarnished by her captor. A widow, of course, had a similarly unhappy decision to make for herself:

> Women, aswel maydens as widdowes and wives, having substance, some in goods moveable, and some in landes and tenements, and some being heires apparant unto their ancesters, for the lucre of such substances beene oftentimes taken by misdoers, contrary to their will, and after married to such misdoers, or to other by their assent, or

defiled, to the great displeasure of God, and contrary to the Kings Lawes, and dispergement of the said women, and utter heavinesse and discomfort of their friendes, and to the evill example of all other.[8]

Sexual violation was not necessary to this crime, because the possibility of its having occurred was sufficient to ruin a woman's value as a commodity in the marriage market.

The economic motive, 'the lucre of such substances', was the principal concern of the statute-makers.[9] English law 'from the beginning of Magna Charta' was interested primarily (almost exclusively) with property rights. In a society where status and access to legal rights depended on the ownership of property, the matter of law was the settlement of property disputes.[10] Rape was no exception. Each of the pertinent statutes identifies it as a crime against family property.

The language of the Henry VII statute quoted above is significant: the woman is subject to *disparagement* – the degradation and dishonour of marrying a social inferior. Her friends suffer 'utter heavinesse and discomfort'. Rape is not so much a physical as a social threat to women, and it is not awful because of the emotional devastation inflicted on *her*, but on account of the distress it causes her family and peers.[11] In general, the rape statutes are designed to redress a wrong committed against a woman's male relatives. These men, rather than the woman herself, are considered to be the victims of a rape.

Ravishment not only threatened the property of men of means, but also threatened to disrupt the divisions between different social strata. Ravishment was viewed by the law as a crime inspired by a desire to move up the social ladder. Whether many ravishers actually succeeded in accumulating money or position from such forced alliances, the strong fear behind the language of the law was that opportunistic men could exploit women sexually to infiltrate the higher classes.[12]

Social mobility was frightening not only because the upper classes sought to exclude outsiders from a closed circle, but also because an undesirable match could in reality lower the status of the woman's family, leaching away their resources and humiliating them before their peers. The costs of a successful ravishment might include a loss of liquid assets to the interloper, a loss of expected assets and alliances from an advantageous match for the ravished daughter, and a lessening of the likelihood of subsequent lucrative matches for the other children of the family.[13] A great deal of symbolic and real capital depended upon the chastity of women.

COMPLICITY AND CONSENT IN RAVISHMENT LAW

Rape law encountered a tremendous difficulty in dealing with the fact that women, unlike other chattels, have wills of their own. A series of increasingly complicated supplemental statutes were passed in England to address the role of women within the crime of rape. What if a woman consented to be ravished? At what age could a woman be held responsible for her consent? What if a woman were forced through violence or threats, but then consented after the fact? Her family was no less damaged. There seems to have been a widespread and continuing sentiment that the common law allowed too many women to go unpunished for their part in crimes that wreaked havoc in their families' lives.

Though it finally climaxed with a flurry of legal manoeuvring in the second half of the sixteenth century, the fervour to close the loopholes in rape law began very early in English juridical history. The Westminster II statutes (1285) suspected that some cases presented as ravishment were, in fact, adultery, and added a punishment for the woman to the judgement against the ravisher. If a wife can be shown to have consented either before or after the fact, Westminster II, cap.34 states that she can be 'barred forever of action to demand her dower, that she ought to have of her husbands lands'. A 1383 law extended this provision to bar from their inheritance *any* 'Ladies, daughters [of noble men], and other women', who 'after such rape doe consent to such ravishers' (6 Richard II, cap.6). It is not sufficient for a woman to have resisted a rape. These laws perceive a danger that she will be seduced by the rape, that her affection and loyalty to her husband or her duty to her father may be swayed by the man who raped her. The Richard II law states its perception that rapists in the fourteenth century were 'offending more violently, and much more then they were wont', but its substance is not directed against the rapists at all. Apparently, what was of real concern was a perceived increase in the number of women who conspired with other men to deceive and defraud their husbands and families. What was violently offensive, then, was the sexual defection of women. [...]

English law had two contradictory responses to women. On the one hand, as we have seen, it attempted to hold them ever more closely accountable for their actions. Simultaneously, however, it viewed them as incapable of managing their own affairs. For the most part, women were not treated as autonomous individuals in the eyes of the law. Young women and married women had limited access to the legal system except through their fathers or husbands, of whom they were merely extensions. While a woman could be brought to trial for committing a crime, she could not bring suit against another on her own behalf. Furthermore, the law tended to see women as having significant moral deficiencies that made them more susceptible to error and more likely to commit crimes than men whose moral sensibilities were more highly developed. This opinion of women creeps into the language of a statute passed in 1453 to address ravishers who trick women into becoming accessories to their own ravishment. The law singles out men who take advantage of the 'innocencie and simplicitie' of women to get the women into their power and force them into marriage or into signing bonds that pay to the extortionist-ravisher (31 Henry VI, cap.9). Women, though responsible for their actions, are strongly suspected of being incapable of acting responsibly.

From the earliest statute (Westminster I, passed in 1275), the law distinguished between a 'damsell within age' and a woman (maid, wife, or widow) who had reached the age of consent (Westminster I, cap.14). The age of consent traditionally had been twelve for women and fourteen for men, and indicated the age at which young people could officially be married. The age of consent was a legal interpretation of the age at which mind and body were fit to enter into marriage.[14] The law estimated that consummation and conception were possible for most adolescents at that age, and it was, therefore, also the age at which they were held accountable for their sexual behaviour. A girl under twelve years old was assumed to be incapable of giving her consent even to relations she might think she desired, and she was believed to be too young to conceive a child even if her vagina proved large enough for penetration to be accomplished.[15] As there was no threat that she would conceive a bastard child, the culture could magnanimously consider a girl 'within years' to be innocent whether she had consented to her ravisher or not. After turning twelve, however, she was held accountable for her sexual decisions because they could compromise her

husband's or future husband's paternity and disrupt the primogeni-
tural flow of wealth from father to child.[16]

[...]

Coke's *Institutes* suggest that the Elizabethan and Jacobean legal
establishments tied themselves in knots with concern over the
sexual conduct of ten- and twelve-year-old women. In *Aristotle's
Master-Piece*, a most popular text on reproductive biology, there is
a caution to parents that attests to the age's concerns about female
sexuality:

> 'Tis a duty incumbent upon Parents, to be careful in bringing up
> their Children in the ways of Vertue; and have ever a regard that
> they fully not[e] their Honour and Reputation, especially the
> Females, and most of all the Virgins, when they grow up to be mar-
> riagable, for if through the unnatural severity of rigid Parents they
> be crossed and frustrated in their love, many of them, out of a mad
> humour, if temptation lies in their way, throw themselves into the
> unchaste Arms of a subtle charming Tempter, being through the
> softness of good Nature, and strong Desire, to pursue their
> Appetites, easily induced to believe Men's Flatteries, and feigned
> Vows of promised Marriage, to cover the shame; and then too late
> the Parents find the effects of their rash Severity, which brought a
> lasting stain upon their Family.[17]

Rigid parents, of course, were not the only ones who feared the
effects of desire on women's honour. If the prevalence of the theme
in literature can be added to the great concern evidenced in these
statutes, we might conclude that subtle charming Tempters lurked
about the dark corners of many a father's and husband's night-
mares. When *Aristotle's Master-Piece* describes 'The softness of
nature, and strong Desire', it pinpoints precisely the same traits that
the law identified as the traits that left women vulnerable to rapists
and made them apt to conspire in their own ravishment.

The dual nature of rape as violation and pleasure was embedded
in the very terms used to identify the crime: rape and ravishment.
Rape, which seems to be derived from the Latin, *rapere*, of which
raptus is also a form, meant in English 'the act of taking anything
by force[, the] violent seizure (of goods), robbery' (*OED*).
Ravishment, from the French *ravissement*, a form of the verb *ravir*,
may derive from the same Latin root as rape. Drawing on the idea
of transportation, both 'rape' (rapture) and 'ravishment' developed
the additional meaning, 'to transport with delight'. The conjunction of meanings embedded in these words corresponds to an

ambivalence about the crime: it was simultaneously understood to be a violent theft and a sexual dalliance. The first was certainly reprehensible; the second might be open to interpretation. In fact, both ravishment and rapture were terms that conspired to suggest that this kind of 'stealing' might hold pleasures for the ravisher – and that the pleasure might even be experienced by the woman raped as well.

Kathryn Gravdal offers a history of the French legal and colloquial terminology for rape. She notes that in France (as in England) the legal definition of rape originally required an abduction to have taken place in order for a sexual assault to be chargeable. When, over time, the law changed to eliminate this requirement, it left the terms *ravir* and *ravissant* 'free to become wholly figurative' in their popular use. It was at this point in England and in France that rapture and ravishment came to connote an emotional or sexual carrying-away. Gravdal points out that

> this transformation is inflected by a shift in gender coding: when *ravir* was literal, it was the male who ravished (carried away or abducted) the female. When the term soars off into the realm of the figurative, it is the female who is ravishing, who causes the male to be 'carried away' and is responsible for any ensuing acts.[18]

What Gravdal notices in the language of rape was part of a larger inclination in the culture of both France and England to blame women for their own violation, which we have seen in the statutory history of English law. [...]

In *The Changeling*, De Flores finds that the thought of a woman 'ravishes' (II.ii.132). He seeks out Beatrice-Joanna's company in order to 'please [him]self with the sight / Of her, at all opportunities' (I.i.104–5). His fantasy is that Beatrice-Joanna will be 'ravished' when he rapes her, that she will find pleasure in what repulses her. 'Methinks I feel ... her wanton fingers combing out this beard, / And being pleasèd with, praising this bad face' (II.ii.147–9). He imagines her an active participant in her rape. The play bears him out. Beatrice-Joanna, beautiful and desirable, is also desirous. She even comes to 'love anon' what she initially 'fear'st and faint'st to venture on' – De Flores, the man she loaths (III.iv.170–1). Middleton and Rowley created an archetype of the woman-driven-by-desire in the character of Beatrice-Joanna.

BEATRICE-JOANNA'S CRIME

The play opens at rape law's critical moment: it introduces Beatrice-Joanna at the precise moment of her sexual awakening. Beatrice-Joanna is a young woman who previously has seen no reason to contradict, or even involve herself in, her father's arrangements for her marriage. Unfortunately for all concerned, Beatrice-Joanna meets a man who creates 'a giddy turning in [her]', which makes her realise that marriage could be a sexually fulfilling union (I.i.159). This new love, Alsemero, is suitable in all respects except for his arriving on the scene five days after Beatrice-Joanna's father has completed negotiations for her marriage to Alonzo de Piracquo. The daughter knows that her father cannot honourably withdraw from the match, and that he will not entertain her objections – so she circumvents his plan and follows her heart, allowing it to lead her into a disastrous spiral of crime and corruption.

The playwrights construct the conflict of interest between Beatrice-Joanna and her father as a contest of wills.[19] *Will* is a term whose significance is made much of by the play. At the close of the first scene there is an exchange that foregrounds this term in order to demonstrate what is at stake in the daughter's sexuality. Boasting to Alsemero of the fine match he has made with Alonzo de Piracquo, the father, Vermandero, vows,

> He shall be bound to me
> As fast as this tie can hold him; I'll want
> My will else.
> B-J (*aside*)   I shall want mine if you do it.
>   (I.i.221–3)

Beatrice-Joanna completes and confutes her father's line with her aside. Her will, that is to say her desire and her intention, conflicts with his intent for her. This daughter asserts herself as having a will separate from her father's. In order to establish Beatrice-Joanna's responsibility for her subsequent actions, Middleton and Rowley deliberately echo the language of ravishment law with its emphasis on the woman's will to have or avoid sexual activity ('with her will or against her will').

When the father speaks of his 'will', the word invokes a second meaning. Here it not only refers to his immediate intentions for his daughter's marriage, but also reminds us that fathers have wills of another sort that concern their children. Her match, of course, has a material part in his will, his legal testament. Beatrice-Joanna is her father's sole heir, and her children will inherit his property. His will for the disposition of his estate requires her faithful participation, a condition with which Beatrice-Joanna wilfully refuses to cooperate.

The term 'will' had a further significance in the period that bears on this exchange in the play. 'Will' also meant sexual desire, a connotation that resonates in Beatrice-Joanna's line.[20] The independence that she asserts is specifically framed in terms of her desire. Furthermore, when De Flores closes the scene with the promise, 'Though I get nothing else, I'll have my will' (I.i.240), his use of the term evokes the contemporary slang in which 'will' was a reference to the erect penis. The intertwined sexual and legal threads of this term underscore the fundamental interconnection of this family's sexual and social welfare, both of which are undermined by Beatrice-Joanna's corruption.

Beatrice-Joanna's discovery that she has a will contrary to her father's is her first step towards betraying his honour, a trespass she compounds with deceit. Beatrice-Joanna never makes her objections known, but undertakes secret steps to subvert her father's plan for her. In the moment of that first aside, her course takes shape.[21] We watch as a woman-child who once made her likes and dislikes painfully clear becomes a woman who disguises her intentions and falsifies her emotions. The aside and soliloquy become her characteristic modes of speech. Beatrice-Joanna's subsequent actions and conversations are marked increasingly by secrecy and disingenuousness.

Beatrice-Joanna has tremendous success with her programme of deception, at least initially. She hides her disobedience from her father, gives Alsemero no reason to suspect her virtue, and even fools Alonzo into a false sense of her faithfulness. Tomazo de Piracquo is the first to see behind her mask. He notices her cool reception of his brother and tries to warn Alonzo to break off the match before he marries an unfaithful wife. Tomazo counsels his brother to:

> Think what a torment 'tis to marry one
> Whose heart is leaped into another's bosom:
> If ever pleasure she receive from thee,
> It comes not in thy name or of thy gift;
> She lies but with another in thine arms,
> He the half-father unto all thy children

> In the conception; if he get 'em not,
> She helps to get 'em for him; and how dangerous
> And shameful her restraint may go in time to,
> It is not to be thought on without sufferings.
>
> (II.i.131–40)

How accurate Tomazo's vision is, the play reveals quickly. Beatrice-Joanna's restraint gives way to danger and shame before Alonzo has a chance to marry her, but Alonzo cannot see his peril and ignores the warning. Alsemero, too, has no inkling that anything is amiss with Beatrice-Joanna until after he has married her, although he might have recognised her love for him – and her corresponding disregard for Alonzo – as an ominous sign if he had considered it carefully. The fact that neither lover picks up Beatrice-Joanna's dangerous signals is precisely the play's point. The danger of women's falseness is its subtlety, its secrecy, its ability to masquerade convincingly as virtue.

Like Tomazo, De Flores can see what her noble lovers cannot, and he uses his knowledge to steal Beatrice-Joanna from the arms of these rivals. When he discovers Beatrice-Joanna in a secret tryst with Alsemero, De Flores observes his advantage:

> ... if a woman
> Fly from one point, from him she makes a husband,
> She spreads and mounts then like arithmetic,
> One, ten, a hundred, a thousand, ten thousand,
> Proves in time sutler to an army royal.
>
> (II.ii.60–4)

This is the same logic applied by Brabantio and Iago to caution Othello against trusting Desdemona's chastity in Shakespeare's play. 'She has deceived her father and may thee' (I.iii.289). If Desdemona was an exception to this rule, Beatrice-Joanna is not.[22] Middleton and Rowley endorse De Flores' analysis of her susceptibility to corruption, and the play confirms the underlying conventional wisdom that a woman false to one might be false to any.

When we consider Beatrice-Joanna, we can see what the law feared. She is wilful and sexual; she is deceitful and unrepentant; she doesn't even recognise her error as she begins her course of immorality. We have seen that ravishment law was concerned that women might lack the moral sense to conduct themselves appropriately. Because their 'innocencie and simplicitie' might be easily abused, women were subject to seduction and to moral error

(31 Henry VI. cap.9). Middleton and Rowley interpret women's wilfulness in much the same way that the statute writers did.

As they have created her, Beatrice-Joanna is a young woman who understands her society's demand that women have sex only within marriage. Until she experiences sexual desire for the first time, she acquiesces to the match with Alonzo that her father designs for her. However, the playwrights place her in a moral dilemma when she meets and begins to desire Alsemero. When she sets about to subvert her father's plans for her marriage, Beatrice-Joanna may be attempting to find a culturally acceptable resolution to the problem she faces. If she could arrange to marry Alsemero, then she could also be an honourable wife. Then she would not desire anyone but her husband. She finds, however, that there is no social mechanism that will allow her to exercise her choice. She refuses to allow Alsemero to practise the one quasi-official means at his disposal to intervene in her marriage. She will not let him challenge Alonzo because she fears that the result will be either Alsemero's death or his imprisonment for murder. Finding no sanctioned means to escape a marriage she does not wish to make, Beatrice-Joanna slides easily into disreputable schemes. When De Flores presents himself to her at the right moment, she leaps at the opportunity to allow him to kill her fiancé for her.

Beatrice-Joanna is both amoral and 'simple'. She does not hesitate to plot Alonzo's murder and apparently does not consider his death to have any moral significance. This ethical blindness also causes Beatrice-Joanna to fall prey to her own 'innocencie and simplicitie' in her dealings with De Flores. She has not the faintest inkling of the kind of obligation she incurs with De Flores through her bargain with him. Beatrice-Joanna believes that De Flores would do anything to serve her, when, in fact, his objective is sex not service. It is Beatrice-Joanna's plan to rid herself of De Flores by getting him to commit murder, so he will have to flee her father's household. She assumes that De Flores wants to earn a large reward for his task, but she cannot conceive of the reward he demands.

> **Beatrice-Joanna**   Thy reward shall be precious.
> **De Flores**   That I have thought on;
>   I have assured myself of that beforehand,
>   And know it will be precious; the thought
>   *ravishes.*
>   (II.ii.130–2; emphasis added)

Beatrice-Joanna assumes that the motive that drives men is desire for property; she overlooks De Flores' sexual desires. Even the law, which assumes that covetousness is the principal motive for crime, does not make Beatrice-Joanna's mistake. In their anxiety over women's consent, the rape statutes always remember that sexual desire is a powerful motivator of men. Instead of taking her gold and running away, De Flores exercises a power over Beatrice-Joanna that she neither realised she had given nor imagined he would take. She marvels that 'He's bold, and I am blamed for it' (III.iv.97).

In fact, Beatrice-Joanna is so unaware of her position that De Flores must explain her predicament to her quite bluntly:

> Though thou writ'st maid, thou whore in thy affection,
> 'Twas changed from thy first love, and that's a kind
> Of whoredom in thy heart; and he's changed now,
> To bring thy second on, thy Alsemero,
> Whom by all sweets that darkness ever tasted,
> If I enjoy thee not, thou ne'er enjoy'st.
>
> (III.iv.142–7)

Beatrice-Joanna does not fathom her complicity in the murder, and, thus, cannot anticipate how De Flores uses it to gain access to her. 'Why, 'tis impossible thou canst be so wicked, / ... / To make his death the murderer of my honour!' (III.iv.120,122). She fails to recognise her responsibility for Alonzo's murder. It has not occurred to her that that act touched her honour in any way.

Middleton and Rowley have designed a heroine who confirms the law's paternalistic concern for women's moral weakness.[23] Beatrice-Joanna's moral compass is fundamentally skewed. In part, her behaviour is guided by flawed interpretations of her culture's gender roles, but her most egregious acts are the product of a criminal disregard for human life. Beatrice-Joanna's assumption that desire might have a meaningful place within marriage or that women might under some circumstances be sanctioned to act on desire simply does not square with Jacobean notions of marriage and sexuality.

Beatrice-Joanna's project to marry the man she desires becomes a diabolic mirroring of Jacobean sexual mores. Her wilfulness is seen to be an all-absorbing focus on herself that threatens everyone else. This self-absorption creates the cock-eyed view by which she sees herself as pursuing a logical course to an honourable marriage.

'A woman dipped in blood', though she surely is, Beatrice-Joanna continues to 'talk of modesty' (III.iv.126).

CHANGELINGS

The law, with its straightforward statements about consent and age, its cold definitions of damage and disinheritance, is completely inadequate either to deter or address the crimes in Middleton and Rowley's play. The most frightening aspect of *The Changeling* is the success with which De Flores and Beatrice-Joanna hide Alonzo's murder and the further betrayal of their sexual alliance. Once she succumbs to De Flores' attack, Beatrice-Joanna actively covers up the crime, hiding her incontinence and counterfeiting chastity in order to proceed with her marriage to Alsemero. In *The Changeling's* nightmare vision, women's desire is deadly and defiling. Middleton and Rowley play masterfully on all the legion fears about women and their traitorous sexuality to which the 'consent and complicity' statutes were a reaction. With its powerful illustration of the corruptibility of women, the play confirms the validity of the statute-makers' concerns, but simultaneously undermines the comfort promised by their strict penalties.

Literature and law both expressed great concern that women might falsify their sexual activity. Rape law, which sought to fix blame and to redress wrong materially, was frustrated by the near impossibility of determining whether a woman had been forced or merely seduced by her ravisher. The maddening characteristic of most rapes, of course, was that they lacked witnesses, and their facts remained obscured in the irreconcilable difference between a woman's accusation and a man's defence.[24] This dilemma drove justices to search for a test that could determine the facts of a rape with certainty.

Michael Dalton, in *The Countrey Justice* (1618), claimed to have just such a test when he advised fellow magistrates that 'if the woman at the time of the supposed rape do conceive with child, by the ravisher, this is no rape, for a woman cannot conceive with child except she do consent.'[25] Dalton's understanding of biology was based in the Galenic medicine still much in use. The author of *Aristotle's Master-Piece* reports the view of this branch of medical wisdom that conception occurs when the male and female seed are released during copulation – a release that had to be accompanied in both sexes by orgasm. Dalton, then, based his legal test on the assumption that if a woman conceives, she must have experienced pleasure in the act of intercourse, which in turn signifies that she consented to the act, if not beforehand, then by virtue of having enjoyed it.

The test was necessary, of course, because women lack the obvious signifiers of desire with which men are equipped. Without penises, which offer visual confirmation of arousal and satisfaction, women could easily counterfeit their experience of the sexual act. Not only did this absence of ocular proof allow women to pretend pleasure when they felt none, it also made it possible for them to conceal their pleasure when it served them to do so.

Even as Dalton was circulating his consent test, however, the medical wisdom on which it was based was becoming obsolete. The *Master-Piece* reports Galenic opinion only to rebut it, proposing, instead, a biology of conception in which the active male seed searches out and fertilises the passive ovum in the woman's body. Among the propositions it explicitly refutes is the Galenic belief that women's orgasm is produced by their ejaculation of seed.[26]

The *Master-Piece* also takes sides in another of the period's disputes over women's sexuality. It maintains that a ruptured hymen is not evidence of lack of virginity, claiming that 'the Learned' affirm that

> such fracture may happen divers ways by accidents, as well as Copulation with Man, *viz* by extraordinary straining, violent coughing, immoderate sneezing, stopping of Urine, and violent motion of the Vessels, inforcibly sending down the humours, which pressing for passage break the Ligatures or Membrane, so that the intireness or fracture of this thing, commonly taken for the Virginity or Maidenhead, is no absolute sign of dishonesty.[27]

After taking away this absolute sign of a woman's falseness, the author of *The Master-Piece* offers a most interesting consolation to his readers. He will have it known that while a woman's sexual activity cannot be proved by her ruptured hymen, an intact hymen is a certain proof that she remains a virgin. He illustrates the importance of this truth with a legal case in which a woman was found to have falsely accused a man of raping her. Her deceit was discovered when a gynaecological exam certified that she was still a virgin. Far from offering reassurance, this illustration demonstrates the dire need for discernible proof of women's sexual status. It cautions that even when women are chaste, they may perpetrate dangerous sexual falsehoods.

The Changeling exploits its culture's anxiety about the difficulty of ascertaining the facts of women's sexuality. Alibius, the subplot's jealous husband, fears that his wife will find opportunities to cuckold him if he allows her to leave his house, so he confines her indoors in the company of the madmen and fools he treats, and entrusts her to the oversight of his wily servant. Were she so inclined, Isabella could find plenty of opportunity to betray her husband without leaving home. Certainly his unreasonable confinement of her gives her ample motive for cuckolding him, but the playwrights maintain Isabella's chastity as a counterexample to Beatrice-Joanna's falseness. The lesson of the subplot is not so much that some women are capable of chastity, but that nothing men can do will guarantee women's honesty.

In the main plot, Tomazo de Piracquo spends the entire play suspecting Beatrice-Joanna of falseness he cannot prove. Alsemero becomes consumed by questions about his bride's chastity. The audience knows all of Beatrice-Joanna's secrets, and it waits for the other characters to realise the magnitude of her hidden sins. The plot is driven toward the moment when the truth will be revealed, but discovery is so slow in coming that it seems entirely possible that Beatrice-Joanna may get away with murder and adultery. The play, which makes its audience privy to all of the facts, builds suspense by postponing discovery until the last possible moment. It teases its audience with the spectre of a woman's successful deception, withholding as long as practicable the reward of her violent punishment and her acceptance of guilt. The audience is as desperate that the truth be known as the characters are to discover that truth.

As soon as he has married her, Alsemero begins to be troubled by hints of Beatrice-Joanna's unfaithfulness. He has, however, come to marriage prepared to deal with such doubts. Alsemero owns a medical kit that contains special preparations with which he can discover whether Beatrice-Joanna is a virgin, and if not a virgin, whether she is pregnant. Such certain tests, if they had existed, would have been worth more to seventeenth-century husbands than possession of the philosopher's stone.[28] The liquid in Glass M, which would allow a man 'to know whether a woman be a maid or not', would settle for once and all the uncertainty that even a woman's body could no longer be trusted to resolve (IV.i.41).

Among its uses, Glass C, 'to know whether a woman be with child', would have allowed Daltonite judges to resolve their cases much sooner, before a pregnancy could otherwise have been detected (IV.i.26). If Beatrice-Joanna were to fail the first test, but were then to claim that she had been raped by De Flores, Glass C might have helped to establish her guilt.

But Alsemero's science is no more successful than Michael Dalton's. Beatrice-Joanna discovers his physician's closet and reads the secret of his procedures there. With this knowledge she is able to counterfeit the signs of chastity when she is put to the test. Alsemero's medicine fails because it relies on the female body to demonstrate symptoms that will indicate the woman's condition. The play asserts what its seventeenth-century audience already suspected, what the law tried so diligently to counteract: that women find it all too easy to counterfeit their reactions, to hide their deficiencies, to mask the signs that their bodies should offer as clear signals for men to read. When forced to swallow the contents of Glass M, Beatrice-Joanna gapes, sneezes, laughs and falls into melancholy just as Alsemero's text predicts a virgin will – but she is an actress, not a virgin. On her wedding night, Beatrice-Joanna supplies a body double to act her part in the darkened bridal chamber. Throughout her short marriage, Beatrice-Joanna plays the spotless bride; her act is a mask to cover the rottenness of her sin and the defilement of her body.

Women are changelings. They are changeable and interchangeable. Not only are women able to counterfeit their actions, they are able to disguise themselves and substitute themselves for one another. Beatrice-Joanna capitalises on the fact that in the darkened bed chamber women's bodies were undetectably replaceable. Alsemero is able to search his bedmate's body for signs of virginity, but cannot discern that he has the wrong woman in his bed. Beatrice-Joanna's successful evasion of his investigations testifies that women's bodies, though fleshly and material, are elusive and undecipherable.

When Alsemero at last obtains ocular proof of Beatrice-Joanna's falseness (he sees Beatrice-Joanna and De Flores in a private tryst in the garden), he realises that instead of a wife he has married a player. He finally sees what lies behind the 'visor' she has worn 'O'er that cunning face' (V.iii.46,47). Her infidelity and her deception and the false testimony of her body are the characteristic untruths of actors. Women's sexuality was, indeed, a puzzle akin to the destabilised image of the transvestite player. Insofar as it was noted, the appearance of the boy beneath the woman's clothes may have been taken as an image of the rotten core at the centre of women, of the inauthenticity of the female sex.[29] Beatrice-Joanna is at last known to be 'the changeling', a counterfeit daughter, a whore masquerading as a bride, an actor in women's clothes.

The play makes self-conscious use of this acting metaphor to call attention to what can be known and what eludes knowledge, what can be seen and what remains hidden. The final scene re-enacts De Flores' rape of Beatrice-Joanna and literalises his 'murder' of her honour, but stages this action where we cannot see it. Alsemero locks Beatrice-Joanna into a room with De Flores, bidding them

> ... rehearse again
> Your scene of lust, that you may be perfect
> When you shall come to act it to the black audience
> Where howls and gnashings shall be music to you.
> (V.iii.114–17)

From behind the closed door of the chamber come the sounds of that rehearsal, 'horrid' sounds which are the climax of their relationship and of the play. This audible, but hidden, scene of lust supplies the moment of revelation for which Vermandero, Tomazo, Alsemero, and their audience have yearned. But even this revelation is unclear. Beatrice-Joanna can be heard uttering ambiguous sounds, perhaps of passion, perhaps of agony. De Flores responds with equally suggestive words, as Alsemero interprets their performance for his father-in-law and Tomazo:

> **Beatrice** [*within*]   Oh, oh, oh!
> **Alsemero**   Hark 'tis coming to you.
> **De Flores** [*within*] Nay, I'll along for company.
> **Beatrice**   Oh, oh!
> (V.iii.139–40)

Alsemero's remark is as much a double-entendre as the rest of the exchange. It is both a bitter taunt directed at Beatrice-Joanna, and a response to Tomazo's demand for 'a recompense, for murder and adultery' (V.iii.138).

Behind that closed door, De Flores is stabbing Beatrice-Joanna, then turning the knife on himself. When he forced Beatrice-Joanna to sleep with him, De Flores murdered her honour; now he finishes his crime with her actual murder. Her body, when De Flores drags her out onto the stage, bears visible signs of his violation, signs which are a literalisation of the violence their sexual union committed on her body and her honour and, by extension, on her family. Beatrice-Joanna makes this connection explicit when she warns her father not to touch her.

> Oh come not near me, sir; I shall defile you.
> I am that of your blood was taken from you
> For your better health; look no more upon't,
> But cast it to the ground regardlessly;
> Let the common sewer take it from distinction.
> (V.iii.149–53)

The daughter, of course, has already defiled her family by her actions. She understands that her body, which was vulnerable to De Flores' assault, must be cut off from the family in order to restore it to honour. Her blood, the biological connection between father and daughter, must be shed to effect this social cure, even as seventeenth-century medicine would prescribe a therapeutic blood-letting in order to remove the defiling humour from a sick patient. In this final moment, Beatrice-Joanna acknowledges the duty accepted so much more gracefully by Lucrece. She realises that, in order to erase the shame she has cast upon her father and her husband, she must die.

The ostracism demanded by the law of seventeenth-century women guilty of consenting to their ravishers' desire is pushed to an extreme on the stage in Middleton and Rowley's play. But Beatrice-Joanna's body – bloody, dead, and cast aside on the stage – is a literalisation of the kind of cutting-off prescribed by the law to separate a family from the daughter whose body has betrayed them. In life as on stage, honour could only be salvaged through a ritual purging of the defiled part: the woman. Once that purge is complete, Alsemero can treat the matter as closed and can encourage his father-in-law to forget it entirely:

> Let it be blotted out; let your heart lose it,
> And it can never look you in the face
> Nor tell a tale behind the back of life
> To your dishonour; justice hath so right
> The guilty hit that innocence is quit
> By proclamation and may joy again.
> (V.iii.182–7)

When he declares, 'I am satisfied, my injuries / Lie dead before me', Tomazo de Piracquo confirms the necessity and accepts the sufficiency of her death as a recompense. In this final scene, the playwrights render Beatrice-Joanna's body readable. While she lived, she was change-able and her body was a cipher. Once dead, her body's signs are clear, straightforward.

In deference to the demands of their genre for dramatic closure, or perhaps out of their own desire to reconcile the dangerous issues their play has addressed, Middleton and Rowley give their play a 'happy' ending. What began as a nightmarish vision of the consequences of a woman's desire and her weakness in defence of her honour, ends like a fairy tale. In this fictional world, the truth finally comes to light and justice holds the guilty parties to account. Death compensates death, and the innocent survivors can see that they will 'joy again'. The family reconstitutes itself as a male circle, no longer vulnerable to the vagaries of women. Alsemero reminds Vermandero that he has 'yet a son's duty living' (V.iii.216). The alliances Vermandero sought to forge with the Piracquo brothers and with Alsemero are realised despite Beatrice-Joanna's betrayal – and those bonds are more fast now that there is no further danger to be feared from her. Beatrice-Joanna's death is framed by these men, her survivors, as the necessary prerequisite to their formation of a more perfect family, an all male family.

The barrenness of this resolution is readily apparent. This 'happy' ending betrays its own artificiality, with its rhymed couplets and self-referential theatricality – and, of course, it doesn't feel happy at all. It offers a manifestly fictional resolution to problems that defied such simplistic treatment. Only on stage could the fifth act be depended on to supply a full confession and a complete recompense to the victims of a ravishment. Of course, the law also sought to supply such a recompense. Ample evidence of the failure of the legal establishment to redress the damage of rape is available in the history of its perpetual tightening of the statutes and in the continued wrangling of judicial authorities over the interpretation and application of those laws. For all of its efforts to define women and to proscribe their sexual behaviour, the law found them to be changelings, whose complicity eluded detection. Middleton and Rowley's play tries to manage what the law could not when it exposes the falseness of a woman for all to see, but it is ultimately no more successful than the law in allaying the fear that a woman might succeed in deceiving her family and friends. It was a fear fed rather than eased by stories like this one. This fear required, but could not be satisfied with, the bloodied bodies of women like Lucrece and Beatrice-Joanna. Its loathing of the vulnerability of the female body demanded scenes of retribution and blame like this one in *The Changeling*. But the self-condemning, willing death Beatrice-Joanna dies could only increase the anxiety of a culture that set women as the sentinels to guard familial honour.

From *English Literary History*, 62 (1995), 759–90.

NOTES

[Deborah Burks's essay works within a familiar new historicist paradigm. This begins with what is known as 'thick description', where a specific case study is researched and described in some detail. The discussion that then follows attempts to extrapolate from the specific case in order to draw more far-reaching conclusions about the culture in which it is situated. So it is here. From the opening account of a fraught arranged 'society' marriage between the young daughter of Sir Edward Coke and Lady Elizabeth Hatton, and Sir John Villiers, Burks proceeds with an investigation of 'issues of property, status and gender' as they are implicated in the 'marriage negotiations of the propertied classes'. There is some detailed historical material on rape laws in Jacobean England, after which the essay moves into a tight, close reading of *The Changeling*. Due to limitations of space in this volume, the opening few pages have had to be cut: a brief summary of Burks's account of the Coke / Villiers affair is included below.

The depth of Burks's scholarship is one of the most striking aspects of the essay. (The voluminous footnotes have been edited here, with excisions marked by an ellipsis. In most cases, omissions are long quotations from works Burks mentions, or else a reduction in the list of references originally included in a particular footnote.) The essay is also exemplary for the way in which it reads a literary (or dramatic) text so thoroughly in relation to other discourses, as Burks draws on legal documents, medical textbooks, and aspects of early modern popular culture in order to locate the play. The essay itself sheds genuinely new light on the sexual politics and dynamics of Middleton's text, in particular challenging us to reassess our reading of Beatrice-Joanna. All references are to Thomas Middleton and William Rowley, *The Changeling*, edited by Russell A. Fraser and Norman Rabkin (New York, 1976).

Deborah Burks begins her original essay with an example of the way in which marriage was frequently used as a means of advancing social status in the seventeenth century, citing the case of Sir Edward Coke's attempt to match his youngest daughter Frances with Sir John Villiers. This took place in 1617, some five years before *The Changeling* was first staged. Coke had offended James I and lost his position as a Chief Justice; an alliance with Villiers meant a step closer to the king, since Villiers's younger brother, the Duke of Buckingham, was a favourite of the king's. Unfortunately, the prospective bride herself objected to the proposal (Villers's sanity was fragile, and he was reputed to be prone to violent outbursts and seizures), and she found an ally in her mother Lady Elizabeth Hatton, who presumed to resist not only her husband's choice of mate for their daughter, but also his plan to provide the dowry out of her own jointure estates. The subsequent tug of war between mother and father was a public sensation, as the parents battled for the right to control their daughter, her marriage, and its financial arrangements. 'The case illustrates a crucial problem in Jacobean gender-relations,' Burks explains. 'Although the law and popular opinion held that men had an exclusive right to control property and to make decisions for all members of their families, it was clear that women as well as men possessed "wills", which prompted them to desire, and to decide, and to act on their own. Where in men, the will was seen as the rightful expression of intention, ownership, and familial authority, in women, it was associated with petulance and indulgence, especially sexual indulgence' (from Burks, *Horrid Spectacle: Violation in the Theater of Early Modern England*, forthcoming). In the Hatton case, the king himself intervened, Lady Hatton was arrested, and the wedding went ahead, but the daughter's resistance did not die at the altar. With a husband insane and apparently impotent, Frances took a lover and became pregnant. The prospective heir was disowned by the Villiers family. 'Though her fate was less cataclysmic than the tragedies that befell so many stage heroines in her day,' Burks concludes, 'the comparison is tempting to draw' (Burks, "'I'll Want my Will Else"', p. 762). Ed.]

1. In *Woman and Gender in Renaissance Tragedy* (Atlantic Heights, NJ, 1989), Dympna Callaghan examines the Renaissance construction of gender and explores the construction of women and of female desire as socially disruptive and dangerous. [...] Susan Dwyer Amussen discusses the substantive as well as metaphorical connections between women's role in the family and social order or disorder in both her book length study, *An Ordered Society* (New York, 1988) and her article, 'Gender, Family and the Social Order, 1560–1725', in Anthony Fletcher and John Stevenson (eds), *Order and Disorder in Early Modern England* (Cambridge, 1985).

2. Middleton's poem, 'The Ghost of Lucrece', was published in 1600. There were actually two dramatisations of *Appius and Virginia*. The first was an early Elizabethan interlude, the second is tentatively credited to John Webster and Thomas Heywood. See Leonard Tennenhouse, *Power on Display: the Politics of Shakespeare's Genres* (New York, 1986), p. 111; Lee Bliss, *The World's Perspective: John Webster and the Jacobean Drama* (New Brunswick, NJ, 1983), p. 6.

3. The Jacobean public was treated to the scandalous tales of a number of real women of this stripe. ... [Burks cites the case of Frances

Howard; for further details of the case and its significance to the play, see Cristina Malcolmson's essay '"As Tame as the Ladies": Politics and Gender in *The Changeling*', reprinted in this volume (in particular pp. 146–7). Burks also cites Margot Heinemann, *Puritanism and Theatre: Thomas Middleton and Opposition Drama under the Early Stuarts* (Cambridge, 1980) as another text linking the Howard scandal with Middleton and Rowley's play – Ed.].

4. See James Sharpe, 'The People and the Law', in Barry Reay (ed.), *Popular Culture in Seventeenth Century England* (New York, 1985). Sharpe discusses popular enthusiasm for litigation in the Jacobean period and the tendency of British subjects to define their legal rights in terms of property holding and in contrast to the prerogative rights asserted by the Stuart monarchs. [...]

5. Penelope Corfield discusses the economic pressures of the early seventeenth century in her essay, 'Economic Issues and Ideologies', in Conrad Russell (ed.), *The Origins of the English Civil War* (New York, 1973). Perez Zagorin sketches out the influence of these pressures on the English social hierarchy in his preliminary chapter on 'Social Structure and the Court and the Country' in *The Court and the Country: The Beginning of the English Revolution* (London, 1969). [...] In her chapter on 'Wealth, Inheritance and the Spectre of Strong Women' in *Still Harping on Daughters* (New York, 1983), Lisa Jardine addresses some of the demographic and economic factors which placed stress on English views of female heirs to substantial estates (pp. 68–98).

6. Edward Coke, *The Institutes of the Laws of England* (London, 1644), cap. 11.

7. Even married women seem to have been vulnerable to this crime if they could be used to extort property from their husbands. They might be held for ransom, or in some cases, the ravishment might be part of a larger theft of a man's property.

8. 'Anno 3, Henry VII, cap. 2', *A Collection in English, of the Statutes Now in Force, Continued from the Beginning of Magna Charta* (London, 1603), 170 c. Unless otherwise noted, all citations of statutes have been taken from this edition.

9. In her essay, ' "The Blazon of Sweet Beauty's Best": Shakespeare's *Lucrece*', in Patricia Parker and Geoffrey Hartman (eds), *Shakespeare and the Question of Theory* (New York, 1985), pp. 95–115, Nancy Vickers finds plentiful evidence in *The Rape of the Lucrece* for the depiction of rape as covetousness in Renaissance England's conception of the crime. [...]

10. Issues of physical assault and character defamation, though covered by statutes against mayhem (maiming) and murder, seem to have been

settled out of court more often than in. Physical retribution continued to be a more direct way of dealing with such matters. The courts, which were slow and costly, were used to obtain monetary settlements in property disputes, but swifter and more personal retaliation was often sought in cases of physical affronts and assaults. Lawrence Stone discusses the continuance of personal violence in the period in *The Crisis of the Aristocracy, 1558–1641* (Oxford, 1965).

11. It is worth noting, too, that ravishment was defined primarily as a crime committed against women of substance, though some of the laws do remember 'others' (the most important of these others being servants who might be ravished away from their employers' service). There were other laws that concerned themselves with the sexual behaviour of poor women: bastardy laws, including a very strict law passed early in James I's reign, punished indigent women for bearing children who would become a drain on their parish's charity. Ravishment statutes might be seen as rich women's bastardy laws. Martin Ingram discusses popular attitudes about fornication and bastardy in 'The Reform of Popular Culture? Sex and Marriage in Early Modern England', in Reay (ed.), *Popular Culture in Seventeenth Century England*, esp. pp. 151–6.

12. Coke, *Institutes*, offers two examples from the Parliament Rolls of widows who were 'shamefully' ravished, and forced by 'dures and menace of imprisonment' to marry men they did not wish to marry (cap. 11).

13. In *Making a Match: Courtship in Shakespeare and His Society* (Princeton, NJ, 1991), Anne Jennalie Cook discusses marriage negotiations and their financial importance to sixteenth- and seventeenth-century families. Cook quotes from the wedding sermon of Lord and Lady Hay (1607) to illustrate the economic and political importance of marriage between propertied families: 'to marry joins sex and sex, to marry at home joins house and house, but your marriage joineth land and land, earth and earth' (p. 239). In 'Rape in England between 1550 and 1700', Nazife Bashar notes that cases which claimed a substantive economic damage to the family of a rape victim were more likely to be successfully prosecuted than claims made by working class families who could not claim much damage. [...] (The London Feminist History Group [ed.], *The Sexual Dynamics of History: Men's Power, Women's Resistance* [London, 1983], p. 42). [...]

14. See William Blackstone, *Commentaries on the Laws of England*, 4 vols (New York, 1841). Blackstone notes that a girl within age 'by reason of her tender years ... is incapable of judgement and discretion', and that 'a male infant, under the age of fourteen years, is presumed by law incapable to commit a rape, and therefore it seems cannot be found guilty of it ... As to this particular species of felony, the law supposes an imbecility of body as well as mind' (vol. 4, p. 212). [...]

15. Coke, *Institutes*, affirms at numerous points [...] that penetration was necessary for a rape to have occurred. Ejaculation near but not within a woman's body did not constitute a crime. Similarly, sodomy was held to have occurred only in cases where anal penetration could be proven.

16. [Burks here provides further details of changes in English law that signal anxiety around the issue of the age of consent for girls – Ed.]

17. *Aristotle's Master-Piece* seems to have been hugely popular, although early editions of it are now extremely scarce. A Latin edition of 1583 and an English translation of 1595 are the earliest known printings of the work which ran through numerous editions and remained in print into the eighteenth century. I quote from the Garland press facsimile of the 1694 edition: Randolph Trumbach (ed.), *Aristotle's Master-Piece: Or, the Secrets of Generation* (New York, 1986), p. 63.

18. Kathryn Gravdal, *Ravishing Maidens: Writing Rape in Medieval French Literature and Law* (Philadelphia, 1991), p. 5.

19. There seems to be almost uniform agreement among critics that Middleton was responsible for the main plot and that Rowley wrote the subplot. [...] The play's action, however, is so carefully integrated that it seems that this collaboration was a close one. For my purposes, I will treat the play as a joint effort, rather than attributing specific aspects to one of its authors or the other.

20. Christopher Ricks, in 'The Moral and Poetic Structure of *The Changeling*', *Essays in Criticism*, 10 (1960), 290–306, discusses the sexual connotation of the world 'will' in the play. He also calls attention to the double meanings of several other recurrent terms, particularly *service*, *blood*, *act* and *deed*, and discusses their function within the play. [Lois E.] Bueler also discusses the rhetorical importance of these terms ('The Rhetoric of Change in *The Changeling*', *English Literary Renaissance*, 14 [1984], 95–113). The *OED* listings for 'will' consume several pages and include most of the senses I have discussed. For the use of will as a reference to the penis (a pun that continues in current British usage), see Eric Partridge's discussion of Shakespeare's use of the term in *Shakespeare's Bawdy* (New York, 1990).

21. Karen Newman observes that women's rebelliousness was often presented as a linguistic protest against patriarchal authority. Beatrice-Joanna's articulate, but secret, rebellion against her father's will might be seen as an alternative to Kate's shrewishness, which is Newman's subject in 'Renaissance Family Politics and Shakespeare's *The Taming of the Shrew*', *English Literary Renaissance*, 16 (1986), 86–100.

22. Jardine also notes the similar assumptions elicited from men by the behaviour of Desdemona and Beatrice-Joanna. Jardine points out the undeniable sensuality of Desdemona's character, often forgotten or glossed over by modern critics (*Still Harping*, p. 75).

23. It is significant that ravishment law does not punish ravished women as felons even when it finds them to be material accessories to the crime. Such women are to be ostracised rather than executed. In other words, the law seems to treat women as incapable of the felonious malice attributed to their ravishers. See Heinemann's discussion of Beatrice-Joanna's moral deficiency (*Puritanism and Theatre*, pp. 175–8).

24. In *Pleas of the Crown*, 2 vols (London, 1678), Matthew Hale reflected on this unknowableness when he explained why juries should be reluctant to convict defendants in rape trials: 'It is true rape is a most detestable crime, and therefore ought severely and impartially to be punished with death; but it must be remembered, that it is an accusation easy to be made and hard to be proved, and harder to be defended by the party accused tho' never so innocent' (vol. 1, p. 634). If *men's* guilt was difficult to establish, *women's* complicity with their rapists, however it might be suspected, even more persistently eluded the kind of proof the law craved. It remained a mystery of the most unsettling kind.

25. G. R. Quaife quotes this statement as part of a larger passage from Dalton in his discussion of sexual violence in *Wanton Witches and Wayward Wives: Peasants and Illicit Sex in Early Seventeenth Century England* (New Brunswick, NJ, 1979), p. 247. J. A. Sharpe also cites Dalton in the course of his helpful survey of rape cases prosecuted during the seventeenth century. See especially his *Crime in Seventeenth Century England, 1550–1750* (New York, 1984), pp. 63–5. Other legal texts promoted this 'conception-equals-consent' rule, including Sir Henry Finch's *Law, or a Discourse Thereof* (1627), E.T.'s *The Law's Resolution of Women's Rights* (1632), and William Lambarde's *Eirenarcha, or Of the Office of the Justices of the Peace* (1611).

26. *Aristotle's Master-Piece*, pp. 22–5. The author of the *Master-Piece* disputes much of this Galenic biology, particularly the notion that women have seed [...] Although he does not specify whether orgasm is necessary to conception in his competing physiology, it seems likely that it is not, as it is his opinion that the woman's ovum is the passive recipient fertilised by the active male seed. [...]

27. *Aristotle's Master-Piece*, p. 89.

28. Alsemero's medical guide seems to be a compilation of experiments selected out of other texts. Beatrice-Joanna mentions the name of one of the authors it cites, Antonius Mizaldus, a French physician whose works included precisely such potions and tests. Dale B. Randall has researched Renaissance metaphysical works for evidence that such tests were not uncommon, and reports a substantive tradition of virginity and pregnancy tests in 'Some Observations on the Theme of Chastity in *The Changeling*', *English Literary Renaissance*, 14 (1984),

347–66. Of particular note is the fact that Randall finds a waning of confidence in such tests by the seventeenth century [...]

29. See, for example, Jardine, *Still Harping*; Kathleen McLuskie, 'The Act, the Role and the Actor', *New Theatre Quarterly*, 10 (1987), 120–30; Phyllis Rackin, 'Androgyny, Mimesis and the Marriage of the Boy Heroine on the English Renaissance Stage', *PMLA*, 102 (1987), 29–41; Jean E. Howard, 'Crossdressing, the Theatre and Gender Struggle in Early Modern Europe', *Shakespeare Studies*, 39 (1988), 418–40; Laura Levine, 'Men in Women's Clothing', *Criticism*, 28 (1986), 121–43; Stephen Orgel's 'Nobody's Perfect or Why Did the English Stage Take Boys for Women?', *South Atlantic Quarterly*, 88 (1989), 7–29; and J. W. Binns's 'Women or transvestites on the Elizabethan stage?', *Sixteenth Century Journal*, 5 (1974), 95–120.

9

Gender, Rhetoric and Performance in *The White Devil*

CHRISTINA LUCKYJ

John Webster's *The White Devil* has long provoked anxiety among its critics. The arraignment scene, in which Vittoria defends herself magnificently against charges of murder and adultery, has been widely celebrated as 'one of the great moments of the English stage'.[1] Yet unlike Desdemona in *Othello* or Hermione in *The Winter's Tale*, Vittoria is clearly implicated in the crimes of which she is accused. Her response to Bracciano's importunities has not in fact been 'frosty' (III.ii.202), as she claims it has; indeed, she has eschewed the 'loathed cruelty' (I.ii.209) of the Petrarchan mistress by embracing her lover openly in the first Act (I.ii. 213). And, while her agency is never entirely clear, she goes on to recount a dream in which (at least according to Flamineo) she instructs Bracciano to 'make away his Duchess and her husband' (I.ii.256). Male villain-heroes may not be uncommon in Jacobean tragedy (viz. Vindice in *The Revenger's Tragedy*), but female figures such as Vittoria who arouse admiration and reprehension are rare indeed. In most early modern drama, as Bracciano puts it, 'Woman to man / Is either a god or a wolf' (IV.ii.89–90). Critics therefore continue to dispute the meaning of Vittoria's performance in the trial scene. Some simply label her a hypocrite and Webster a moralist: D. C. Gunby, for example, asserts that 'we should acknowledge the truth of his [Monticelso's] asseveration that "If the devill / Did ever take good shape, behold his picture" '.[2] Others find hypocrisy not in Vittoria but in Webster himself, who thus commits 'an artistic insincerity – a lie in the poet's heart',[3] and indulges his penchant for 'vivid sympathetic insights at the expense of ethical coherence.'[4] More recently, Catherine Belsey has deflected blame from the dramatist to his culture, associating Vittoria's 'discursive mobility' with the unstable and discontinuous place of women in early modern England, when 'in the family as in the state women had no single, unified, fixed position from which to speak'.[5] From different perspectives, then, critics have identified the trial scene with disjuncture and dissembling (Vittoria's, Webster's or the culture's), despite its powerful impact on the stage. I shall argue that such anxieties about performance, especially as it constitutes gender identity, are in fact self-consciously articulated and managed by *The White Devil* itself.

Like many early modern texts, *The White Devil* invests its anxieties about performance in women. 'O ye dissembling men!' cries Vittoria, who is promptly corrected by Flamineo: 'We suck'd that, sister / From women's breasts, in our first infancy' (IV.ii.179–80). Women are 'politic' (I.ii.21) performers whose pretence to virtue masks a voracious sexual appetite and whose apparent tears are 'but moonish shades of griefs or fears' (V.iii.187). Despite the proliferation of male disguises, in the rhetoric of *The White Devil* performance is frequently gendered female. To Isabella's plea that he exhibit some marital affection, Bracciano cries, 'O dissemblance' (II.i.171); seeing Vittoria's tears at his ill-treatment, he remarks scornfully, 'Procure but ten of thy dissembling trade, / Ye'd furnish all the Irish funerals / With howling' (IV.ii.93–5). Female theatricality is of course a common misogynist trope in early modern texts; in *Much Ado about Nothing*, Claudio mouths an anti-feminist cliché in his indictment of Hero's 'performance': 'O, what authority and show of truth / Can cunning sin cover itself withal!' (IV.i.35–6). If theatricality in men could be a powerful means of 'self-fashioning', Weidemann points out that 'theatricality in a woman suggests that her identity has somehow become inauthentic or alienated, akin to that of a professional actor'.[6] Joseph Swetnam's notorious *Araignment of lewde, idle, froward and unconstant women* (1615) recycles commonplaces in declaring that 'a woman which is faire in showe is foule in condition, she is like unto a glow-worme which is bright in the hedge and black in the hand'.[7] Such a construction relies on a stable and privileged masculine capacity to 'see through' feminine dissimulation, and make clear distinctions between outside and inside.[8] *The White Devil*, however, problematises this masculine privilege. In this play, as I shall argue, men are as implicated as women in the theatrical practices they abhor; women appropriate theatre as a form of power; and performance is revealed as constitutive, as the 'true' and the 'adulterate' become indistinguishable (I.i.49–50).

'I account this world a tedious theatre,' cries the Duchess of Malfi, 'For I do play a part in't 'gainst my will' (IV.i.83–4). Like the Duchess, Vittoria in her trial and Isabella in her rejection of Bracciano 'play a part'. Unlike the Duchess, however, whose participation in her brother's sadistic 'spectacle' (IV.i.57) is involuntary, the women of *The White Devil* embrace theatricality, offering extraordinarily self-conscious performances. In the trial scene, Vittoria constructs herself as an actor both in the courtroom and on the stage. When she rejects the lawyer's use of Latin, for example, on the grounds that 'amongst this auditory / Which come to hear my cause, the half or more / May be ignorant in't' (III.ii.15–17), her remark applies to the Red Bull audience rather than to the learned ambassadors. When Isabella almost slavishly repeats Bracciano's ceremony of divorce, she at first appears to be masochistically increasing the anguish of her 'piteous and rent heart' by acting out her 'sad ensuing part' (II.i.223–4) in a script that has been written by her husband. But Bracciano's declaration that 'this divorce shall be as truly kept / As if the judge had doomed it' (II.i.196–7) becomes in Isabella's version 'And this divorce shall be as truly kept, / As if in thronged court a thousand ears / Had heard it' (ll. 255–7) – a remark that glances at the Red Bull audience itself. Why do both women, victims in the fictional world, display this kind of metadramatic awareness? And why, at the height of their performances, do both women threaten to violate established gender boundaries? 'O that I were a man, or that I had power / To execute my apprehended wishes' (II.i.242–3), cries Isabella. Similarly, at a central moment of self-assertion, Vittoria declares that her 'defence, of force, like Perseus / Must personate masculine virtue to the point' (III.ii.135–6). 'Personate' had by the early seventeenth century become a new and specifically theatrical term.[9] Webster himself uses it in his character of 'An Excellent Actor' to assert that 'what we see him personate, we thinke truely done before us'.[10] While it could mean 'represent, embody', it was also commonly used to mean 'imitate, feign, counterfeit'.[11] The verb again foregrounds Vittoria's theatricality: in the theatre one cannot represent without counterfeiting. But why, for both Isabella and Vittoria, is metatheatre so closely associated with crossing gender lines? In part, it is clear that to become tragic subjects (authors and agents of their own choices), women must *act* in both senses of the word – take action and play a (male) role. Yet even as they appropriate masculine power, they also exceed mere role-playing to reveal a heightened awareness of the theatre itself, and this has important implications for the play.

Despite Flamineo's proposal that Vittoria be attired 'in a page's suit' (IV.ii.209) to facilitate her escape from the house of convertites, literal crossdressing – with its potential for playful masquerade and the destabilising of gender[12] – never occurs in *The White Devil*. By this time, as Michael Shapiro points out, such transvestism had become a distinctly old-fashioned device.[13] And when Isabella and Vittoria crossdress rhetorically, they appear at first to mirror the many other women in early modern plays whose expressed longing to turn into men emphasises by contrast their immutable and essential 'feminine' natures. In *The Duchess of Malfi*, the Duchess may defy Bosola with 'Were I a man / I'd beat that counterfeit face into thy other' (III.v.117–18), but her fantasy of masculine violence must give way to her gently controlling, indirect tale of the feminised salmon/victim. In Middleton and Rowley's *The Changeling*, Beatrice-Joanna may sigh, 'Would creation ... Had form'd me man', but her attempt to realise the 'freedom' of a man (II.ii.107–8,109)[14] actually delivers her into the power of De Flores, who fetishises and essentialises her virginal female body. Similarly, in Shakespeare's *Much Ado about Nothing*, Beatrice may cry repeatedly, 'O that I were a man!' (IV.i.303, 306, 317), but she must finally acknowledge that she 'cannot be a man with wishing' (ll. 322–3), and she defers to Claudio's agency. Such fantasies of crossing gender lines are destined to remain merely fantasies partly because these women endorse a gender system from which they are necessarily excluded. Like the anonymous author of the crossdressing pamphlet *Haec Vir*, who finally defends female transvestism as a reification of traditional masculine value,[15] Beatrice laments a world in which 'manhood is melted into curtsies, valour into compliment, and men are only turned into tongue, and trim ones, too' (IV.i.319–21). Women seek to turn into men only because men are not doing their job; the value of that job is never in question. Similarly, in *The White Devil*, Isabella's cry, 'O that I were a man' (II.i.242), draws attention not only to what she lacks but also to her

brother's ineffectual defence on her behalf. The jealous tirade that
follows appears to confirm her irrational feminine nature: while
Francisco associates her with the (typically female) 'fury' (l. 244),
Bracciano implies that her 'humour' (and perhaps her forced absti-
nence from marital intercourse) has led to the rising of her
'stomach' (ll. 271–2), akin to the rising womb, a common symptom
of hysteria. In the trial scene, Vittoria tenders her 'modesty / And
womanhood' (III.ii.132–3) before she reluctantly, 'of force' (l. 135),
adopts a masculine pose in her own defence. At first glance, rhetorical 'crossdressing' appears to be a conventional means of heightening the illusion of femininity that is crucial to an all-male theatrical
company.

In *The White Devil*, however, the simple dichotomy between essential feminine identity and masculine disguise is problematised by
metatheatrical presentation. For one thing, Isabella is deliberately
constructing and playing out a female stereotype; the feminine is
clearly a matter of performance here. For another, the violent fantasies of a 'foolish, mad, / And jealous woman' (II.i.263–4) are also
constructed as the 'apprehended wishes' of a 'man' (ll. 242–3):

> To dig the strumpet's eyes out, let her lie
> Some twenty months a-dying, to cut off
> Her nose and lips, pull out her rotten teeth,
> Preserve her flesh like mummia, for trophies
> Of my just anger!
>
> (II.i.245–9)

Here is a fantasy of dismemberment which parodies the Petrarchan
blazon (already parodied by Flamineo at I.ii.114–18) and anticipates Bracciano's own later rage against Vittoria, his threat to 'cut
her into atomies' (IV.ii.40). As the scene builds in tension, Isabella's
breathless rage gives way to an increasingly firm control of the
stage, as she directs the movements of the male characters
(ll. 250–2) and repeats, even as she parodies, Bracciano's vow of
divorce. Isabella's performance, despite its apparently 'feminine' irrationality, actually gets her the 'power' (l. 242) of a man: whereas
earlier she attempts to placate Bracciano gently when he commands
her to 'take [her] chamber' (l. 154), here she defies her brother's
issue of the same command (l. 269) and refuses to 'stay a minute'
(l. 270). The fetishised kiss that Isabella earlier desires (ll. 156–7)
and Bracciano refuses and then transfers to her hand to mark perversely the 'latest ceremony of ... love' (l. 193) is finally bestowed at

Isabella's command (l. 252). After making him kiss her, she re-inscribes his discourse: whereas he refers to her 'love' (l. 200) for him, she recasts it sardonically as her 'former dotage' (l. 259). Francisco identifies Isabella as both a madwoman and a male cuckold who merits 'horns' (l. 266). The final impact of the scene is to illuminate a double standard at work: while the male characters construct Isabella's divorce ceremony as quixotic feminine ravings to be easily dismissed (ll. 273–4), Bracciano's vow – cast in the same words – is 'fixed' (l. 205) and immutable. In her 'part' (l. 224), however, Isabella plays out both the hysterical impotence of the jealous woman and the tyrannical potency of the au-tonomous male. The contrived theatricality of the scene exposes both as culturally authorised modes of self-display.

In *The White Devil*, perspective is frequently shifting and unreli-able, and subjectivity frequently foregrounded – this is a world in which, as Flamineo says, 'men at sea think land and trees and ships go that way they go' (I.ii.154–6), and 'they that have the yellow jaundice, think all objects they look upon to be yellow' (ll. 108–9). That Isabella can play masculine and feminine parts at once, blur-ring gender boundaries, exposes gender as a matter of perception as well as self-construction. Similarly, in the trial scene Vittoria repre-sents herself simultaneously as a railing shrew taking a 'woman's poor revenge / Which dwells but in the tongue' (III.ii.283–4) and as a commanding rhetorician, usurping 'masculine virtue' (l. 136). Both Isabella's and Vittoria's performances deconstruct traditional gendered antitheses and expose them as contingent on subjective construction.[16]

It is worthwhile here to recall briefly some of the cultural debate surrounding real crossdressed women: it was common, for example, to assume, as does Richard Brathwait's *English Gentlewoman* (1631), that crossdressed women 'labour to purchase them opinion of *esteeme*, by their unwomanly expressions of valour'.[17] Female transvestism was clearly constructed as a desire to imitate masculine modes. Imitation, however, also opens a space for masquerade, parody, and caricature. Judith Butler points out that 'in imitating gender, drag implicitly reveals the imitative structure of gender itself'.[18] In *As You Like It*, for example, Rosalind imagines herself with 'a swashing and a martial outside / As many other mannish cowards have / That do outface it with their semblances' (I.iii.120–2). Her imitation of masculinity promises to expose its artificial construction through parody. Indeed, masculine extravagance (the sartorial equivalent of the braggadocio) was frequently displaced onto women in a burgeoning consumer economy; Karen Newman suggests that 'the furor over cross-dressing may owe more to an objection to women's sharing in the male privilege of *excess in dress* than to specifically masculine attire'.[19] Thus female transvestites are horrifying partly because they figure *masculine* theatricality, read here not as power but as degeneration. In *Hic Mulier* (1620), the author finds in female transvestism a critique of masculine behaviour when s/he denounces women who desire to be 'man in body by attire, man in behaviour by rude complement, man in nature by aptness to anger, man in action by pursuing revenge, man in wearing weapons, man in using weapons,' and rails against crossdressed women for imitating the worst aspects of men: 'The long hair of a woman is the ornament of her sex ... the long hair of a man, the vizard for a thievish or murderous disposition. And will you cut off that beauty to wear the other's villainy?'[20] Along with this pamphlet's clear anxiety about women's access to male privilege is a hint that such behaviour functions as a critique of men. If, as Valerie Lucas points out, this pamphlet 'betrays how men fashion the female transvesite as a mirror image of masculine violence',[21] the female transvestite may in turn appropriate that mirror image and reflect it back at men. Crossdressed women, like the effeminised men discussed by Laura Levine, threaten to reveal 'that there is no masculinity in itself but only masculinity insofar as it is staged and performed'.[22]

Similarly, the women of *The White Devil* who usurp masculine rhetoric are positioned not only to gain access to male privilege but also to offer a savage critique of that privilege. Isabella's repetition of Bracciano's vow, for example, apparently intended to salvage his reputation, actually exaggerates and caricatures his pose: she parodies his autocratic appropriation of the authority of a 'judge' (II.ii.197) by upping the ante to 'a thousand ears' and 'a thousand lawyers' (II.256–7).[23] Her performance of Bracciano's machismo foregrounds its inherent theatricality. At the centre of her trial, Vittoria claims that her 'defence, of force, like Perseus / Must personate masculine virtue' (III.ii.135–6). Heightening the artifice of her performance, she self-consciously alludes to Ben Jonson's 1609 *Masque of Queens* in which Perseus, 'expressing *heroicall* and *masculine Vertue*',[24] arrives to rout the anti-masque of witches and usher in twelve famous queens dressed as warriors for battle. As

Perseus, Vittoria by implication represents her opponents as witches (demonised masculine women) from whose 'cursed accusation' – *maleficia* – she is justified in defending herself; at the same time she identifies herself not with the idealised and disempowered Queen Anne but with the King, the controlling extratheatrical presence in the masque embodied by Perseus.[25] Furthermore, Vittoria 'cross-dresses' to emulate masculinity – like real seventeenth-century women modelling themselves on heroic hermaphrodites – while she constructs it as a theatrical performance of the most distant and artificial kind. (The Red Bull, of course, catered to an audience at the other end of the social spectrum than the court masque.) Since the line is unpunctuated in the quarto, her offer to 'personate masculine virtue to the point' suggests a perfectly detailed ('to the point') portrait of masculinity – a theatrical sketch, perhaps even a 'character' to vie with Monticelso's character of a whore presented earlier.[26]

While it is difficult to attribute a parodic impulse to Vittoria herself, it is possible to trace in Vittoria's masculine theatricality Webster's profound ambivalence toward his male hero. It is surely important that, even as Vittoria invokes 'masculine virtue', this commodity is in short supply in the play. When, for example, Bracciano intervenes as Vittoria's 'champion' (III.ii.180) during the trial, his rhetoric is grossly fraudulent and self-aggrandising. His claim to have been motivated by 'charity ... which should flow / From every generous and noble spirit, / To orphans and to widows' (ll. 161–3) is a cowardly attempt at inventing an alibi. He then resorts to violent threats and lordly Latin tags, finally exiting on the line, 'Nemo me impune lacessit' (l. 179) and abandoning his lover so that (as Vittoria herself points out) '[t]he wolf may prey the better' (III.ii.180). However, perhaps the play's most obvious exposure of masculinity as a precarious and risible construction comes earlier, when Bracciano's son, the young prince Giovanni, dons a suit of armour and tosses his 'pike' (II.i.110) – a common euphemism for penis – while declaring his plan to press the women to the war / And then the men will follow' (ll. 135–6). Though Francisco announces that 'a good habit makes a child a man' (l. 137), Giovanni makes the swaggering Bracciano of the second act by analogy look like a child.[27] Similarly, Vittoria's accomplished performance of masculinity exposes those cultural paradigms that underlie the rhetorical posturing of the men in this play.

Indeed, the main thrust of Vittoria's trial scene is that no one is exempt from performance, and that all performance is contingent on interpretation. Monticelso, for example, offers to read Vittoria's flushed cheeks as a sign of her inauthenticity: 'I shall be plainer with you, and paint out / Your follies in more natural red and white / Than that upon your cheek' (III.ii.51–3). Vittoria's deceptive show is like the whore's use of cosmetics; the Cardinal invokes a misogynist commonplace which metonymically figures a gilded exterior masking a corrupt interior. However, since the boy actor used paint to play a woman,[28] the Cardinal's charge (however true) loses its misogynist force and becomes simply antitheatrical. Moreover, he participates in the performance he condemns when he adopts the metaphor of applying cosmetics to describe his own rhetorical strategies. Vittoria then contests his reading: 'O you mistake,' she corrects him. 'You raise a blood as noble in this cheek / As ever was your mother's' (ll. 53–5). 'The shameful blush,' writes Bevington, 'may represent one of two opposite responses: dismay and confusion at an undeserved accusation or admission of guilt.'[29] By foregrounding this sign, Vittoria exposes its contingency on perception and on theatrical representation: it is as likely to manifest the confused dismay of a noblewoman as the cheap artifice of a whore. Later, the Cardinal draws attention to her sumptuous attire by charging: 'She comes not like a widow: she comes armed / With scorn and impudence. Is this a mourning habit?' (ll. 121–2). In reply, Vittoria points out: 'Had I foreknown his death as you suggest, / I would have bespoke my mourning' (ll. 123–4) – in her case, mourning attire would signify not grief but guilt. Far from simply exposing Vittoria as a hypocrite or avoiding the problem altogether (as critics suggest), the trial scene of *The White Devil* openly contests the intelligibility of performance.

Despite her metatheatrical awareness, then, Vittoria is consistently anti-theatrical. She begins the scene by pointedly invoking an 'auditory' (III.ii.15), thus taking the part of playwrights such as Webster who sought 'full and understanding' ('To the Reader', ll. 6–7) listeners rather than the gaping spectators of the common stages.[30] By contrast, the Cardinal insistently foregrounds the visual in a protracted display of misogynistic scopophilia, alternately inviting and rejecting 'ocular proof' of Vittoria's corruption. 'Observe this creature' (l. 57), 'look upon this creature' (l. 120), 'See my lords' (ll. 63, 129), he instructs the ambassadors (and the theatre audience). On the one hand, the Cardinal continually draws attention to Vittoria's appearance. On the other hand, he insists that her appearance is no guide to her inner reality:

> You see my lords what goodly fruit she seems,
> Yet like those apples travellers report
> To grow where Sodom and Gomorrah stood:
> I will but touch her and you straight shall see
> She'll fall to soot and ashes.
>
> (III.ii.63–7)

This kind of standard anti-feminist fare is reiterated in the Cardinal's description of a whore as 'Sweet meats which rot the eater: in man's nostril / Poisoned perfumes' (ll. 81–2). What is significant here is the paradox underlying his rhetoric: what he seeks to prove by *sight* can never be *seen*, and must always therefore be subject to doubt. The final absurdity comes when he both invokes and dismisses his audience's visual sense: 'If the devil / Did ever take good shape behold his picture' (ll. 216–17). The Cardinal depends not only on the stability of outward signs but also on their utter deceptiveness; Vittoria consistently foregrounds the latter. At the same time, she challenges the misogynist notion that men can penetrate women scopically by splitting herself into subject and object: as, in Act I, she is both controlling narrator and terrified victim of her own dream (I.ii.230–48), in the trial scene she is both the detached observer who offers to 'give aim' to guide her enemies' shots and the object of those shots, 'at the[ir] mark' (III.ii.24). This puts Vittoria, rather than the Cardinal, in control of the object of representation, herself.

Continually focused on the crudely visual spectacle, the Cardinal himself is as deeply implicated in performance as the woman he condemns. Vittoria points out, 'It doth not suit a reverend cardinal / To *play* the lawyer thus' (III.ii.60–1, emphasis added). In his construction, Vittoria is a 'counterfeit' jewel (l. 41) whose adulterous affair 'would be played o'th'stage, / But that vice many times finds such loud friends / That preachers are charmed silent' (ll. 249–51). The line repays closer examination: from his predictable opening equation of illicit sexuality with promiscuous theatre, the Cardinal moves surprisingly to ally himself *with* the theatre, an instrument used by 'preachers' to expose 'vice'. His anti-theatricality doubles back on itself, as he fashions himself as supporter, rather than opponent, of the stage.

In response, Vittoria foregrounds her own theatricality – theatricality which signals not her hypocrisy but the conditions of performance itself. For the theatre can stage only outward signs of inner truths; as Katharine Maus points out, 'spectacle depends upon, sometimes betrays, but never fully manifests a truth that remains shrouded, indiscernible, or ambiguous'.[31] After insisting on the ambiguity of visible signs, Vittoria significantly lays claim to an interiority that is simply impregnable: 'For know that all your strict combined heads, / Which strike against this mine of diamonds, / Shall prove but glassen hammers, they shall break' (III.ii.143–5). Vittoria's only real defence against the Cardinal's two-pronged attack is to withdraw into unknowable inwardness, to lay claim to 'thoughts' (l. 230) to which outward signs can bear no witness. This interiority is, however, quite different from Hamlet's 'that within which passes show' (*Hamlet* I.ii.85), which intimates an 'authentic inner reality'[32] or private subjective space. 'This mine of diamonds' is defined not by what is within but by what is without – dense and impenetrable, it dazzles the eye of the beholder without giving him a point of access. In other words, Vittoria foregrounds not only the indeterminacy of those signs used to define and incriminate her but also the inaccessibility of subjectivity itself. She thus reappropriates misogynist notions of feminine indeterminacy for her own ends.[33] By fashioning herself as a performer, Vittoria can distance herself from her own self-representation and open a space for her subjectivity, a subjectivity defined by negation and absence, by what cannot be represented. It is hardly surprising that she later withdraws into a silence which defies exegesis (IV.ii.188). By foregrounding Vittoria's unintelligibility, the play challenges its own production of theatrical spectacle.

Anxiety about theatrical spectacle – its constitutive power, its possible duplicity – haunts *The White Devil* far beyond its representations of gender. The conjurer, for example, before revealing the double murder in dumb show to Bracciano, unexpectedly agonises about the distinction between his own 'strong-commanding art' (II.ii.22) and mere 'juggling tricks' (l. 14), inauthentic performances. His overanxious insistence on the authenticity of his conjuring betrays an anxiety not only about the tenuous distinction between black and white magic but also about the art of theatre itself. After the dumb shows, in which the two murders are played out before his eyes, Bracciano inexplicably remarks: ''Twas quaintly done, but yet each circumstance / I taste not fully' (II.ii.38–9). Does his commendation of acts 'quaintly done' apply to the murders, or the means of their discovery, and are these separable? Is it nagging uncertainty about the gap between representation and reality that underlies his need for further confirmation? This moment is followed by the conjurer's assurance that the real will immediately impinge on them as guards 'come with purpose to apprehend / Your mistress' (ll. 48–9), but his words are never confirmed; instead, the stage is cleared and reality elided by theatrical convention. The conjurer's initial distinction between legitimate theatre – making the real visible – and illegitimate theatre – manufacturing illusion – is made only to be confounded. A similar moment recurs in Act IV, when Isabella's ghost is 'conjured' by Francisco. Is the ghost in fact an objectively 'real' ghost of revenge tragedy erroneously dismissed by a new Machiavellian revenger? Or is the ghost a figment of Francisco's 'melancholy' (IV.i.108), of 'Thought, [which] as a subtle juggler, makes us deem / Things supernatural which have cause / Common as sickness' (IV.i.106–8)? The issue is never resolved for the audience. Underlying all this is of course a theatrical joke: such uncertainty imitates theatre itself, which is both as real as actors on a stage (the ghost exists) and as illusory as their playing of roles (the ghost never exists). With Flamineo's mock suicide in the final Act, Webster daringly forces his audience to confront the constitutive power of illusion when it is finally revealed as mere theatre – theatre in which pistols never hold bullets and death never occurs, yet in which audience desire and expectation are transformative. Antonelli recognises this when he advises Lodovico at the opening of the play:

> Perfumes the more they are chafed, the more they render
> Their pleasing scents, and so affliction
> Expresseth virtue fully, whether true,
> Or else adulterate.
>
> (I.i.47–50)

His casual remark hints at the play's underlying trope: that 'expression' (literally, the action of pressing out; figuratively, the manifestation or performance) finally effaces distinctions between the 'true' and the 'adulterate'. Outward signs and performances are not only unreliable guides to inner essences, they also transform them, rendering any distinction between enactment and pretence meaningless.

That life itself is theatre, theatre thus an image of theatre, was of course a commonplace of the age. The *theatrum mundi* conceit is pithily expressed by that 'laboured and understanding' playwright admired by Webster ('To the Reader,' ll. 40–1), Ben Jonson: 'I have considered our whole life is like a play, wherein every man, forgetful of himself, is in travail with expression of another. Nay we so insist in imitating others, as we cannot, when it is necessary, return to ourselves.'[34] The power inherent in theatrical modes of 'self-fashioning' has been frequently emphasised by new historicist critics; recently, however, some critics have exposed the anxieties hinted at by Jonson that inevitably accompany such a contingent construction of identity. Maus argues that 'in a culture in which truth is imagined to be inward and invisible ... theatrical representation becomes subject to profound and fascinating crises of authenticity.'[35] Laura Levine attends to the 'profound sense of powerlessness' generated by the notion that 'things lack or are believed to lack an independent existence apart from their own theatricalisations'; her study identifies such contingency with masculine identity in particular.[36] Theatre may actually have dangerous constitutive power, as Jonson suggests. Virtue is 'fully' expressed by affliction; whether it is 'true' or 'adulterate' virtue may be irrelevant. Such fears and fantasies about performance are crucial to *The White Devil* and especially to its representations of gender.

I have argued that *The White Devil* is as theatrically self-aware as its female characters; like them, it pushes anxieties about gender and performance to the surface by exposing all its characters – male and female – as implicated in performance. Furthermore, it challenges the notion that such performances can be easily decoded; rather, they are exposed as contingent on fallible, subjective interpretation. The deepest fear haunting the play is, of course, the fear that there is nothing behind or beneath the performance, no fixed self or gender.[37] *The White Devil* provisionally manages this fear by illuminating performance as a necessary and useful component in the construction of identity. If, in this play, perspectives are shifting and no single reading is definitive, then identity is as fluid and malleable as the performance which 'expresseth' it. In Isabella's case, for example, the 'piteous and rent heart' (II.i.223) supposed to underlie her 'part', is effectively expressed in her decision to 'rail and weep' (l. 230); self and performance are effortlessly elided. What we see is a study in the actor's 'personation' of his part; while we are always aware of his artifice, if the performance is good we are simultaneously convinced by his 'real' passion. However she attempts to close off her performance and reintroduce distinctions between self and part, between silent 'killing griefs' (II.i.277) and loquacious tirade, Isabella succeeds only in revealing the constitutive power of theatre. Similarly, that Vittoria is invariably remembered in the theatre for her heroic posture – for 'something fine, proud and wonderfully defiant'[38] – is not accidental: it is proof of the same constitutive power. Her performance actually shapes her identity, if only because we as spectators participate in the shaping.[39] Paradoxically, Vittoria's anti-theatricality helps her stage herself successfully. And, though *The White Devil* exposes the theatricality of gender, Bracciano dies like the 'princes' (V.iii.35) of *de casibus* tragedy and Vittoria can claim she is 'too true a woman' (V.vi.221) to feel fear at the prospect of death. However, *The White Devil*'s self-consciousness about crossdressing and theatre, so often articulated explicitly by Vittoria, should make us aware of the provisional and contingent nature of identity, gender, and performance for all the characters in this play.

From *Enacting Gender on the Renaissance Stage*, ed. Viviana Comensoli and Anne Russell (Urbana, IL, 1999), pp. 218–32.

NOTES

[Christina Luckyj's essay is notable for the way it draws on elements of performance theory, as well as more familiar literary critical discourses, feminism and cultural materialism in particular. The citation of the performance theorist Judith Butler alongside a literary critic such as Karen Newman is indicative of Luckyj's approach.

We are familiar with the convention of cross-dressing that was standard practice in the early modern English theatre, where all female roles were played by boys. Readings of the implications of that convention have proliferated over the past twenty years or so. Luckyj, however, chooses to focus on another kind of impersonation, where female characters problematise their femininity, as well as received notions of masculinity, by destabilising gender differences. Luckyj points out how, at crucial moments during the play, both Vittoria (and to a lesser extent Isabella) describe their behaviour in metatheatrical terms. They are acutely aware of that behaviour as *performance*, and often articulate it with reference to gender. These descriptions, frequently expressed as fantasies of crossing gender boundaries, Luckyj refers to as 'rhetorical "crossdressing" ' (p. 194).

Luckyj's reading opens up a subversive space in the play. Many critics have discussed Webster's shifting moral perspective in *The White Devil* (see Introduction), and for Luckyj, this has significant ramifications for the means by which the play interrogates gender: the way in which Vittoria problematises gender distinctions can be read as a critique of male privilege (which the play exposes most starkly when Bracciano and Flamineo walk free from the court, leaving Vittoria as the one to face punishment). Webster's insistence on multiple perspectives, coupled with the contingency and fluidity that is inherent in performance, leaves plenty of room for the interrogation and even subversion of established gender categories, with far-reaching implications for the political *status quo*.

All references are to the New Mermaid edition of *The White Devil* edited by Christina Luckyj (London, 1996). References to *The Duchess of Malfi* are taken from the New Mermaid version edited by Elizabeth Brennan (London, 1964), and quotations from Shakespeare's plays are taken from G. Blakemore Evans (ed.), *The Riverside Shakespeare* (Boston, 1974). Ed.

1. Jack Landau, 'Elizabethan Art in a Mickey Spillane Setting', *Theatre Arts*, 39 (1955); reprinted in R. V. Holdsworth (ed.), *Webster: 'The White Devil' and 'The Duchess of Malfi': A Casebook* (London, 1975), p. 234.

2. D. C. Gunby, 'Critical Introduction' to *The White Devil*, in D. C. Gunby, David Carnegie, Antony Hammond and Doreen Delvecchio (eds), *The Works of John Webster*, vol. 1, p. 76.

3. Ian Jack, 'The Case of John Webster', *Scrutiny*, 16 (1949); reprinted in G. K. Hunter and S. K. Hunter (eds), *John Webster: A Critical Anthology* (Harmondsworth, 1969), p. 162.

4. Madeleine Doran, *Endeavours of Art: A Study of Form in Elizabethan Drama* (Madison, WI, 1954), p. 355.

5. Catherine Belsey, *The Subject of Tragedy: Identity and Difference in Renaissance Drama* (London, 1985), p. 160.

6. Heather L. Weidemann, 'Theatricality and Female Identity in Mary Wroth's *Urania*', in Naomi J. Miller and Gary Waller (eds), *Reading Mary Wroth: Representing Alternatives in Early Modern England* (Knoxville, TN, 1991), p. 194.

7. Joseph Swetnam, *Arraignment of lewd, idle, froward and unconstant women* (London, 1615), pp. 12–13. Webster was fond of the image of the glow-worm for the deceptiveness of appearances, and used it twice: in *The White Devil*, Flamineo ironically uses the phrase to praise Mulinassar (the disguised Francisco) for his ability to distinguish reality from illusion (V.i.41–2); in *The Duchess of Malfi*, Bosola repeats it in an attempt to strip the Duchess of her illusions of greatness (IV.ii.144–5). In both cases the speaker's own claim to penetrate theatrical appearance to uncover a plainer truth is problematised.

8. Carol Cook makes a similar observation about Shakespeare's *Much Ado About Nothing*: 'Masculine privilege is contingent on the legibility of women, and the ambiguous signifying power of women's

"seeming" is the greatest threat to the men of Messina' (' "The Sign and Semblance of Her Honour": Reading Gender Difference in *Much Ado About Nothing*', Deborah Barker and Ivo Kamps [eds], *Shakespeare and Gender: A History* [London, 1995], p. 76).

9. Andrew Gurr, *The Shakespearean Stage, 1574–1642*, 3rd edition (Cambridge, 1992), p. 99.

10. John Webster, 'An Excellent Actor', F. L. Lucas (ed.), *The Complete Works of John Webster*, 4 vols (London, 1927), vol. 4, p. 43.

11. Gunby, Carnegie, Hammond, and Delvecchio point out that '*personate* was used in widely divergent senses at this time', though they find in its metatheatrical usage an anti-feminist agenda: 'Vittoria is passing herself off fraudulently as a man' (*Works*, vol. 1, pp. 298–9).

12. Much has been written about the potential for subversion when boy actors play women crossdressing as men, particularly in Shakespeare's comedies: see, for example, Jean E. Howard, 'Crossdressing, the Theatre and Gender Struggle in Early Modern England', *Shakespeare Quarterly*, 39 (Winter, 1988), 418–40 and Catherine Belsey, 'Disrupting Sexual Difference: Meaning and Gender in the Comedies', in John Drakakis (ed.), *Alternative Shakespeares* (London, 1985), pp. 166–90.

13. Shapiro comments that Flamineo's 'suggestion might even be a shared joke among the three characters, for by 1612 the female page had become a cliché on the English stage' (*Gender in Play on the Shakespearean Stage: Boy Heroines and Female Pages* [Ann Arbor, MI, 1994], p. 25).

14. Citation from N. W. Bawcutt (ed.), Thomas Middleton and William Rowley, *The Changeling* (London, 1958).

15. *Haec Vir*, while offering a spirited defence of women's right to cross-dress, nonetheless ends with a reassertion of the gender hierarchy: 'Cast then from you ornaments and put on your own armour; be men in shape, men in show, men in words, men in actions, men in counsel, men in example' (in Katherine Usher Henderson and Barbara F. McManus [eds], *Half Humankind: Contexts and Texts of the Controversy about Women in England 1540–1640* [Urbana, IL, 1985], p. 288.

16. Sheryl A. Stevenson also notes the moments of female impersonation in *The White Devil*, and suggests that these contribute to a blurring of gender distinctions (' "As Differing as Two Adamants": Sexual Difference in *The White Devil*' in Carole Levin and Karen Robertson [eds], *Sexuality and Politics in Renaissance Drama* [Lewiston, NY, 1991], p. 164). Her conclusion, however, differs from mine; she claims that 'In Isabella and Vittoria, masculinity becomes a mask which seems at the same time a hidden aspect of self' (p. 166). I am suggest-

ing that, far from turning into men, Isabella and Vittoria problematise both masculinity and notions of a hidden self.

17. Richard Braithwait, *The English Gentlewoman* (London, 1631), p. 24.

18. Judith Butler, *Gender Trouble: Feminism and the Subversion of Identity* (London, 1990), p. 137.

19. Karen Newman, *Fashioning Femininity and English Renaissance Drama* (Chicago, 1990), p. 21.

20. *Hic Mulier* in *Half Humankind*, p. 270.

21. Valerie Lucas, '*Hic Mulier*: The Female Transvestite in Early Modern England', *Renaissance and Reformation*, n.s.12 (1988), 73.

22. Laura Levine, *Men in Women's Clothing: Anti-theatricality and Effeminization, 1579–1642* (Cambridge, 1994), p. 56.

23. Stevenson points out that 'Isabella's duplication of Bracciano's mocking, ceremonial divorce offers evidence that the play's women deliberately mirror men' (' "As Differing as Two Adamants" ', p. 164).

24. *The Masque of Queens* in C. H. Hereford et al. (eds), *Ben Jonson*, 11 vols (Oxford, 1941), vol. 7, p. 302, 1.365.

25. Suzanne Gossett suggests that in the *Masque of Queens*, 'Perseus represents King James' (' "Man-maid, Begone!": Women in Masques', in Kirby Farrell, Elizabeth H. Hagemann and Arthur Kinney [eds], *Women in the Renaissance: Selections from 'English Literary Renaissance'* [Amherst, MA, 1990], p. 123).

26. The line has often been repunctuated by editors. Both the new Cambridge edition (*Works of John Webster*, vol. 1, ed. Gunby, Carnegie, Hammond and Delvecchio) and John Russell Brown's Revels edition of *The White Devil* (London, 1960), following Lucas, add a break in the line so that it reads. 'Must personate masculine virtue – to the point!' (III.ii.126). The unbroken line in the quarto, however, heightens its theatrical self-consciousness.

27. Giovanni is still a child, and so his dependence on women is childishly and charmingly overt, even as he dons the apparel and attitudes of early modern men (just illustrated in the swaggering confrontation between Francisco and Bracciano). Coppélia Khan comments on the 'disparity between men's social dominance and their peculiar emotional vulnerability to women' in the construction of early modern manhood (*Man's Estate: Masculine Identity in Shakespeare* [Berkeley and Los Angeles, 1981], p. 12).

28. I thank Brian Gibbons for bringing this to my attention.

29. David Bevington, *Action is Eloquence: Shakespeare's Language of Gesture* (Cambridge, MA, 1984), p. 96.

30. Gurr points out that Renaissance playwrights 'valued their poetry much more than the "shows" of the common stage, and consequently rated hearing far above seeing as the vital sense for the playgoer' (*Playgoing in Shakespeare's London* [Cambridge, 1987], p. 85).

31. Katharine Eisaman Maus, *Inwardness and Theatre in the English Renaissance* (Chicago, 1995), p. 210.

32. Catherine Belsey, *Subject of Tragedy*, p. 41.

33. Elizabeth Harvey points out that 'there is a difference between being consigned to a marginalised position by the patriarchal order and voluntarily (and self-consciously) occupying that position as a strategy for subverting the dominant discourse' (*Ventriloquized Voices: Feminist Theory and English Renaissance Texts* [London, 1992], p. 57).

34. Jonson, 'Timber, or Discoveries', in Ian Donaldson (ed.), *Ben Jonson* (Oxford, 1985), p. 551.

35. Maus, *Inwardness and Theatre*, p. 32.

36. Levine, *Men in Women's Clothing*, pp. 7, 70–1.

37. This fear is one of the central concerns discussed by Levine.

38. Benedict Nightingale, 'Snared by a Sinister World', *The Times*, 19 June 1991, p. 18. Nightingale is praising Josette Simon's Vittoria in the 1991 National Theatre production directed by Philip Prowse.

39. The claim I am making here for Webster's demand that his audience recognise both the constitutive power of theatre and its deceptive instability is similar to Dena Goldberg's argument: 'And just as the play warns us not to believe everything we hear or see, it demands, nonetheless, that we make a judgement of some kind. To demand that an audience be both active and sceptical in relation to one's own play is remarkable in itself and is asking a great deal, even of a Jacobean audience' (' "By report": The Spectator as Voyeur in Webster's *The White Devil*', *English Literary Renaissance*, 17 [Winter 1987], p. 84).

10

'Tis Pity She's a Whore: Representing the Incestuous Body

SUSAN J. WISEMAN

I

Soranzo	Tell me his name!z
Annabella	Alas, alas, there's all.
	Will you believe?
Soranzo	What?
Annabella	You shall never know.
Soranzo	How!
Annabella	Never; if you do, let me be cursed.
Soranzo	Not know it strumpet! I'll rip up thy heart and find it there.
Annabella	Do, do.

(IV.iii.49–53)

In this speech from Ford's mid-seventeenth-century play *'Tis Pity She's a Whore* there are a number of gaps between what is presented on stage and what might be called the 'meanings' of what is happening in relation to cultural contexts.[1] The story so far is that Soranzo is one of Annabella's suitors. She agrees to marry him because she is pregnant with her brother's child. Soranzo has discovered Annabella's pregnancy, but he does not know that the father is Giovanni. This exchange, therefore, draws our attention to several aspects of the play. Firstly, Soranzo's questioning dramatises the impossibility of knowing about incest from the evidence of the pregnant body; for the body does not of itself disclose the identity of the child's father, let alone the nature of the relationship between the two parents. Secondly, the conversation alerts us to the marital and legal structures governing the body, especially the female body, as the reference to a curse suggests the religious strictures which regulated sexual behaviour. Thirdly, and more generally, Annabella's body is subject to violent handling. The dialogue calls attention to the physical body, and its sexual significance is displayed to the theatre audience. Additionally, the idea of ripping up Annabella's heart to discover the name of the child's father there reminds the audience of the earlier incestuous exchange of vows between Annabella and her lover/brother Giovanni, while simultaneously echoing the rhetoric used in a lovers' exchange of hearts. The audience are in possession of these facts, but they also watch scene after scene in which the knowledge of incest is denied, concealed or re-read through the linguistic and dramatic structures of the text.

'Tis Pity She's a Whore was written for the theatre, but the relationship between the making of meaning in the theatre and its cultural context is problematic. Meaning in the theatre is itself destabilised by the complexity of theatrical representation and its use of a written or spoken text in combination with other sign systems (gesture, staging, etc.), which may support or contradict the linguistic text (obviously these contradictions are sometimes inscribed within the script itself). One way of formulating this is to separate linguistic and other signifiers. As the theatre semiotician Veltrusky put it, 'In theatre, the linguistic sign system, which intervenes through the dramatic text, always combines and conflicts with acting, which belongs to an entirely different sign system.'[2] An example of this is the way in which, in Act I, scene i, we see Annabella make a choice of Giovanni after a sequence of lovers have appeared and either been discussed or themselves paid suit. We, the audience, know that the 'truth' of any liaison between sister and brother must be an incestuous one, but as Kathleen McLuskie says, the script's 'structure of the lovers rejected and a lover chosen leads the audience to accept Annabella's choice in spite of the startling danger of incest'.[3] However, this pattern of theatrical structure which makes Giovanni into a lover (and Giovanni's later use of language which makes their love into a platonic union) operates throughout in tension with the audience's knowledge of

the confounding of nature and culture, self and other, which takes place in the incestuous act. It could be argued that the theatre, because of its specific representational status, offers a case study in the containing and naturalising function of sexual discourse. All the way through 'Tis Pity She's a Whore the audience hear words and see actions on stage which do not correspond to what they 'know' in terms of culture. Although the experience of an audience depends on specific historical circumstances, for both a contemporary and an early modern audience, this play would present a contradiction or paradox between a script (using or gesturing towards legal, religious, platonic or civil language to misdescribe incest) and the problem of assignable cultural meanings attached to a body on stage.

'Tis Pity She's a Whore offers a reworking of the familiar family drama of Renaissance tragedy. It extends the complex triangles of desire and specifically the sister–brother relations found in plays including Measure For Measure, The Duchess of Malfi (published in 1623 with a commendatory verse by Ford), James Shirley's The Traitor and Ford's own The Broken Heart. This essay uses 'Tis Pity She's a Whore to examine the relationship between the body and the languages (of, for example, love, law and sin) used to describe it in the English Renaissance. A central question is: what was the significance of incest and the incestuous body in the mid-seventeenth century? Moreover, what relationship can be seen between incest in a theatrical text and in other kinds of writing about sexuality, such as legal and religious discourse, or conduct manuals? Although the play is set in Parma, it is used here to raise questions about English theatre and the regulation of sexuality.

During the Renaissance, a range of (masculine) discourses and institutions claimed to give the body symbolic meaning. Peter Burke's definition of 'culture' as 'a system of shared meanings, attitudes and values, and the symbolic forms (performances, artefacts) in which they are expressed or embodied' offers some scope for the discussion of dramatic and particularly theatrical representation in relation to other 'symbolic forms'.[4] Access to the past, however, is notoriously problematic, and different sign systems cannot easily be read as equivalent or arbitrarily connected. There must inevitably be important differences in the ways in which legal documents and dramatic and theatrical texts treat and utilise the symbolic representations of incest.[5]

It has been argued by both historians and cultural historians that during the seventeenth century privacy became an issue for the individual, while at the same time it also became evident that the body of the individual was claimed not only by the individual her-or-himself and by the church, but also by the state.[6] Michel Foucault and Robert Muchembled have argued that the period 1500–1700 saw a cultural change which produced a nexus of new ideas about family life and licit and illicit sexual behaviour.[7] More cautiously, Martin Ingram concludes that 'these changes add up to a significant adjustment in popular marriage practices and attitudes to pre-marital sexuality'.[8] What the historians do not address is the relationship between these societal shifts and Burke's 'performances'. Incest is often represented in early-modern cultural production (theatrical examples include *Hamlet, Women Beware Women, The Revenger's Tragedy*), and incestuous scenarios seem to have been part of the theatre's appeal to public interest. This crime is mentioned in sacred, legal and other secular official discourses, but such discourses differ in the ways in which they consider incest, and therefore, the meanings assigned to incest differ between legal documents and dramatic or theatrical texts.

Writers including Stephen Greenblatt, Natalie Zemon Davis and Lisa Jardine have tried, in different ways, to negotiate the relationships between different kinds of texts within a field of discourse. Stephen Greenblatt writes of sexual discourse as 'a field which in the early modern period includes marriage manuals, medical, theological and legal texts, sermons, indictments and defences of women; and literary fictions'.[9] Granted that most texts in this field attempt to keep the meanings of sexuality stable and ordered, are all these different writings on sexuality equivalent? Can the semiological systems of a theatrical text 'read' in the theatre be equated with a marriage manual?

One of the most obvious discourses about sexuality is found in conduct books by writers such as Gouge and Tilney which describe and prescribe marital arrangements and the proper ordering of sexuality within the domestic sphere.[10] The discussion of incest in Bullinger's *Christian State of Matrimony* (1541) mediates between Biblical meanings of incest and the implications of the incestuous body in Christian civil society:

> he that hath not a shameless and beastly heart doth sure abhorre and detest the copulations in the said forbidden degrees. Honesty, shame-fastness, & nurture of it self teacheth us not to meddle in such: therefore sayeth god evidently and playnly in the often repeated chap. Levi. xviii Defile not your selves in any of these things, for with all these are the heathen defiled, who I will cast out before you. The

land also is defiled therethrowe: & I will visit their wickedness upon
them, so that the land shall spew out the inhabitours thereof.[11]

Here both nature and 'nurture' are outraged by incest and associate
it with both the heathen and with the rebellion of the land itself,
which casts out those who commit it. For the literate these words
would echo the commonplace interdictions of Leviticus and the
tables of consanguinity and affinity found on church walls. It is a
helpful passage in that, like *'Tis Pity She's a Whore*, it discusses
copulation rather than attempted marriage, as tends to be the focus
of legal documentation, which concentrates on relationships of
affinity rather than consanguinity. The connections between texts
like this one, prescribing the regulation of the body, with legal
records and theatrical representation constitute the complex formation through which ideas of sexuality circulate in language.

In a seventeenth-century context, incest became known through
the religious language of confession, as it does in Ford's play
through Giovanni's and Annabella's confessions to the friar, and
Putana's secular confession to Vasques (IV.iii). Confession is needed
for the church and law to assign meaning to an individual body in
its social context, as the mere body in front of an audience is not
self-explanatory. Even a pregnant body does not tell all its own
secrets, and incest is undiscoverable from external evidence.
Nevertheless, contemporaries did link sexual irregularity to external
signs: in the early-modern period what was perceived as sexual
laxity or deviance was associated with monstrous births. According
to manuals of sexual conduct, such as the later *Aristotle's Master-
Piece*, these births indicated indulgence in sexual extravagance or
misbehaviour, for example intercourse at an 'inappropriate' time in
a woman's menstrual cycle. Manuals such as the *Master-Piece* did
not link incest explicitly to monstrous birth, but their illustrations
do mythologise the dangers of forbidden liaisons, picturing, for instance, the offspring of a woman and a dog.[12]

Incest was of two types: affinity (sexual relations or intermarriage
with non-blood relatives with whom there was a problem because
of inheritance) and consanguinity. Lawrence Stone concludes that
incest 'must have been common in those overcrowded houses where
the adolescent children were still at home'.[13] He also writes that 'all
known societies have incest taboos, and the peculiarity of them in
England was the restriction of their number at the Reformation to
the Levitical degrees'. Moreover, he suggests that the fact that the

punishment for incest was 'surprisingly lenient' indicates that sodomy and bestiality were accounted crimes of greater seriousness. Incest was not declared a felony until 1650, before which – like adultery and fornication – it was investigated, tried and punished by ecclesiastical authorities. Furthermore, incest tends to appear in the records only when people were caught or accidentally married within prohibited degrees, for which latter offences pardons were granted. In 1636 Sir Ralph Ashton in Lancashire was punished for having adulterous sex with a woman and her niece. In the same year Elizabeth Sleath and her father, by whom she had had a second child, received 'severe chastisement' at the house of correction before being sent for further punishment.[14]

As Stone reminds us, information about 'sexual conventions' is hard to find. However, the law does offer certain insights into the possible fate of sexual offenders and particularly the female body. Bastardy provides a paler analogue for it in that the single woman's pregnant body partly confesses her crime; fornication and bastardy were meanings attendant upon her pregnancy, but the body of a woman would not reveal the father to whom the parish might turn to require economic support for the child. If a woman had committed fornication, she might be declared a common whore and punished with banishment by some church authorities.[15] She might be put on good behaviour for a year, fined, whipped, put in the stocks and required to confess, wearing a white sheet in front of the church. Such punishments appear to reflect the economic, familial, physical, social and symbolic values associated with cases of women contravening the imperative to be chaste. The nature and sites of the punishment indicate the issues at stake.

In cases of bastardy where children were actually born rather than merely conceived outside wedlock, paternity was investigated by two Justices of the Peace. In 1624 a statute was passed whereby women who gave birth to an illegitimate child that would be dependant on the parish might be sentenced to one year's hard labour. Collective dishonour and financial burden seem to have been the crux of the matter for the parish, and the Justices were entitled to find ways of keeping the child off parish relief. As the body of the woman did not reveal the child's father, pregnant women could be subjected to mental and physical torture to elicit a confession of paternity. The Justices were also entitled to punish the parents by whipping, which could be done in the marketplace or in the street where the offender lived, as well as in the house of correction.[16] In cases of fornication and bastardy, illegal sexual conduct is revealed physically in the pregnancy of the woman. The symbolic *meaning* of bastardy, however, like incest, was only made evident by the woman's confession and in the demonstration of her body and her physical punishment at church and market, sites of central importance in civil and religious society. For example, in 1613 one Joan Lea was to be 'openly whipped at a cart's tail in St John Street ... until her body be all bloody', and in 1644 Jennett Hawkes was ordered to be 'stripped naked from the middle upwards, and presently be soundly whipped through the town of Wetherby'.

Incest, however, is a much more extreme and confused crime, in which the woman must confess paternity in order that the crime be known. Her body does not reveal the implications of its condition. Without confession the meaning of incestuous sexuality remains hidden. Without confession the sin cannot be identified and confirmed by the religious, financial, civil and familial discourses which converge to declare the (female) body sinful and which look for signs of its crime in the way Soranzo does in the speech quoted at the beginning of this essay. When incest is confessed, however, it merely exposes further and greater confusions surrounding the means of reproduction. Unlike the confession of paternity in the case of bastardy when the naming of the father clarifies a situation and enables the child to be socially placed, the naming of the father in the case of incest multiplies familial and social connections in incompatible ways. Incest and the child of an incestuous relationship have too many, contradictory meanings.

One theorisation of the meanings of incest is offered by Jacques Derrida, who takes incest as the example of a sign which confuses the oppositional status of 'nature' and 'culture'. Incest troubled Lévi-Strauss because it fitted the categories of *both* nature and culture, and Derrida comments, 'It could be perhaps said that the whole of philosophical conceptualisation, which is systematic with the nature/culture opposition, is designed to leave in the domain of the unthinkable the very thing that makes this conceptualisation possible: the origin of the prehistory of incest.'[17] One of Derrida's aims here is to attack the truth value of philosophical concepts, which he sees as created by the pre-conditions which govern how any given discourse produces knowledge. We might see this remark as offering a way to read incest in *'Tis Pity She's a Whore*, where different discourses converge to make meanings around Annabella's and Giovanni's sexual relationship which actually serve to *conceal* the 'truth' of their incest.

For example, Giovanni's language in the early part of the play has two results. It confuses the categories of nature and culture and erases the confusions caused by incest through an appeal to 'beauty' as a 'natural' producer of desire and therefore as an endorsement of that desire. Where other signifiers such as 'heart' are expanded in the play to operate at a complex and ambiguous level of meaning, the idea of incest constitutes what we might call the absent centre in Giovanni's discourse, the hidden precondition of his platonic language.

II

In '*Tis Pity She's a Whore* the female body is represented as an ethical, financial, spiritual, amatory and psychological territory. Annabella's body, the procreative feminine corpus, is located and relocated within these competing ways of looking at the body. The poetic language of love and service used by Soranzo and Giovanni serves to conceal or blur the illicit nature of the physical love that they describe, and to misrepresent the social and economic position of the women courted. It is the relationship of women to sex, money and language that actually determines the outcome of the sexual relationships presented in the play.

This is made evident in Act II when Soranzo in his study considers adapting an encomium to Venice for Annabella.

> Soranzo   Had Annabella lived when Sannazar
> Did in his brief encomium celebrate
> Venice, that queen of cities, he had left
> That verse which gained him such a sum of gold,
> And for one only look from Annabell
> Had writ of her, and her diviner cheeks.
> (II.ii.12–17)

Economic exchange is here implicit in the rhetoric of praise. Part of the project of courtly love is to redefine transgressive, physical acts of love and to transform what is, say, adultery in the discourse of civil society, into platonic union in the language of patronage.[18] This language operates within an economy of patronage in which 'service' and 'duty' are rewarded. We might think of the contract of the luckless Pedringano in *The Spanish Tragedy*, or Beatrice-Joanna in *The Changeling*. In '*Tis Pity She's a Whore* this ends with literary language made literal in the ripping up of Annabella's heart.

The play indicates the duplicitous implications of the language of courtly love in the words of Soranzo and Giovanni. Soranzo appeals to Annabella in terms of courtly love (e.g. III.ii and the scene with Hippolita in II.ii). Giovanni similarly employs the comparative language of courtly love, notably in a scene of courtship (I.ii). It is here that two important metaphors are first encountered, that of the power of the gaze and the trope of the heart on which truth is written. The power of the gaze is attributed, in the terms of courtly love, to the mistress / sister (although, of course, the agent of attribution is Giovanni). Moreover, the scene suggests the legend of Prometheus, another myth of origins, crime and death:

> Giovanni   ... The poets feign, I read,
>   That Juno for her forehead did exceed
>   All other goddesses: but I durst swear
>   Your forehead exceeds hers, as hers did theirs.
> Annabella   Troth, this is pretty!
> Giovanni   Such a pair of stars
>   As thine eyes would, like Promethean fire,
>   If gently glanced, give life to senseless stones.
>   (II.ii.192–8)

This culminates in Giovanni baring his breast:

> Giovanni   And here's my breast, strike home!
>   Rip up my bosom, there thou shalt behold
>   A heart in which is writ the truth I speak.
>   (II.ii.209–11)

It is, however, Annabella's body rather than Giovanni's which comes to bear the meaning of their transgression. In this text the word 'heart', and her heart in particular, is a nexus of several different discourses. Moreover, the significance of Annabella's body is repeatedly transformed during the play by the powerful discourses which are here beginning to define it. This process locates the meaning of the female body within the dominant discourses of religion and courtly love, and her act of will in committing incest with her brother is ultimately subsumed into the civil discourse of whoredom.

If the language of courtly love serves as a structure to conceal, by reinterpreting, Giovanni's and Annabella's incest, where does the act of incest appear in the discourses of the body which permeate 'Tis Pity She's a Whore? Perhaps it is closest to being openly articulated in Act I. This introduces the 'uncanny' disclosure of hidden desire in Annabella's recognition of her sexual attraction to her brother (her platonic 'mirror' as he later notes) when she sees his 'shape' momentarily as an object of her desire without recognising it as her brother.[19]

> **Annabella**   But see, Putana, see; what blessed shape
> Of some celestial creature now appears?
> What man is he, that with such sad aspect
> Walks careless of himself?
>
> (I.ii.131–4)

When Putana looks and tells Annabella that it is her brother, she exclaims 'ha!' Quite the reverse of Giovanni's confessional disquisition on his incestuous passion, this exclamation marks textually the recognition of desire but also the danger attendant upon it. This moment of recognition of 'something secretly familiar' is reminiscent of the repeated moments of recognition in the story of the Sand-man retold by Freud in his essay on the uncanny.[20]

Also, like Oedipus's self-blinding, it suggests the dangerous closeness of the double, more fully articulated at a linguistic level in the scene of the vows (I.ii.253–60). The association between sight and desire is made explicit here but receives fuller elaboration later in the play when it is Putana who is blinded. For she has both 'seen' (metaphorically) Annabella's and Giovanni's act of love and has spoken of it. For Freud, blindness and damage to the eyes is a metaphor for castration. Putana, in seeing, sanctioning *and* speaking about the sexual union of Giovanni and Annabella, appropriates the rights of the law, the father and the Church. She takes over the role of the receiver of confessions and maker of meanings in relation to the incestuous union. However, she also recognises that the meanings she offers for incest (in which female desire is of paramount importance) cannot be spoken in the public sphere. Putana's language is that of the individual acting pragmatically in civil society, but outside the law, as at Act II, scene i where she joins with Annabella in concealing the incest, saying, 'fear nothing, sweetheart; what though he be your brother? Your brother's a man, I hope, and I say still, if a young wench feel the fit upon her, let her take anybody, father or brother, all is one' (II.i.46–9).

Thus during most of the play the languages of courtly love, platonism and pragmatism are substituted for that of incest. Simultaneously, in a series of episodes, blame and punishment are transferred from the central figures of higher social class on to the bodies of those of lower or more marginal status. These threads in the plot act almost as substitute punishments: lesser transgressions receive harsh punishment while incest remains at the centre of the play, invisible and unspoken.

An example of such a replacement can be found in the figure of Hippolita and the language associated with her. Hippolita, the 'lusty widow', has been drawn by Soranzo's seduction into adultery and attempted murder. She has previously entered into a relationship with Soranzo, and in the play we watch and hear Soranzo redefine their relations, *not* in the codes of courtly love but in the sacred (and civil, or pragmatic) vocabulary of adultery, sin and repentance. She appears in Soranzo's study when he is composing the courtly encomium we saw earlier:

> **Hippolita**   'Tis I:
> Do you know me now? Look, perjured man, on her
> Whom thou and thy distracted lust have wronged.
> ...
> Thine eyes did plead in tears, thy tongue in oaths
> Such and so many, that a heart of steel
> Would have been wrought to pity, as was mine:
>   (II.ii.26–38)

In this first interview with her Soranzo exchanges the language of courtly love, used to compose the poem to Annabella, for that of Christian repentance, used to justify giving up Hippolita:

> **Soranzo**   The vows I made, if you remember well,
> Were wicked and unlawful: 'twere more sin
> To keep them than to break them.
>   (II.ii.86–8)

He appropriates whichever code serves his purpose, and the abandoned mistress of the language of courtly love becomes the 'whore' (a term which might signal a casual partner) and an adulteress in that of Christian repentance. The language of service and courtship reappears strangely distorted when Soranzo says, 'Ere I'll be servile to so black a sin, / I'll be a corse' (II.ii.97). The dramatic irony implicit in this speech reminds us that Hippolita's crime and punishment contrast with the greater, central significance accorded culturally to incest. Soranzo's service to adultery is substituted by his service to incest. Once more what we see and hear is in tension with what we know.

The scene demonstrates masculine control over the discourses which produce the meanings of female sexuality. This example of femininity defined and redefined by masculine control of the languages of religion and law is repeated at Act IV, scene i. Momentarily, Hippolita appears to have taken control of the meaning of the masque for her own vengeful intentions. She and the audience discover at the same moment that she has been betrayed by the language of revenge, through the agency of Vasques, the manipulator. Her attempt to control the codes of masque and revenge for her own ends causes her to be, in Vasques's words, a 'mistress she-devil', whose 'own mischievous treachery hath killed you' (IV.i.68–9). Although she is defeated, the language of her final curse on Soranzo is prophetic: 'Mayst thou live / To father bastards, may her womb bring forth / Monsters' (II.i.97–9). Yet again a substitution occurs in the dramatic irony of the prophecy. The audience recognises the displacement of the central issue, incest, by the peripheral and structurable issue of bastardy, and the reference to 'monsters' reminds us of other criminal expressions of sexuality.

The replacement of incest by other language in the play as a whole is indicated most obviously by the fact that the word is rarely enunciated. Just before the play opens Giovanni has confessed incestuous desire to the Friar and made himself 'poor of secrets', though he remains rich in desire. During his post-confessional conversation with the Friar, Giovanni begins to elaborate the secular theory of beauty, fate and desire which is soon to find its elaborate ritual expression in the vows he and Annabella take by their mother's 'dust'.

The lovers themselves do not name their incest, though the Friar finally names it to Annabella in Act III, scene vi. Annabella does not utter a description of her own actions until she repents in Act V, and then she speaks of Giovanni: 'O would the scourge due to my black offence / Might pass from thee, that I alone might feel / The torments of an uncontroll'ed flame' (V.i.21–3). The language describing Annabella's body and interpreting the incestuous desires and actions of the siblings (for actors and audience) has for most of the play been that of courtly love, Neoplatonism and the pragmatic discourse of Putana. Annabella here confesses her actions:

> **Annabella** My conscience now stands up against my lust
> With depositions charactered in guilt, [*Enter Friar*]
> And tells me I am lost: now I confess,

> Beauty that clothes the outside of the face
> Is cursed if it be not clothed with grace.
>
> (V.i.9–13)

This moment not only offers us access to Annabella's subjectivity, in which lust and conscience are coterminous, but refers us to signifiers which also existed culturally during the Renaissance; the pun on guilt/gilt points to the interpretation of incest in society by returning us to the tables of consanguinity figured in the prayer book and on church walls. Annabella's confession fuses for a moment the problematic language of the play which refuses to reconcile incest and the interdiction available to any church-goer. Moreover, we find in this speech not an opposition of inner and outer, but a contrast of surfaces in which grace becomes a kind of clothing. In its concentration on surface and externals the language serves to call attention to the social and cultural construction of the sequence of sin and repentance, further underlined by the entrance of the Friar as eavesdropper/audience.

In the final act of the play the word 'incest' is used in the discourse of Parmesan society. Vasques says the word, and so does the Cardinal: its articulation by these two ambiguous figures is accompanied by the ritual punishment of offenders. Giovanni at this point makes literal the discourse of courtly love using the symbolism of the exchange of hearts in describing his murder of Annabella. His reappearance bearing the bloody organ cannot be interpreted by the characters on stage. For on the one hand the appearance of the real heart makes literal on stage the discourse of courtly love, yet on the other hand it makes evident the inability of this discourse to contain, explain or give meaning to incest, which has a meaning so much more illicit than that of, say, adultery.

The enigmatic but mobile figure of Vasques plays a central role in exposing the faults of women, especially in the final stages of the play. It is only in Act V that we find that Vasques, who hears the confessions of both Hippolita and Putana, is acting for the Father – for Soranzo's father, thence for Soranzo, and therefore for the determination of meaning in relation to the father, law and religious discourse. When, at last, Vasques offers an 'explanation' (or confession) of himself, he says 'this strange task being ended, I have paid the duty to the son which I have vowed to the father' (V.vi.111–12). In a short prose speech he 'explains' his conduct:

> **Vasques**   For know, my lord, I am by birth a Spaniard, brought forth my country in my youth by Lord Soranzo's father,

whom whilst he lived I served faithfully; since whose death I have been to this man, as I was to him. What I have done was duty, and I repent nothing but that the loss of my life had not ransomed his.

(V.vi.115–21)

Vasques's manipulation of language has permitted him to act as a confessor to the women, who are lured into telling him their secrets and thence, through language, brought to their downfall. It is he who has already (at this point) ordered Oedipus's punishment to be inflicted not on Annabella or Giovanni but on Putana.

The uncanny recognitions of incestuous desire in Act I are mapped more fully here when Giovanni reveals to his father the doublings brought about by incest – 'List, father, to your ears I will yield up / How much I have deserved to be called your son' (V.vi.37–8). The Oedipal punishment for incest is transferred from the male to the female body, as well as down the social scale. Vasques names Putana as 'of counsel in this incest', and he renders up Putana, 'whose eyes, after her confession, I caused to put out' (V.vi.127–8). In Act I Giovanni endowed the eyes of his mistress with the power to give life, linking this to Promethean fire. In Act V, the only possible reason that Putana's eyes are burnt out is because she has been witness to the incestuous passion. The importance accorded to knowledge at this point in the play suggests the power of incest to confound the boundaries of nature and culture and thus elide any clear distinctions between self and other. The maiming of Putana keeps incest hidden by removing it 'from sight'. [...]

How can the body of Annabella be read in the final scene? Her brother has taken her heart and the significance of this is explored in metaphors of consumption:

> Giovanni You came to feast, my lords, with dainty fare;
> I came to feast too, but I digged for food
> In a much richer mine than gold or stone
> Of any value balanced; 'tis a heart,
> A heart, my lords, in which mine is entombed:
> Look well upon 't, d'ee know 't?
> Vasques What strange riddle's this?
> Giovanni 'Tis Annabella's heart, 'tis; why d'ee startle?
> I vow 'tis hers: this daggers point ploughed up
> Her fruitful womb, and left to me the fame
> Of a most glorious executioner.

(V.vi.23–33)

We know that Giovanni and Annabella have been lovers for 'nine moons', but we do not know when she conceived. It would be possible to play Acts IV and V with her very heavily pregnant. Annabella's body is first exposed to violence when she becomes pregnant, and the wound by which she was murdered might run from her womb to her heart in the cut an anatomist might use to open a body. Many signifiers converge on Annabella's body. It is food, or has food buried within it. It is simultaneously a mine, an evidently vaginal image, in which Giovanni has 'digged' and found something more exotic than the minerals yielded by mining in distant places, a heart. The heart is her body, but it also signifies his heart within her breast. Her body is a rich vagina-womb-mine, but also a burial ground (ploughed up) from which Giovanni must disinter *his* buried heart. The uncanny doublings of the vows come to a mordant fruition here. The child is cut off and the womb invaded, not by a doctor extracting a child but by the brother-lover in search of her heart which signifies him, his identity. The vows, sworn by Annabella 'by our mother's dust', by Giovanni 'by my mother's dust' (I.iii.254, 257), are fulfilled here as Giovanni possesses and consumes singly all those relations which have become so doubly double.

The opposition here is between inner and outer, and between surface and depth (unlike the metaphors in Annabella's speech of repentance above). The heart, now exposed, is endowed by Giovanni's public confession with all the private and confused meanings of incest. At one level, of course, it is a religious emblem and the emblem of the lover's heart, but like Annabella's dangerously pregnant body, the flesh itself cannot be completely interpreted without language.[21] Giovanni stands on stage with a dripping heart, but the meaning of the murder is constructed by language. Even Vasques, that underminer of plots and reader of signs, cannot answer this sphinx's incestuous riddle. He, however, returns to the stage to inform the feasters that Giovanni has, indeed, ripped out Annabella's heart. It is possible to read Giovanni's final confession, or explanation, of her heart as once again re-inventing the meaning of his love, and of Annabella's body, for he concentrates the illicit multiplicity of relations on her heart. If we read the end of the final act this way, it comes as no surprise to find that when the Cardinal finally mentions Annabella's sin, he does not speak of all those double meanings Giovanni had elicited from her body in that half-emblem, half-meat, her heart.

The Cardinal's address transforms the incest once again into something containable within the single realm of culture when in the closing words of the play he pronounces, ' 'tis pity she's a whore'.

This phrase reconstitutes the dominant position of family, state and the church within society. Simultaneously, however, it calls attention to the failure of the secular and sacred languages used in the play to contain or reinterpret incest.[22] The bodies of the incestuous couple have been represented by the lovers themselves (particularly Giovanni) in the languages of courtly love and Platonism. The Cardinal's words appear to be a bid for closure, marking a point at which the irreconcilable nature of the conflicting claims of church, state, family and economics on the body – particularly the reproductive body – fail to be resolvable and fail to verify and stabilise the meaning of incest.

Incest, which is the central concern of the play, disappears once more in the Cardinal's words which reinstate the social placing implicit in the designation 'whore'. The centre, for Derrida, is 'the point at which the substitution of contents, elements or terms is no longer possible',[23] and incest signals the collapse of the structure of separateness between bodies and families. Instead of substitution there is doubling. In the Cardinal's closing line of the play (also the title) the waters of language return to cover incest and to substitute a crime which allows the meanings of femininity to remain stable. Annabella is returned from incest to the dangerous (but less dangerous) general category for the desirous female. As a 'whore' Annabella once again signifies within the problematic of endless female desire.

However, the Cardinal's closing words leave unresolved the theatre of competing demands which the play has articulated. The tension between what we hear ('whore') and the incest which we 'know' to have taken place remains. His words present another riddle which, by asserting one of the meanings of Annabella's dead body, throws into relief all the others which remain unspoken.

III

The competing discourses of the play are interwoven with its context, but are not reducible to 'sources': they are re-invested with new meanings in the 'symbolic performance' of theatre.[24] The body alone has no meaning. But the question of what happens to the body in a play such as *'Tis Pity She's a Whore* and what gives that body meaning is complex. How is a critic to interpret the body in a play? For an anatomist, meanings exist within the body, but in the theatre only the combination of script and other codes makes the meaning of the theatrical figure. Obviously, much depends on production decisions, but the relationship between text and context is important, if fraught. As Roger Chartier says;

> To understand a culture ... is above all to retrace the significations invested in the symbolic forms culture makes use of. There is only one way to do this: to go back and forth between texts and contexts; compare each specific and localised use of one symbol or another to the world of significance that lends it meaning.[25]

Put this way, the relationship of text to context is very complicated for symbolic bodies in the theatre, with all their precarious and slippery meanings. The context can only be other texts, other bodies in texts and the field of discourse within which these textual bodies exist.

Of course, it is not possible to talk with the dead, or to fully reanimate a field of discourse of which literary language is only a part.[26] Nor is it possible to work out exactly how the seventeenth-century theatre audience for *'Tis Pity She's a Whore* made the leap from their own experience of sexual crimes in the community to an analysis of a symbolic performance. According to Derek Hirst, policing of 'the proper order of personal relationships' in early modern England was part of the role of neighbours, and this included regular denunciations for sexual deviance. Hirst suggests that as many as one person in seven might have been denounced by neighbours for sexual deviance.[27] This might lead us to ask how we can begin to imagine the relationship between an audience who participated in such a very active neighbourhood policing and the incestuous bodies in *'Tis Pity She's a Whore*.

One answer must be to compare the play with other texts in a similar field (what, for instance, might a theatrical text share with legal texts, conduct books, etc.?). Another might be to attempt to identify the specific purposes and investments of a particular discourse, which might not be shared with other texts in the field. For example, Michael MacDonald's recent study of suicide suggests that the significance of self-murder changed with the rise of the newspaper. He suggests that eighteenth-century newspapers 'altered the reader's relationship to events: attitudes to crime, like suicide,

were increasingly determined by reading, rather than by direct experience and by rumour'.[28] The newspaper, with its pretensions to
forensic veracity, might fix and report 'facts' for private consumption; the theatre, with its reputation for tempting fictions, might
endow the body with an ephemeral plethora of meanings. Thus, evidence from texts in a similar field helps to illuminate the script of
the play, and we can to some extent move between text and context
to map a loose set of relationships between punishments in the ecclesiastical courts and the significance of the body in the theatre.
Yet, in both the theatre and the church court the body on display
does not reveal its own significance. Without explanation from
script, set and costume the body of a pregnant woman cannot be
fully 'read' either by the figures on the stage or by the audience.
Veltrusky, quoted at the beginning of this essay, suggested that
script and the actions of the body on stage were parts of independent discourses. He went as far as to say that the body on stage
and the dramatic text (language) belong to completely different sign
systems; as he sees it, the dramatic text, where it exists, can control
everything except the actor.[29] This makes it possible to regard the
incestuous body in *'Tis Pity She's a Whore*, with the attendant gaps
and misrepresentations in the script, as being constituted by the cultural understandings of the audience in relation to the interdepen-
dent contexts of analogous texts and theatre practice.

From *Renaissance Bodies*, ed. Lucy Gent and Nigel Llewellyn
(London, 1990), pp. 180–97.

NOTES

[Reading literary texts in relation to non-literary texts – legal, historical
and clerical documents, letters and journals – has become an established
principle of new historicism and other related schools of criticism. This collection provides plenty of examples. Susan Wiseman's essay is important
for the way in which it insists, however, on addressing Ford's *'Tis Pity
She's a Whore* as a text written for performance, rather than simply as a literary text. Her stress upon the play's theatrical dimension, and constant reminders that we are dealing with a signifying *body* on stage, is instructive.
This signifying body – Annabella's – simultaneously reveals (her pregnancy)
and conceals (the identity of the father, and so, for a while, the incestuous
relationship with her brother). In one sense, the dramatic text itself seeks to
circumvent the language of incest, as the essay makes clear, using instead
the discourses of courtly love and platonism. However, at the climax of

the play, there is a single stark signifier – the 'half-emblem, half-meat' of Annabella's heart, ripped from the 'vagina-womb-mine' that is her body. It is around this signifier that the complex meanings cluster, meanings determined by the convergence of a number of sign-systems, linguistic, visual and cultural, within the 'symbolic performance of theatre'. Wiseman's essay explores these systems while at the same time demonstrating the rich dramatic effect Ford's play secures through its staging and action. Quotations are taken from Derek Roper (ed.), *'Tis Pity She's a Whore* (Manchester, 1975). Ed.]

1. The dates of first performance are between 1615 and 1633, when the play was first printed.

2. Jiri Veltrusky, 'Dramatic Text as Component of Theatre', in Ladislav Matejka and Irwin R. Titunik (eds), *Semiotics of Art: Prague School Contributions* (Cambridge, MA and London, 1976), pp. 94–117, esp. p. 114.

3. Kathleen McLuskie, *Renaissance Dramatists* (Hemel Hempstead, 1989), pp. 129–30. [...]

4. Peter Burke, *Popular Culture in Early Modern Europe* (London, 1978), p. xi.

5. For a critique of arbitrary connections between texts within a field of discourse see Walter Cohen, 'Political Criticism of Shakespeare', in Jean E. Howard and Marion F. O'Connor (eds), *Shakespeare Reproduced: the Text in Ideology and History* (London, 1987), pp. 37–8.

6. See for example Francis Barker, *The Tremulous Private Body: Essays on Subjection* (London, 1984), pp. 3–4.

7. Michel Foucault, 'The Repressive Hypothesis', *The History of Sexuality*, trans. Robert Hurley (Harmondsworth, 1981), vol I, pp. 17–21. [...]

8. Martin Ingram, 'The Reformation of Popular Culture? Sex and Marriage in Early Modern England', in Barry Reay (ed.), *Popular Culture in Seventeenth Century England* (London and Sydney, 1985), p. 157.

9. Stephen Greenblatt, 'Fiction or Friction', *Shakespearean Negotiations: The Circulation of Social Energy in Renaissance England* (Oxford, 1988), p. 75. See also the essays in Natalie Zemon Davis, *Society and Culture in Early Modern France* (Cambridge, 1987); her *Fiction in the Archives* (Cambridge, 1987); Lisa Jardine, *Still Harping on Daughters* (Brighton, 1983).

10. William Gouge, *Of Domestical Duties* (London, 1622); Edmund Tilney, *A Brief and Pleasant Discourse of Duties in Marriage* (London, 1568).

11. Heinrich Bullinger, *The Christian State of Matrimony*, trans. Miles Coverdale (London, 1541), ch. viii, 'Of matrimony', p. xviii. Bullinger also refers critically to the stringent Roman Catholic laws on incest within the degrees of affinity in ch. xix.

12. *Aristotle's Master-Piece* (London, 1690), p. 177.

13. Lawrence Stone, *The Family, Sex and Marriage* (Harmondsworth, 1979), p. 309. See also Peter Laslett, *Family Life and Illicit Love in Earlier Generations* (Cambridge, 1977).

14. Lenore Glanz, 'The legal position of English women under the early Stuart kings and the interregnum, 1603–1660', unpublished PhD dissertation, Loyola University of Chicago, 1973, p. 195; *C.S.P.D. Chas. I*, IX, pp. 190, 500–1. Other recorded punishments included fines: see Glanz, 'The legal position of English women', p. 196; *C.S.P.D. Charles I*, V, pp. 41, 62, 90, 91, 102, 108.

15. Glanz, 'The legal position of English women', p. 202.

16. Ibid., pp. 202–9.

17. Jacques Derrida, 'Structure, Sign and Play', in his *Writing and Difference*, trans. Alan Bass (London and Henley, 1978), p. 284.

18. See Joan Kelly, 'Did women have a Renaissance?' in her *Women, History and Theory* (Chicago and London, 1984), pp. 30–6. Reprinted from Renate Bridenthal and Claudia Koonz (eds), *Becoming Visible: Women in European History* (Boston, 1977).

19. Plato, *Phaedrus*, 255d, 'he appears to have caught the infection of blindness from another; the lover is his mirror in whom he is beholding himself, but he is not aware of this.' *The Dialogues of Plato*, trans. B. Jowett (Oxford, 1953), III.

20. Sigmund Freud, *The Standard Edition of the Complete Pyschological Works of Sigmund Freud*, ed. J. Strachey et al., vol. XVII: 1917–1919 (London, 1955), 'The Uncanny', pp. 217–52, esp. p. 245.

21. See for example Christopher Harvey, *The School of the Heart* (1647), in Alexander Grosart (ed.), *The Complete Works* (London, 1874). See also Michael Neill, ' "What Strange Riddle's This?": Deciphering *'Tis Pity She's a Whore*' in Neill (ed.), *John Ford: Critical Re-visions* (Cambridge, 1988) [essay 11 in this volume – Ed.] [...]

22. Jacqueline Rose, 'Sexuality in the reading of Shakespeare: *Hamlet* and *Measure for Measure*', in John Drakakis (ed.), *Alternative Shakespeares* (London, 1985), p. 118.

23. Derrida, 'Structure, Sign and Play', p. 279.

24. See Derek Roper's introduction to [the play], pp. xxvi–xxxvii, for summary discussion of sources.

25. Roger Chartier, *Cultural History*, trans. Lydia G. Cochrane (Cambridge, 1988), p. 96.

26. Greenblatt, *Shakespearean Negotiations*, pp. 1–3. Greenblatt begins, 'I began with the desire to speak with the dead', and goes on to explore the difficulties around this idea.

27. Derek Hirst, *Authority and Conflict* (London, 1987), p. 49.

28. Michael MacDonald, 'The Secularisation of Suicide in England 1660–1800', *Past and Present*, 111 (May 1986), 50–100, esp. p. 51; see also D. T. Andrew's comment and MacDonald's reply in *Past and Present*, 119 (May 1988), 158–70.

29. Veltrusky, 'Dramatic Text as Component of Theatre', p. 115: 'the general function of drama in the shaping of the semiotics of theatre can be brought out only by means of confronting the two sign systems that are invariably present, that is, language and acting'. See also Patrice Pavis, 'Notes Toward a Semiotic Analysis', trans. Marguerite Oerlemans Bunn, *The Drama Review*, 84 (1979), 93–104, esp. p. 104: 'Very often it is the *out of sync*, the absence of harmony between parallel scenic systems, that ... produces meaning.'

11

'What Strange Riddle's This?': Deciphering *'Tis Pity She's a Whore*

MICHAEL NEILL

I

A Devise is nothing else but a rare and particular way of expressing oneself; the most compendious, most pleasing, most efficacious of all other that humane wit can invent. It is indeed most compendious, since, by two or three words it surpasseth that which is contained in the greatest volumes. As a small beame of the Sun is able to illuminate and replenish a cavern be it ever so vast, with the rays of its splendor: So a Devise enlightens our whole understanding.

(Henri Estienne, *The Art of Making Devices*)[1]

The glory of my deed / Darkened the mid-day sun, made noon as night.

(Giovanni)

The Renaissance belief in the capacity of images to seize and possess the mind is endlessly reflected in Tudor and Stuart dramaturgy. Memory, the ancients had taught Ford's contemporaries, was particularly responsive to visual impressions, especially those created by 'striking' and 'active' images of a violent or grotesque character. Such mnemonic devices achieve their greatest effectiveness, according to the influential treatise, *Ad Herennium*, 'if we assign to them exceptional beauty or singular ugliness ... or if we somehow disfigure them, as by introducing one stained with blood'.[2] To this belief was added the conviction that the density of compacted meaning in symbolic images, emblems, devices and imprese, endowed them with a persuasive potency beyond the reach of mere words. In play after play the most powerful climaxes are marked by stage pictures whose intensity produces an effect of startling arrest. Borrowing a term from the epic theatre of Brecht, Michael Hattaway has described these tableau-like episodes as 'gests' – 'moments when the visual elements of the scene combine with the dialogue in a significant form that reveals the condition of life in the play'.[3] Often they are best approached as elements in a carefully orchestrated structural sequence; but in certain outstanding instances a single stage picture of peculiar complexity and force can seem to contain, in the tightly enfolded manner of an emblem or device, the meaning of a whole work.

Something of the hold which such powerful iconic spectacles exercised upon the contemporary imagination is suggested by the crude, but often expressive woodcuts chosen to adorn the title pages of early seventeenth-century quartos. The 1616 text of *Dr Faustus*, for example, shows the great conjuror as we see him in Act I, scene iii of Marlowe's play, in the act of raising the devil. Although the text appears to locate the scene in 'some solitary grove' (I.i.154), the artist understandably imagines it in the study which provides the symbolic locus for so much of the play's action, the little room from which this pursuer of the infinite never truly escapes.[4] He is shown surrounded by the learned volumes and scientific instruments that are the tokens of his insatiable *libido sciendi*; in one hand he holds the necromantic book whose spells have raised the demon that rears in front of him, in the other he clasps his magician's staff of power, thrust forward in a gesture of command as though to hold the menacing creature at bay. Around him on the floor, marked with those astrological figures and potent anagrams that identify it as a kind of widdershins model of the universe, is the mighty circle whose ambiguous symbolism makes it not only an instrument of power and a protective enclave but also an image of confinement – at once a sign of the infinite and a cipher of nothingness, a reminder of that futile circularity which (by a kind of diabolic quibble) seems to reduce the twenty-four years of Faustus's career to the twenty-four hours of a natural day. This magician is a figure at once splendid and pitiable, a lord of creation and a slave of desperate limitation, circumscribed by an intellectual prison of his own making; and the whole play of *Dr Faustus* can be viewed as an exfoliation of the paradoxes contained in this deceptively simple icon. Similarly, in the woodcut commissioned for the 1615 quarto of Kyd's *The Spanish Tragedy* we are offered something much more than what at first sight appears – a naïve representation in the old serial fashion of one of the more sensational episodes of the play, Horatio's clandestine murder. The foregrounding of the arbour, that desecrated garden with its 'fruits of love' (II.iv.55) – a body 'hanging on a tree' (IV.iv.111) – draws attention to the powerful religious and political resonances of this emblematically conceived scene.[5] In it are concentrated the key meanings of Kyd's tragedy.

It was part of the retrospective quality of Ford's art that he, more than most dramatists of the Caroline period, liked to build his plays towards climactic 'gests', resembling the densely compacted 'speaking pictures' represented in these illustrations – one can think of the great dance episode (V.iii) in *The Broken Heart*, or the tomb scene that concludes *Love's Sacrifice* with its bizarre mock-resurrection; most strikingly of all, there is the final banquet scene of *'Tis Pity She's a Whore* where Giovanni makes his extraordinary entry with Annabella's heart impaled upon a dagger. For audiences and readers alike this is the most shocking, eloquent and unforgettable of all the play's stage pictures; and the frantic scrutiny to which it is subjected by the baffled onlookers at Soranzo's feast makes it inevitable that it be read in metaphoric terms. Indeed, as D. K. Anderson long ago pointed out, it gains a strange hallucinatory power as the enacted culmination of Ford's obsessive heart and banquet imagery; and this alone is enough to identify it as of decisive significance for the whole play.[6] No adequate account of Ford's dramaturgy can avoid coming to terms with this scene; yet its air of melodramatic extravagance has made it the object of more critical embarrassment than intelligent scrutiny. Artaud might extol the dramatist's magnificent extremism, but to Ford's detractors, and even to some of his admirers, his coup for a long time seemed to epitomise the gratuitous sensationalism associated with the so-called Caroline 'decadence'.[7] It is true that since Muriel Bradbrook first drew attention to the scene's emblematic character[8] the climate of response has gradually become more sympathetic, but there is still no general agreement as to how this crucial episode is to be judged or interpreted.

For some, whether they read it in moral or psychoanalytic terms, the spectacle is simply a way of representing Giovanni's diseased inner condition: in Mark Stavig's severely moralistic scheme it shows 'the ultimate depravity of a man approaching madness';[9] while Derek Roper takes it as a quasi-Freudian symbol defining Annabella's murder as 'a sadistic version of the sexual act'.[10] For others, who see in it an extreme version of the apocalyptic denouement characteristic of Jacobean tragedies of blood, its significance is primarily social: Ian Robson, for example, finds Giovanni yielding to 'the savage ethics of his native culture';[11] while Brian Morris sees the mutilated heart as an emblem of the hidden corruption beneath the surface of Parmesan social order, 'the perfect, final, visual image, for what has been going on, privately, secretly, in their midst'.[12] For Ronald Huebert, on the other hand, it is a piece of self-conscious symbolisation contrived by the hero himself: this is Giovanni's 'last grotesque attempt to unlock the truth as he sees it ... He carves a martyr's heart out of the breast of a sinner ... The word has become flesh. The poetic metaphor has become a transcendental symbol ... Annabella's heart is torn from her body in order to confirm Giovanni's belief in her purity, just as the entrails of the sacrificial lamb are torn and scattered to confirm the Hebrew belief in a pure Messiah.'[13]

How, faced by such various and proliferating opinions, ought one to read the scene? It may help to begin with a pair of anecdotes that place it in a more strictly contemporary context. On 16 November 1600, a minor courtier, Philip Gawdy, wrote to his brother with a mildly sensational story from the court:

> There is news besydes of the tragycall death of M[rs] Ratclifie the mayde of honor who ever synce the deathe of S[r] Alexander her brother hathe pined in such straunge manner, as voluntarily she hathe gone about to starve her selfe and by the two dayes together hath receyved no sustinaunce, which meeting with extreame griefe hathe made an end of her mayden modest dayes at Richmond uppon Saterdaye last, her Mae[tic] being [present?] who commaunded her body to be opened and founde it all well and sounde, saving certaine stringes striped all over her harte. All the maydes ever synce have gone in blacke. I saw it my selfe at court.[14]

If someone suspected suicide, they were disappointed, for the body bore no trace of poison; instead they found what must have seemed like incontrovertible evidence of a broken heart, physical proof of an emotional crisis whose status normally hovered between metaphor and medical fact. In the process a pathological investigation had become something else: the officiating surgeons had

become archaeologists of feeling – it was as if they had quite literally plucked out the heart of the dead woman's mystery, uncovering
an emblem of extraordinary and disconcerting vividness, in which
the boundaries of the real and the metaphorical were spectacularly
abolished.

This display of Margaret Ratcliffe's mortally injured heart serves
as a reminder of the curious double existence enjoyed by the human
body in early modern culture: it was both a biological entity and an
assembly of emblematically arranged parts each with its own allegoric meanings, among which the heart as the supposed seat of the
affections had a peculiar prominence. Its twofold role was vividly
brought home in the ingeniously contrived indignities inflicted upon
the body in the iconographic theatre of public executions.[15] In the
course of the drawing and quartering of traitors, for example, it
was customary for the executioner to cut out the victim's heart and
display it for the execration of the crowd. John Aubrey describes
the death of the Gunpowder conspirator, Sir Everard Digby: 'When
his heart was pluckt out by the Executioner (who, *secundum
formam* cryed, Here is the heart of a Traytor!) it is credibly reported, he replied, Thou liest!'[16] If one asks why such demonstrations did not arouse the same moral disgust as, say, the superficially
similar eviscerations conducted by the 'barbarous' priests of Meso-
America, the answer must be that the symbolic life of the body
enabled the atrocity to be absorbed as part of a comprehensible
ritual language. The horror of the occasion, while necessary to its
sensational impact, was carefully contained by the ceremonial
framework which identified the mutilation as belonging to a recog-
nisable mode of public discourse. The point of the ceremony was to
demonstrate the power of the monarch, and it did so through its
very ability wholly to reduce the living body to a system of abstract
signs: Digby's heart was less a vital organ than the sign of that inner
truth which his false face had kept hidden from the world. On every
person's heart, so the metaphors went, was inscribed the truth of
their feelings: the executioner made the metaphor real at the same
time as ritual cloaked the mutilated flesh in the decency of
metaphor – and in Aubrey's story even the defiant body plays its
part by answering as though it belonged to some emblematically
conceived picture or device.

The highly theatrical nature of such spectacles made them naturally attractive to dramatists accustomed to working with emblematic images and with a taste for the sensational: the extraordinary

moment at the end of *The Atheist's Tragedy*, where D'Amville is made to dash out his own conniving brains with the very axe that is about to accomplish his travesty of justice, is a case in point. At first sight anyway, Giovanni's vision of himself as a 'glorious executioner' offering his sister's heart as a token of the 'justice' he has achieved (V.vi.33, 102) invites a reading of his device in the same straightforward emblematic terms; and it is worth noticing that two plays which contributed significantly to the shaping of Ford's tragedy (and whose outlines the audience were perhaps expected to discern behind his work), Robert Wilmot's *The Tragedy of Tancred and Gismund* and John Fletcher's *The Mad Lover*, feature just such metaphoric transformations of the human heart. *'Tis Pity*, however, subjects the metaphorising process itself to intense ironic scrutiny.[17]

[...]

[In *Tancred and Gismund* (see note 17), the lover's eviscerated heart is at once a brute physical object and the site of an ingenious semiotic contest between a vindictive father and his bereaved daughter. In *The Mad Lover*, by contrast, Fletcher's witty revision transforms Wilmot's hideously substantial impresa to a mere conceit: grisly appearances to the contrary, the bleeding organ in the golden chalice turns out to be a heart and no heart – in effect nothing more than a metaphor of exceptional vividness.]

One way of accounting for the climactic tableau in *'Tis Pity* would be to see it as taking this process of witty reversal one step further and reinvesting Fletcher's emblem with the shockingly literal life it had in *Tancred and Gismund*; and such an explanation would be fully in accord with Ford's mannerist delight in startling revisions of his predecessors.[18] But the effect is more perplexing than this purely formal explanation might allow. By comparison with Wilmot's, the symbolism of Ford's tableau seems both diffuse and obscure: where Wilmot offers a simple choice between the rival readings imposed on Guiszard's heart by the tyrant and his resilient victim, Giovanni's feverishly excited language exposes his sister's heart to a bewildering variety of competing interpretations. At times he can seem to resemble the exulting Tancred – as in that grotesque moment when he offers Annabella's once-doting husband his murderous parody of the petrarchan exchange-of-hearts conceit: 'Soranzo, see this heart which was thy wife's: / Thus I exchange it royally for thine. [*Stabs him.*]' (V.vi.72–3). When, on the other hand, he presents himself as the devourer of Annabella's heart 'I came to feast too, but I digged for food / In a much richer mine than gold or stone ...' (ll.24–5) – it is the Gismund role he assumes. Yet in the same breath he seeks to identify himself as the the passive Guiszard-or-Memnon-like victim of a fatal passion, holding up to the company 'a heart ... in which is mine entombed' (l. 27).

If the echoes of Wilmot and Fletcher seem to point towards an interpretation of the heart gest in terms of the familiar iconography of Love's Cruelty, Giovanni's insistence on the sacredness of Annabella's love serves as a reminder that this, like much erotic imagery, was readily adapted to devotional purposes.[19] Indeed he has already sought to dress the murder in the sainted trappings of a martyrdom which will carry her to 'a throne / Of innocence and sanctity in Heaven' (V.v.64–5), creating a context in which the audience may invest the wounded heart with its traditional devotional significance. Carried by a saint, the heart was symbolic of love and piety; when pierced, it stood for 'contrition and devotion under ... extreme trial'.[20] More specifically, for anyone familiar with Catholic hagiography, it would have recalled the ecstatic suffering of St Teresa, whose visionary *mors osculi* took the form of a fiery spear thrust into her heart. In this scheme Giovanni is the 'glorious executioner' of Annabella (V.vi.33) rather as Divine Love is Teresa's executioner in the highly erotic versions of her martyrdom by Bernini and by Ford's admirer, Richard Crashaw.[21]

There is, one is bound to think, an aspect of deliberate mystification about Giovanni's construction of this profoundly ambivalent symbol, which helps to account for the bafflement it provokes in his stage audience. Annabella's horrified puzzlement at the wild, blasphemous-sounding fantasy of eclipse which announces her impending death: 'What means this?' (V.v.83) is echoed in the frantic interrogatories of the banqueters at Soranzo's feast. It is the same question that starts to the Cardinal's lips as Giovanni, tricking himself out in the rhetoric of Marlovian hubris, makes his melodramatically timed entrance:

> Soranzo   But where's my brother Giovanni?
>   *Enter* **Giovanni** *with a heart upon his dagger.*
> Giovanni   Here, here, Soranzo! trimmed in reeking blood
>   That triumphs over death; proud in the spoil
>   Of love and vengeance! Fate or all the powers
>   That guide the motions of immortal souls
>   Could not prevent me.
> Cardinal   What means this?
>   (V.vi.9–14)

It is as though the Cardinal felt the need for some metaphoric explanation to abate the literal horror of that bleeding flesh; and Giovanni, a self-proclaimed 'oracle of truth' (l.52), is quick to respond, hinting at a bewildering set of alternative meanings, though the glosses and mottoes he supplies, like those of a true mystagogue, are gnomic, obscure and even contradictory. It is, he pronounces, with an eye to his own theatricality, a mere 'idle sight', a spectacular token of 'the rape of life and beauty / Which I have acted' (V.vi.19–20); or it is a symbol of profane sacrifice ('The glory of my deed / Darkened the mid-day sun, made noon as night', ll.21–2), a sacramental offering that turns the banquet into a bizarre erotic parody of the eucharist:

> You came to feast, my lords, with dainty fare;
> I came to feast too, but I digged for food
> In a much richer mine than gold or stone
> Of any value balanced.
>
> (V.vi.23–6)

It may be either a conventional petrarchan emblem of his own passion, or a 'glorious executioner's' bitter quotation from the spectacular imagery of public justice – though in the light of Giovanni's vindictive rage against his rival, the audience may be more inclined to recognise in it the often-used emblem of Envy devouring a heart.[22] Above all, Giovanni endows it with a powerful erotic suggestiveness, which harks back to the overheated conceits of the murder scene itself. In that scene Annabella's wry reference to her 'gay attires' (V.v.20) makes it clear that she faces death clad in the bridal robes which Soranzo commanded her to put on (V.ii.10–11); like Desdemona's wedding sheets, they provide a bitterly ironic visual commentary on a murder which Giovanni imagines not merely as amatory climax (killing her in a kiss), but also, in a weird compression, as a deadly caesarian section ('the hapless fruit / That in her womb received its life from me, / Hath had from me a cradle and a grave', V.v.94–6). Now he presents the heart almost as though it were the newly delivered offspring of their passion:[23]

> 'Tis Annabella's heart, 'tis; why d'ee startle?
> I vow 'tis hers: this dagger's point ploughed up
> Her fruitful womb ...
>
> ...
>
> For nine months' space, in secret I enjoyed
> Sweet Annabella's sheets; nine months I liv'd

A happy monarch of her heart and her.
(V.vi.30–2, 43–5)

Vasques' sarcastic incomprehension ('What strange riddle's this?'
l. 29) is understandable; for the effect of this proliferation of
metaphoric suggestion, this layering of riddle upon riddle, is finally
to defeat the exegesis it seems to invite. The greater the load of alternative meanings heaped upon it, the more the heart seems to assert
its atrocious physicality, driving a wedge between sign and
signification, word and thing. The strangely over-insistent repetition
of the word 'heart' through the last two scenes of the play (V.v.56,
78, 102, 105; V.vi.3, 16, 26, 45, 59, 63, 72) emphasises this discrepancy, forcing a perplexed concentration on the mere raw meat in
Giovanni's hand. The effect is not altogether unlike that achieved
rather more crudely in *Titus Andronicus* with its pitiless exposure of
the problematic relation between words and things. The action of
Shakespeare's tragedy is built around successive spectacles of dismemberment, beginning with the offstage lopping of Alarbus's limbs,
continuing through the mutilations of Lavinia and Titus and the be-
heading of Martius and Quintus, and climaxing in the Thyestean
banquet where Tamora is made to feast upon the heads of her
butchered sons. In retrospect, as a number of critics have shown, all
of this may be read as an elaborate analogy for the progressive disintegration of the Roman state, whose 'broken limbs' must be 'knit
again ... into one body' at the end of the play (V.iii.70–2).[24] But at
any given point in the play the metaphoric status of the spectacle
seems much less stable; for when the language of mutilation no
longer expresses the overriding power of a monarch but only the ferocious competition of individual wills, the body becomes a site of
discursive conflict, and its wounds the indecipherable script of political babel. The more the play's elaborate Ovidian rhetoric struggles to
subject its horrors to the decencies of metaphoric control, the more
its brute realities resist ritual confinement.[25] However much Titus
persuades himself that his daughter's maimed body is a 'map of woe'
which talks 'in signs' (III.ii.12), its meanings are ones that he alone
must struggle to impose upon her mangled flesh:

> Thou shalt not sigh, nor hold thy stumps to heaven,
> Nor wink, nor nod, nor kneel, nor make a sign,
> But I, of these, will wrest an alphabet,
> And by still practice learn to know thy meaning.
> (*Titus Andronicus*, III.ii.42–5)

The body he so desperately scans belongs to a world made 'wilderness', a 'barbarous' world without comprehensible order, and therefore ultimately inaccessible to language. For all the rhetorical sound and fury surrounding them, its mutilated limbs are signs that run the danger of signifying nothing. In Ford's play, Annabella's heart becomes, from the very excess of hermeneutic pressure to which it is subject, just such another disturbingly unmetaphored sign.

II

The plague takes dormant images, latent disorder and suddenly carries them to the point of the most extreme gestures. Theatre also takes gestures and develops them to the limit. Just like the plague, it reforges the links between what does and does not exist in material nature. It rediscovers the idea of figures and archetypal symbols which act like sudden silences, fermata, heart stops, adrenalin calls, incendiary images surging into our abruptly woken minds. It restores all our dormant conflicts and their powers, giving these powers names we acknowledge as signs. Here a bitter clash of symbols takes place before us, hurled one against the other in an inconceivable riot. For theatre can only happen the moment the really inconceivable begins, where poetry taking place on stage, nourishes and superheats created symbols ... In theatre, as in the plague, there is a kind of strange sun, an unusually bright light by which the difficult, even the impossible suddenly appears to be our natural medium. And Ford's 'Tis Pity She's a Whore is lit by the brilliance of that strange sun.

(Antonin Artaud)[26]

Other critics have noticed the metaphoric overstrain which seems to push Ford's last scene beyond the allowable limits of emblematic representation. Huston Diehl finds a 'tension between the grisly, literal thing and its metaphoric significance';[27] and Ronald Huebert suggests that it results from the inherent improbability of the analogy on which the scene is founded, the explanation for which he finds in the 'baroque' nature of Ford's style. 'Ripping up the bosom', he suggests, 'is the vehicle which stands for discovering the truth about Giovanni's intentions', but the connection between vehicle and tenor is fundamentally illogical:

The only convincing grounds for drawing any comparison between ripping up the bosom and discovering a secret are, it appears, psychological ... Discovering somebody's thoughts is, under any normal circumstances, so unlike ripping up his bosom that it is both logically questionable and linguistically audacious to suggest the comparison.[28]

In this account the impaled heart forms the culminating image in a series of characteristically 'baroque' metaphors, whose psychological power depends precisely on their suggestive refusal 'to define, to outline, to limit'.[29] What is extravagant about *'Tis Pity*, however, is not so much its metaphors themselves as Giovanni's violent literalisation of them; and what renders the final tableau enigmatic is not so much its associative vagueness as the welter of competing definitions and explanations it invites. In the absence of any controlling ritual context, no one of these can be confirmed; so that the heart always threatens to become nothing more than itself, a grisly tautology – a piece of offal *en brochette*, brutally stripped of all vestiges of metaphor.

However, Huebert's implication that the gest is meant as a way of representing some hidden truth, a secret of the hero's psyche which lies beyond easy or rational articulation, is worth further attention. It is a view put even more forcefully by Carol Rosen in her Artaudian account of the play: 'the heart of Annabella', she writes, '... serves the drama concretely as well as emblematically ... [it] envelops the action in a truly concrete physical language which, according to Artaud, is "truly theatrical only to the degree that the thoughts it expresses are beyond the reach of the spoken laguage" '.[30]

Although Jonathan Dollimore and others have recently argued powerfully for an anti-essentialist reading of Renaissance tragedy,[31] it remains true that in their growing fascination with the human psyche, Elizabethan and Jacobean dramatists characteristically wrote *as though* the self were a distinct entity that could be located at the hidden core of being. Again and again it is to some such irreducible fortress of psychological privacy that their characters retreat when confronted by the prospect of their own ending. In Kyd's *The Spanish Tragedy*, for example, after his mocking epilogue seems to have explained at length the whole 'mystery' of his theatrical revenge, Hieronimo nevertheless insists on guarding one last enigmatic secret:

Urge no more words, I have no more to say.

...

What lesser liberty can kings afford
Than harmless silence? Then afford it me.

...
Thou may'st torment me, as his wretched son
Hath done in murdering my Horatio
But never shalt thou force me to reveal
The thing which I have vowed inviolate.
(*Spanish Tragedy*, IV.iv.151, 180–1, 185–8)

The attempts by the author of the Fifth Addition to clear up the apparent illogicality of Hieronimo's resistance (what more, practically, *could* he reveal?) are surely beside the point: what the revenger seeks to keep inviolate is something else again – its importance consists precisely in the fact that it *cannot and must not be spoken*, and in the elaborately rhetorical world that is *The Spanish Tragedy* this unspoken thing is nothing less, we might say, than the core of the hero's essential selfhood. To protect it he bites out his own tongue.[32] Hieronimo's stepchild, Hamlet, for all his anxiousness that his story be told aright, finally withdraws into the heart of his own mystery, behind the walls of a 'silence' as impenetrable as that claimed by an Iago ('Demand me nothing; what you know, you know: / From this time forth I never will speak word', *Othello*, V.ii.303–4) or a Flamineo ('Leave thy idle questions. / I am i' the way to study a long silence ... at myself I will begin and end', *White Devil*, V.vi.204–5, 259). Their truth, in Polonius's phrase, remains 'hid within the centre'.

Among later Stuart dramatists, however, a subtle modification of such defiant attitudes sometimes brings us closer to the materialist scepticism that Dollimore argues for. 'Our citadels / Are placed conspicuous to outward view, / On promonts' tops, but within are secrets', declares Vermandero in *The Changeling* (I.i.167–9), announcing what is to be the major theme of Middleton and Rowley's play; its action carries us through the winding passages of his castle as it unlocks the labyrinthine recesses of Beatrice-Joanna's and De Flores' hidden selves. 'Secret' is perhaps the play's most obsessively repeated word, and keys are among its most prominent symbolic properties: a key gives access to that narrow and secret passage where Piracquo meets his death, a key opens the closet where Alsemero hides his 'Book of Experiment, Call'd Secrets in Nature' – the same closet where Beatrice-Joanna and De Flores will achieve their murderously final consummation. But the 'Nature' exposed here, as De Flores makes sardonically clear, is socially not metaphysically conceived: Beatrice-Joanna is 'what the act has made [her]', 'the deed's creature', nothing more (III.iv.135–7); and if De

Flores, in a mood of sour triumph, retreats into the castle of his skin it is a place defined by emptiness and absence, as ultimately *indifferent* as that 'common sewer' which will carry Beatrice-Joanna 'from distinction': 'I have drunk up all,' he boasts, 'left none behind / For any man to pledge me' (V.iii.170–1).

'Tis Pity She's a Whore, too, is much preoccupied with unlocking psychological truths, but is arguably even more radical in its challenge to essentialist 'distinction'. The preoccupation with inner secrets is announced at the very beginning of the play, opening as it does in the midst of Giovanni's confession to Friar Bonaventura:

> To you I have unclasped my burdened soul,
> Emptied the storehouse of my thoughts and heart,
> Made myself poor of secrets; have not left
> Another word untold, which hath not spoke
> All what I ever durst or think, or know.
> (I.i.13–17)

In a subtle way that private unclasping of the soul and emptying of the heart anticipate the ferociously public stripping of the self exhibited in the play's catastrophe. Even more strikingly proleptic is scene ii where Giovanni makes his second confession, this time to Annabella:

> Rip up my bosom, there thou shalt behold
> A heart in which is writ the truth I speak
> (I.ii.210–11)

The violence of his gesture with the dagger – like Soranzo's violence when he threatens to 'rip up [Annabella's] heart' to uncover the name of her seducer (IV.iii.53–4) – suggests a curiously literal application of the stock metaphor. For Giovanni in particular the truths of the self are something hid within the centre, as though the heart of his mystery were something inalienably bound up with the physical sources of life itself. It is an assumption which underlies his entire performance in the final scene – where, however, he carries it to the point of an insane travesty that ends by decisively undermining the very metaphysic of identity it means to express. He forces open the heart of her mystery to find there is *nothing there*: the frenzy of physical sensationalism announces a psychological *horror vacui*.

Annabella's heart is in a way the opposite of Margaret Ratcliffe's (or Calantha's); bearing none of the secret signs of inner truth, it is marked only with the violence of Giovanni's solipsistic passion. In its appalling blankness, its resistance to allegoric inscription, it becomes a sign of indistinction and undifferentiation:[33] in contrast to the traditional devices which it superficially resembles, this seeming hieroglyph is neither a way of compacting orthodox meanings nor even a means to articulate the inexpressible, but a sign of semantic annihilation. It is this cancellation of meaning that Giovanni inadvertently expresses in the wild oxymoron of a deed whose 'glory ... darkened the mid-day sun, / Made noon as night' – an act whose fierce illumination appears to quench the light of reason itself. At this point we are closer to the flickering 'brilliance' of Artaud's 'strange sun', his 'inconceivable riot' of bitterly clashing symbols, than to the steady rays with which Henri Estienne's refulgent devices illuminate the cavern of understanding.

But if Giovanni's frenzy makes of his sister's heart a symbolic object drained of symbolic content, an emblem obdurately resistant to confident allegorical reading, his spectacular gesture nevertheless continues to act upon audiences with the force of those 'incendiary images' which Artaud described as 'surging into our conscious minds' from a zone of darkness and silence: the 'strange sun' of the play, in his analysis, is like the harsh light to which civilised beings are exposed by the depredations of the plague, stripping away their social personae to uncover the occulted violence and cruelty beneath.[34] One way of penetrating that dark zone and accounting for the final scene's power to disturb, I am going to suggest, is through an examination of Ford's reworking of yet another earlier drama – Webster's magnificent tragedy of repressed desire, *The Duchess of Malfi*.

Ford's admiration for Webster's play is a matter of record: he contributed encomiastic verses upon its publication in 1623; and that it was among the many plays in his mind as he worked on *'Tis Pity* has already been demonstrated through the various verbal echoes noted by Dorothy Farr.[35] Less readily illustrated but even more eloquent testimony to Webster's influence can be found in the dramaturgical technique of some of Ford's most striking scenes. It was surely from Webster that Ford learned to write the spare, broken dialogue, stumbling between prose and irregular verse, which he turns to such moving effect in the courtship of brother and sister that brings the first act of *'Tis Pity She's a Whore* to its climax. Indeed the entire episode seems to be closely modelled upon the equivalently placed scene in *Malfi* (I.i.368–477) where the Duchess and her steward pick their hesitant way towards mutual confession of their love.[36] In sequences like this, Webster had shown himself a master of the language of barely contained emotion: half-lines seem to stumble into silence; and the fear of what might fill that silence is hinted at in the sudden rushes of speech, registered by the rapid cueing of shared lines. The couple's nervous repartee provides the thinnest of ironic masks for anxiety so acute that the most delicate of rhythmic adjustments can threaten to release a torrent of ungovernable emotion, for whose consequences neither will be answerable – a cataclysm that seems only just held off by the ceremonial restraints of ring-giving and kneeling. Ford's scene depends on the same tense conjunctions of effect, the dialogue stretching and swaying like a tightrope over an abyss:

> Giovanni   Come sister, lend your hand, let's walk together.
>   I hope you need not blush to walk with me;
>   Here's none but you and I.
> Annabella   How's this?
> Giovanni   Faith, I mean no harm.
> Annabella   Harm?
> Giovanni   No, good faith; how is't with 'ee?
> Annabella   [*aside*] I trust he be not frantic. [*To him*]. I am very
>   well, brother.
> Giovanni   Trust me, but I am sick; I fear so sick
>   'Twill cost my life.
> Annabella   Mercy forbid it! 'Tis not so, I hope.
> Giovanni   I think you love me, sister.
> Annabella   Yes, you know I do.
> Giovanni   I know't, indeed. – Y'are very fair.
> Annabella   Nay, then I see you have a merry sickness.
>
> (*'Tis Pity*, I.i.176–91)

Like Webster's, Ford's scene concludes in an improvised wedding ritual in which the couple kneel and exchange vows before retiring to 'kiss and sleep';[37] and, as in *Malfi*, the ritual is produced as a response to – a way of putting in check – the explosion of emotion threatened by a moment of sudden physical intensity. In *Malfi* it is the Duchess whose feelings can no longer abide the tension between her familiar social role and the unnatural part of wooer she is forced to play; she breaks out in a 'violent passion' that rises to an

astonishingly direct confession of her own desire – demanding that
Antonio recognise the warmth and vulnerability of her merely
human flesh:

> Go, go, brag
> You have left me heartless, mine is in your bosom,
> I hope 'twill multiply love there. You do tremble.
> Make not your heart so dead a piece of flesh
> To fear, more than to love me. Sir, be confident,
> What is't distracts you? This is flesh, and blood, sir,
> 'Tis not the figure cut in alabaster
> Kneels at my husband's tomb. Awake, awake, man,
> I do here put off all vain ceremony,
> And only do appear to you, a young widow,
> That claims you for her husband.
>   (*Malfi*, I.i.448–58)

What is so remarkable and touching about this speech is the way
the Duchess manages the emotionally terrifying transition from the
delicacies of conventional petrarchan metaphor to an extraordinary
sexual frankness: she moves with singular grace from a heart considered purely emblematically ('mine is in your bosom'), though an
image that hovers between metaphor and concrete physicality
('Make not your heart *so dead a piece of flesh* / To fear, more than
to love me'), to that arresting assertion – it is surely an implicit
stage direction, inviting him to feel her living warmth – of her own
sensual presence ('This is flesh, and blood, sir'). The equivalent
moment in *'Tis Pity* comes when Giovanni, struggling to find a language for his unspeakable desire, turns to the eloquence of much
more violent gesture. His first attempts to articulate his love are
hedged about in a self-conscious petrarchising artificiality which
Annabella's irony only too easily laughs off: 'The lily and the rose,
most sweetly strange, / Upon your dimpled cheeks do strive for
change' (*'Tis Pity*, I.ii.200–1). 'D'ee mock me, or flatter me?' she
teasingly responds, 'O, you are a trim youth' (ll.204, 208).
Giovanni's response is at once shocking and oddly prophetic –
without warning, he draws his dagger and offers it to his sister:

> Giovanni   Here!
> Annabella   What to do?
> Giovanni   And here's my breast, strike home!
>   Rip up my bosom, there thou shalt behold
>   A heart in which is writ the truth I speak.
>   (*'Tis Pity*, I.ii.209–11)

This is Giovanni's wild equivalent of the Duchess's delicate assertion of her sensuality: and for her gently understated metaphor of
Love's Cruelty ('go, brag / You have left me heartless, mine is in
your bosom'), he offers a histrionic gesture ('Rip up my bosom,
there thou shalt behold / A heart ...') which strikingly anticipates
the ferocious literalisation of the play's catastrophe. Part of the
menacing power of Ford's scene, however, derives from the reworking of a very different, though closely connected episode in
Webster's tragedy – that startling moment just before the wooing
scene, when Ferdinand first hints at his incestuous passion for the
Duchess. After the two brothers have completed their antiphonal
lecture upon the 'luxurious' iniquity of remarriage, Ferdinand is left
alone with the Duchess, who mocks him for the studied artificiality
of their diatribe. His reply is strangely enigmatic – a gesture of murderous threat, cloudily wrapped in dark sentences:

> You are my sister,
> This was my father's poniard: do you see,
> I'd be loth to see't look rusty, 'cause 'twas his.
> (*Malfi*, I.i.337–9)

How are we to understand the oddly antithetical linking of 'my
sister' and 'my *father's* poniard'? Only, it would seem, via the
explicitly phallic suggestiveness of his concluding lines:

> fare ye well:
> And women like that part, which, like the lamprey,
> Hath never a bone in't.
> (*Malfi*, I.i.342–4)

Ferdinand's dagger is both a sign of his phallic aggression, and of
the lethal hostility that issues from the subliminal recognition of
such unspeakable desire – just as the obsessive preoccupation with
his sister's 'blood' registers both a fascination with her sexuality,
and a longing to purge it with bloodletting.[38] Like the blood it
seeks, the murderous paternal heirloom is at once a symbol of
Ferdinand's bond with his sister, and a reminder of the fearful pro-
hibition that keeps them apart; it is both a sign of the phallic power
he claims from their father, and a token of the patriarchal authority
that stands between him and the satisfaction of his desires; and in
those tormenting contradictions may be sensed the ultimate source
for that strange conflict of frenzy and inertia by which Ferdinand is
gripped for the first three acts of Webster's play. The dagger

remains potent in imagination – it is the blade that truly belongs in the Duchess's 'loose ... hilts', the instrument that will hew her 'to pieces', tap her 'whore's blood' and serve to make 'of her bleeding heart ... a sponge' to wipe away his choler (II.iv.3,31,49,15) – but impotent in practice. It reappears in the bedchamber scene, significantly at that chilling instant when Ferdinand silently substitutes himself for Antonio. Turning to face the husband she is about to bed, the Duchess confronts instead the motionless figure of her brother, poniard in hand: 'Die then, quickly!' (III.ii.71).[39] But that dagger-blow, whether sexual or actual, remains for some reason beyond Ferdinand's power to inflict: the weapon is simply presented to the Duchess, a menacing but uncertain token, upon whose significance she and Antonio are left to speculate (III.ii.149 ff.); and the murder, when it does come in the mock wedding-masque of Act IV, scene ii, is a proxy consummation which, in the light of Ferdinand's murderous phallic innuendo, may well seem curiously anti-climactic: 'Strangling is a very quiet death' (V.iv.33).

Evidently Ford recognised in the powerful theatricality of Webster's two dagger scenes a compelling expression of the destructive will-to-sexual-power anatomised in his own tragedy of incest. In *'Tis Pity She's a Whore* Giovanni's dagger does indeed become the agent of a grotesque final consummation, a 'rape of life and beauty' in which both love (revealingly inflated as 'my fate') and 'revenge' are satisfied: 'this dagger's point ploughed up / Her fruitful womb' (V.vi.19–36). Far from being a potentially castrating symbol of paternal authority, Giovanni's knife is made into an instrument and sign of his impious assault on the very foundations of patriarchal order and power: 'Monster of children, see what thou hast done, / Broke thy old father's heart!' (V.vi.62–3).

It is no accident that this weapon should make its first appearance in the wooing scene, and the language which frames the weapon's introduction deserves scrutiny: 'If you would see a beauty more exact / Than art can counterfeit or nature frame, / Look in your glass and there behold your own ... Here! ... And here's my breast, strike home! / Rip up my bosom, there thou shalt behold / A heart in which is writ the truth I speak.' What is striking is the way in which that repeated 'here', 'there' and 'look / behold' have the effect of rhetorically confusing dagger and looking-glass – indeed the flash of its steel may be meant to produce a momentary double-take in the audience. Uppermost in Giovanni's mind no doubt – and following naturally from the conscious poeticising of his preceding speeches – is the neo-platonic idea of lovers' hearts as mirrors of one another's authentic being.[40] But the momentary ambiguity is appropriate, since (as the subsequent action will reveal) the dagger *is* in some sense a metaphoric speculum for the destructive passion to which Annabella is about to surrender. Combining this metaphor with that stock figure of Love's Cruelty, the lady's theft of her inamorato's heart, Giovanni gives the whole complex figure a wildly theatrical twist that may seem to recall Richard of Gloucester's sardonic parody of courtly devotion before Lady Anne. Unlike the histrionic Richard's, however, Giovanni's posturing is in a kind of deadly earnest, marked by that sudden explosion of emotion; and so that it shall not be forgotten, the language of the play keeps the old emblems of Love's Cruelty constantly active in the audience's mind.

Both Giovanni (II.i.4–5, 32; V.v.56–8) and Soranzo (III.ii.23; IV.iii.106–8) present themselves as potential martyrs to Annabella's cruel disdain, having surrendered their hearts into her keeping. Even more graphically, the dying Hippolita calls down upon Soranzo's perfidious heart all the tortures her own is suffering:

> Take here my curse amongst you: may thy bed
> Of marriage be a rack unto thy heart,
> Burn, blood, and boil in vengeance – O my heart,
> My flame's intolerable!
>
> (IV.i.94–7)[41]

Racked, burning and and variously impaled hearts feature prominently in a fifteenth-century German woodcut illustrating the Tortures of Love, but that print may also serve to highlight one striking difference between conventional representations of Love's Cruelty and Ford's climactic tableau: in the iconographic tradition the victim is almost invariably male. In some versions it is the goddess Venus who tears out his heart and inflicts it with the piercing torments of desire;[42] in others it is the mistress herself who is imagined in the act of triumphant evisceration,[43] and even when (as in *King René's Book of Love*) it is a male God of Love who unrips the lover's bosom and delivers his heart to the masculine figure of Desire, the image is still one of passive male suffering.[44] In Ford's version of the motif, however, the roles are strikingly reversed: stabbing his sister 'in a kiss', Giovanni makes of her death a profane *mors osculi* – a grotesque variation upon the Friar's vision of her sufferings in hell: 'Then you will wish each kiss your brother gave / Had been a dagger's point' (III.vi.27–8). Mortally wounded by Vasques, Giovanni greets his own end with a wry recollection of the old monitory emblem of Death at the Feast: 'Death, thou art a guest long looked-for' (V.vi.104); perhaps the last irony of his tableau is that it presents him precisely in the guise of Feasting Death as he appears, for example, in Francis Quarles's *Argalus and Parthenia* (1629). In Quarles's poem the heroine imagines her wedding to this grisly bridegroom: 'His hand shall hold a Dart, on which shall bleed / A pierced heart, wherein a former wound / With *Cupid's* Javelin enter'd, shall be found.'[45] Giovanni's usurpation of the panoply of Death's erotic triumph converts it to a spectacular assertion of male power over the submissive female, that 'rape of life and beauty' of which he defiantly boasts to the assembled banqueters (V.vi.19). It can be no surprise that the dramatist who created this astonishing and disturbing image of the sexual will-to-power should also emerge, in plays like *The Broken Heart* and *Perkin Warbeck*, as the celebrant of a passive and profoundly feminised version of tragic heroism.[46]

From *John Ford: Critical Re-visions*, ed. Michael Neill (Cambridge, 1988), pp. 153–74.

NOTES

[Michael Neill's essay focuses attention on the climax of Ford's play, unpacking the symbolic significance of Giovanni's appearance in the final scene with his sister's heart impaled on his dagger. After some general discussion of the emblematic device, he explores two plays which probably influenced Ford: Robert Wilmot's *The Tragedy of Tancred and Gismund* and John Fletcher's *The Mad Lover* (this section has had to be cut for inclusion in this volume; I have provided a brief summary of the salient points at the ellipsis). The introductory discussion also makes reference to anecdotal material which is revealing about early modern understandings of human pathology – a field that Jonathan Sawday has surveyed in magisterial fashion in his *The Body Emblazoned: Dissection and the Human Body in Renaissance Culture* (London, 1995).

Neill makes reference to a number of other plays covered by this volume – *The Changeling*, *The Spanish Tragedy* and, especially, *The Duchess of Malfi*, where he demonstrates Ford's considerable debt to Webster, reflecting on the parallels between the Giovanni / Annabella and Ferdinand / Duchess relationships. Neill's willingness to read characters such as Giovanni in psychological terms is in some ways a departure from the anti-essentialist approaches of critics like Jonathan Dollimore, and it is worth comparing this approach with the extract of Dollimore's *Radical Tragedy* (1989) in this volume (see essay 5, and see also the Further Reading section).

In his classic study of the birth of the prison, *Discipline and Punish* (first published in French in 1977), Michel Foucault interprets the ritual of public execution as a reduction of the human body to a sign system. Neill reads Giovanni's violation of Annabella – the removal and display of her heart – in Foucauldian terms; he identifies the climax of the play as a moment that is on the one hand violently and unequivocally literal, but on the other hand stubbornly enigmatic, in view of the sheer number of possible interpretations it invites. Quotations are cited from the New Mermaid edition of *'Tis Pity She's a Whore*, edited by Brian Morris (London, 1968). References to other non-Shakespearean texts are taken from Russell A. Fraser and Norman Rabkin (eds), *Drama of the English Renaissance*, 2 vols (New York, 1976). Quotations from Shakespeare are from G. Blakemore Evans (ed.), *The Riverside Shakespeare* (Boston, 1974). Ed.]

1. Cited from E. H. Gombrich, *Symbolic Images: Studies in the Art of the Renaissance* (London, 1972), p. 162.

2. Quoted in Frances A. Yates, *The Art of Memory* (London, 1969), pp. 25–6. For comment which links the grotesque imagery of Ford's final scene to the Herennian tradition, see Huston Diehl, 'The Iconography of Violence in English Renaissance Tragedy', *Renaissance Drama*, n.s. 11 (1980), 27–44, esp. p. 34.

3. Michael Hattaway, *Elizabethan Popular Theatre: Plays in Performance* (London, 1982), p. 57.

4. For an account of John Barton's brilliant theatrical demonstration of this perception in his 1974 RSC production, see Michael L. Greenwald, *Directions by Indirections: John Barton of the Royal Shakespeare Company* (Newark, DE, 1985), p. 202.

5. For discussion of the emblematic significance of this episode, see S. F. Johnson, '*The Spanish Tragedy*, or Babylon Revisited', in Richard Hosley (ed.), *Essays on Shakespeare and Elizabethan Drama in Honour of Hardin Craig* (London, 1963), pp. 23–36.

6. See D. K. Anderson, 'The Heart and the Banquet: Imagery in Ford's *'Tis Pity* and *The Broken Heart*', *Studies in English Literature*, 2 (1962), 209–17.

7. For a more comprehensive treatment of this issue, see Richard Madelaine, ' "Sensationalism" and "Melodrama" in Ford's Plays' in Michael Neill (ed.), *John Ford: Critical Re-visions* (Cambridge, 1988), pp. 29–54, esp. pp. 29–33, 41–2.

8. M. C. Bradbrook, 'John Ford's *'Tis Pity She's a Whore*', *Cambridge Review* (1940), 401–2.

9. Mark Stavig, *John Ford and the Traditional Moral Order* (Madison, WI, 1968), p. 119.

10. See Derek Roper (ed.), *'Tis Pity She's a Whore* (London, 1975), p. 117, nn. 31 and 32; Dorothy Farr's *John Ford and Caroline Theatre* (New York, 1979) combines the two positions, describing the impaled heart as 'both a sex symbol implying absolute possession and, more important, a gathering together ... of the sense of strong physical, moral and spiritual violation which has run through the entire action' (p. 52).

11. Ian Robson, *The Moral World of John Ford's Drama* (Salzburg, 1983), p. 102.

12. Brian Morris (ed.), *'Tis Pity She's a Whore*, New Mermaid edition (London, 1968), p. xxiii.

13. See Ronald Huebert, *John Ford, Baroque English Dramatist* (Montreal and London, 1977), pp. 145–7.

14. E.g. 2804, f.127; quoted from I. H. Jeayes (ed.), *Letters of Philip Gawdy* (London, 1906), p. 103. For a suggestion that Ford was familiar with this anecdote, see Michael Neill, 'New Light on "The Truth" in *The Broken Heart*', *Notes and Queries*, n.s. 22 (1975), 249–50.

15. See Michel Foucault, *Discipline and Punish: The Birth of the Prison*, trans. Alan Sheridan (New York, 1979), pp. 44–5 on the way in which the 'symbolic' tortures applied to appropriate parts of the body formed a decipherable script in which the truth of the victim's crime might be discerned: 'As Vico remarked, this old jurisprudence was "an entire poetics".' Foucault's entire chapter on 'The Spectacle of the Scaffold' (pp. 32–69) is a mine of information on the semiotics of what he calls this 'theatre of terror' (p. 49). For a suggestive application of Foucault's ideas to the 'sensationalist' techniques of Jacobean drama, see Francis Barker, *The Tremulous Private Body: Essays on Subjection* (London and New York, 1984), pp. 21–5, 89–90; Barker lists Annabella's bleeding heart among those images of violent dismemberment in which the stage articulated a '[spectacular] corporeality ... structural to its age' (p. 23).

16. Oliver Lawson Dick (ed.), *Aubrey's Brief Lives* (London, 1962), p. 186.

17. [Michael Neill discusses *Tancred and Gismund* and *The Mad Lover* at this point. In the former, Tancred, motivated by unconsummated incestuous feelings for his daughter Gismund, has her lover Guiszard killed and disembowelled, and his heart sent to Gismund in a golden goblet. Gismund adds poison to the cup and drinks its contents, and Tancred commits suicide on discovering her body. In *The Mad Lover*, Memnon agrees to deliver his own heart to his cruel beloved, at her request, in a goblet; he is persuaded by his brother Polidor to substi-

tute a piece of offal, which Polidor delivers, maintaining the pretence that it is Memnon's own heart. Ed.]

18. As a number of recent critics ... have demonstrated, the problematic aspects of Ford's writings are often most fruitfully approached through his ingenious play with dramatic convention and his creative engagement with the work of contemporaries and predecessors. Nowhere is this trait more apparent than in the wholesale reworking of *Romeo and Juliet* which has long been recognised as forming the groundwork of *'Tis Pity She's a Whore* – to the point where the incest theme might be seen as inverting that perversely exogamous compulsion which so entangles the rival houses of Capulet and Montague.

19. The iconography of Love's Cruelty itself was frequently interpreted by Renaissance Platonists as a Christian mystery: the emblem books are full of tortured hearts, while the erotic image of the heart as a love's tomb becomes an emblem of Divine Grace. [Neill cites a number of references here, and also includes in the original essay a series of plates. One of these, an anonymous fifteenth-century Florentine engraving, 'The Cruelty of Love', is representative: it depicts a young man tied to a tree, with a young woman standing before him with one hand on the side of his opened chest cavity; in the other hand she is holding his heart in front of his face – Ed.]

20. G. W. Ferguson, *Signs and Symbols in Christian Art* (New York, 1961), pp. 48–9 ... Cf. also the use of the pierced heart as a symbol of the Sorrows of the Virgin referred to in Madelaine, ' "Sensationalism" and "Melodrama" ', p. 52, 11. [A plate in the original essay reproduces the title page to John Hayward's *The Sanctuary of a Troubled Soul* (London, 1616), which depicts a heart held in chains by figures named Faith and Hope, while Fear pierces it with a sword, Grief scourges it, and Love simultaneously pierces it with a spear and pours what appears to be a healing balm upon it – Ed.]

21. Though Huebert makes considerable play with Bernini's and Crashaw's treatments of St Teresa's ecstasy in the course of his attempt to define the Baroque, he oddly fails to capitalise on their imagery in his analysis of *'Tis Pity*. For the *mors osculi* and the related *dulce amarum* theme, see Edgar Wind, *Pagan Mysteries in the Renaissance* (London, 1967), ch. 10, 'Amor as a God of Death'; Wind's analysis of this traditional paradox interestingly illuminates Giovanni's double role as avatar of both Love and Death.

22. See, for example, Andreas Alciatus, *The Latin Emblems* (ed. Peter M. Daly, Virginia W. Callahan and Simon Cuttler, Toronto, 1985), emblem 71, where Invidia appears as a hag gnawing at the heart torn from her own breast; and cf. Diehl, 'Iconography of Violence', p. 37 for other versions of this motif.

23. Both images telescope the acts of coition / fertilisation, parturition and death in a fashion that Carol Rosen finds characteristic of the play's climax: 'As various meanings merge in a single moment, Annabella's heart's blood compresses the ritualistic occasions of *'Tis Pity* into a single ceremony of innocence, combining aspects of communion, child-birth, and marriage rites.' See Carol C. Rosen, 'The Language of Cruelty in Ford's *'Tis Pity She's a Whore*', *Comparative Drama*, 8 (1974), 356–68, esp. p. 362.

24. The same analogy between body and state is at work in *Coriolanus*, not merely in Menenius's Fable of the Belly, but even in the ending of the play where the mob's 'Tear him to pieces', announces another grim literalisation of the metaphor.

25. The extraordinary word-play on 'hands' in Act III, scene ii, for example, draws attention to the bleeding stumps of Lavinia and Titus with such grotesque insistence that word, symbol, and physical object become almost ludicrously dissociated.

26. Quoted from Antonin Artaud, *The Theatre and its Double* (London, 1970), pp. 18, 21.

27. Diehl, 'Iconography of Violence', p. 34.

28. Huebert, *John Ford*, p. 145. Huebert's insistence on the forced oddity of Ford's analogy would surely have puzzled Mary Tudor, whose claim to die with Calais engraved upon her heart quite unselfcon-sciously adapted one of the most well-tried tropes in Renaissance love poetry.

29. Huebert, *John Ford*, p. 155.

30. Rosen, 'Language of Cruelty', p. 360. Although Huebert cites Artaud with approval, Rosen's article is virtually alone in its attempt to offer a systematic application of the French seer's suggestive, but often obscure, remarks about the play.

31. Jonathan Dollimore, *Radical Tragedy: Religion, Ideology and Power in the Drama of Shakespeare and his Contemporaries* (Brighton, 1984); Catherine Belsey, *the Subject of Tragedy: Identity and Difference in Renaissance Drama* (London, 1985); and Barker, *Tremulous Private Body*. [A chapter from Dollimore's book is in-cluded in this volume, pp. 107–20. See also Introduction to this volume, pp. 11–12 – Ed.]

32. One more attempt is made to penetrate Hieronimo's silence when Castile insists he be made to write. Hieronimo calls for a penknife with which he dispatches both the Duke and himself: like de Flores' suicidal penknife in *The Changeling*, the weapon makes these gestures into a murderous travesty of utterance.

33. My argument here owes something to the thinking of René Girard; see in particular *To Double Business Bound* (Baltimore, 1978), ch. 7, 'The Plague in Literature and Myth'.

34. See Eric Sellin, *the Dramatic Concepts of Antonin Artaud* (Chicago and London, 1968), pp. 38–42.

35. Farr, *Caroline Theatre*, pp. 50, 55, 171 (nn. 1, 12) cites a number of parallels and specific echoes, but oddly ignores the incest motif.

36. Webster's wooing scene was clearly a favourite with Ford: he also imitated it in *Love's Sacrifice* and *The Lover's Melancholy*; see Kathleen McLuskie, ' "Language and Matter with a Fit of Mirth": Dramatic Construction in the Plays of John Ford', pp. 104, 106, 107, 115; and Martin Butler, '*Love's Sacrifice*: Ford's Metatheatrical Tragedy', pp. 214–15, both in Michael Neill (ed.), *John Ford: Critical Re-visions* (Cambridge, 1988).

37. There is even an echo of the business with the Duchess's ring, which she vowed 'never to part with … / But to my second husband' (*Malfi*, I.i.413–14), in Act II, scene vi when Florio asks his daughter for 'the ring, / That which your mother in her will bequeathed, / And charged you on her blessing not to give't / To any but your husband' ('*Tis Pity*, II.vi.35–8), Annabella reveals that she has given it to Giovanni. Not only are both rings marked with the familiar sexual symbolism of wedding rings, the provenance of each exactly reflects the social taboo that its owner is breaking: the Duchess's supposed lasciviousness in marrying a second time is symbolised by her giving away a ring that is identified as the gift of her first husband and the sign of his continuing claim to her person; Annabella's surrender to incest is symbolised in the yielding up of a ring that is identified as the gift of the mother from whose womb she and Giovanni were born.

38. See, for example, Act II, scene v, lines 23–6, 47–9.

39. In the light of the evasion by which he sought to disclaim the bawdy innuendo of his lamprey – 'I mean the tongue' (I.i.345) – it is tempting to find a significance in the line that cues his entry, 'have you lost your tongue?' (III.ii.68). The bedroom scene also contains Ferdinand's own peculiarly morbid variation upon the exchange of hearts/cruelty of love motif: 'thou hast taken that massy sheet of lead / That hid thy husband's bones, and folded it / About my heart' (III.ii.113–15).

40. See S. R. Jayne (ed. and trans.) *Marsilio Ficino's Commentary on Plato's Symposium* (Columbia, 1944), II, viii, p. 146.

41. Roper's repunctuation of this sentence in the Revels text so as to make it clear that the phrase 'Burn … vengeance' is addressed to her own blood seems beside the point; the demented syntax deliberately conflates her present sufferings with those she wishes on her betrayer.

42. [Neill refers here to an anonymous fifteenth-century woodcut, reproduced in the original essay, which depicts Venus piercing the lover's
heart with a sword; in her other hand she carries a spear on which
another heart is impaled – Ed.]

43. [See note 19, above – Ed.]

44. [Neill here refers to a painting, reproduced in the original essay, depicting Amour plucking out the heart of King René and giving it to
Ardent Desire – Ed.] Compare the ludicrous conceit contrived by the
fool Mauruccio in *Love's Sacrifice*: he proposes to send Fiormonda a
portrait of himself with the bosom opened to expose a heart of pure
crystal, set in a blood-red velvet, which (in a ridiculously literal application of Ficino's metaphor of lovers as one another's mirrors) he
imagines her using as a looking-glass.

45. Francis Quarles, *Argalus and Parthenia* (London, 1629), sig. H⁵.

46. See Harriet Hawkins, 'Mortality, Morality, and Modernity in *The
Broken Heart*: Some Dramatic and Critical Counter-Arguments', in
Neill (ed.), *Critical Re-visions*, pp. 129–52; ' "Effeminately Dolent":
Gender and Legitimacy in Ford's *Perkin Warbeck*', in Neill (ed.),
Critical Revisions, pp. 261–79.

Further Reading

EDITIONS

Colin Gibson's *Six Renaissance Tragedies*, published by Macmillan – now Palgrave (Basingstoke, 1997), includes an excellent general introduction, some rather brief introductory notes to each play, and fairly full explanatory notes at the end of each text. The volume is comprised of *The Spanish Tragedy*, *The Revenger's Tragedy*, *The Changeling*, *The Duchess of Malfi*, *'Tis Pity She's a Whore* and Christopher Marlowe's *Doctor Faustus*.

Also recommended is Katharine Eisaman Maus (ed.), *Four Revenge Tragedies*, Oxford World's Classics series (Oxford University Press, 1995), which collects *The Spanish Tragedy*, *The Revenger's Tragedy*, *The Revenge of Bussy d'Ambois* (Chapman) and *The Atheist's Tragedy* (Tourneur) in an informative, up-to-date edition.

Gamini Salgado (ed.), *Three Jacobean Tragedies*, Penguin edition (London, 1965; revised 1969) comprises *The Revenger's Tragedy*, *The White Devil*, *The Changeling*. This is now out of date in terms of its introduction, but representative of this period of literary criticism with a focus on moral issues, character 'psychology' and tragic flaws.

Martin Wiggins has edited a collection of *Four Jacobean Sex Tragedies* in the Oxford World's Classics series (Oxford University Press, 1998): *The Insatiate Countess* (Marston), *The Maid's Tragedy* (Beaumont and Fletcher), *The Maiden's Tragedy* (Middleton), and *The Tragedy of Valentinian* (Fletcher). These are texts not covered by this volume, but they all explore similar territory, particularly in terms of gender, power and violence. *The Maiden's Tragedy* is particularly worthy of attention in relation to *The Revenger's Tragedy*.

The standard series of non-Shakespearean early modern plays in single volume form remains the Revels Plays series, currently published by Manchester University Press:
Philip Edwards (ed.), *The Spanish Tragedy* (1977)
R. A. Foakes (ed.), *The Revenger's Tragedy* (1975)
N. W. Bawcutt (ed.), *The Changeling* (1975)
John Russell Brown (ed.), *The White Devil* (1977)
Derek Roper (ed.), *'Tis Pity She's a Whore* (1975)

At the time of writing, many in the series were being reprinted in paperback at reasonable prices. In addition, a Revels Student Edition series was launched in the mid-1990s, using the same authoritative text, but with a slimmed down editorial apparatus:

David Bevington (ed.), *The Spanish Tragedy* (1998)
R. A. Foakes (ed.), *The Revenger's Tragedy* (1996)
N. W. Bawcutt (ed.), *The Changeling* (1998)
John Russell Brown (ed.), *The White Devil* (1996)
Derek Roper (ed.), *'Tis Pity She's a Whore* (1997)

The New Mermaid series, published by A. and C. Black (London), is also recommended. Several of their titles have been revised in recent years:

J. R. Mulryne (ed.), *The Spanish Tragedy* (1989)
Brian Gibbons (ed.), *The Revenger's Tragedy* (1991)
Christina Luckyj (ed.), *The White Devil* (1996)
Joost Daalder (ed.), *The Changeling* (2nd edition, 1990)
Brian Morris (ed.), *'Tis Pity She's a Whore* (1988)

There are other individual editions worthy of note, such as Simon Barker (ed.), *'Tis Pity She's a Whore*, Routledge English Texts series (London, 1997) and an old spelling version of *The Spanish Tragedie* ed. Emma Smith for Penguin (London, 1998).

For those looking for collections of writers' works, the Oxford World's Classics series is the most up to date, although their introductions tend to be fairly brief:

John Webster, '*The Duchess of Malfi' and Other Plays*, ed. René Weis (Oxford University Press, 1998)
John Ford, '*'Tis Pity She's a Whore' and Other Plays*, ed. Marion Lomax (1998)
Thomas Middleton, '*Women Beware Women' and Other Plays*, ed. Richard Dutton (1999) (includes *The Changeling* but not *The Revenger's Tragedy*)

The Penguin edition of John Webster, *Three Plays*, ed. David Charles Gunby (Harmondsworth, 1972) is in need of updating. On the other hand, *Five Plays* by Thomas Middleton, ed. Bryan Loughrey and Neil Taylor (London: Penguin, 1988) is relatively up to date and includes both *The Changeling* and *The Revenger's Tragedy*.

TRADITIONAL CRITICISM

The following are either standard works of reference for those researching the genre, or individual essays or books that are seminal in, or representative of, the criticism of the period. For obvious reasons, their approaches tend to differ from the kind of perspectives represented in this volume.

Michael Cameron Andrews, *This Action of Our Death: The Performance of Death in English Renaissance Drama* (Newark: University of Delaware Press, 1989). Relatively traditional in approach, but usefully focusing on the representation of death in plays of the period.

F. T. Bowers, *Elizabethan Revenge Tragedy 1587–1642* (Princeton, NJ: Princeton University Press, 1940). Remains the most comprehensive survey of the genre, discussing a number of obscure plays alongside the more familiar ones.

M. C. Bradbrook, *Themes and Conventions of Elizabethan Tragedy* (Cambridge: Cambridge University Press, 1935). Second part includes chapters on Tourneur, Webster, Middleton; Ford is discussed in the final chapter, tellingly entitled 'The Decadence'.

Nicholas Brooke, *Horrid Laughter in Jacobean Tragedy* (London: Open Books, 1979). Provides some revisionist perspectives on the notion of moral order in the plays, and is excellent for further research into the juxtaposition of the comic and the horrific.

Lily B. Campbell, 'Theories of Revenge in Renaissance England', *Modern Philology*, 38 (1931), 281–96. Good, 'old historicist' discussion of revenge in its early modern context.

T. S. Eliot, *Essays on Elizabethan Drama* (New York, 1932, 1960). Considers Senecan influence on Kyd and Tourneur.

Una Ellis Fermor, *The Jacobean Drama*, 5th edn (London: Methuen, 1965, first published 1936). Posits a familiar argument at the time that praises writers like Webster and Middelton for their insight into female psychology – a position vigorously attacked by feminist critics; see for example Jardine, *Still Harping*, below.

Charles A. Hallett and Elaine S. Hallett, *The Revenger's Madness: A Study of Revenge Tragedy Motifs* (Lincoln: University of Nebraska Press, 1980). Attempts to 'universalise' the genre by seeking out motifs and patterns, with the view that revenge tragedy conveys an archetypal human experience.

R. V. Holdsworth (ed.), *'The White Devil' and 'The Duchess of Malfi': A Casebook* (Basingstoke: Macmillan – now Palgrave, 1975). A collection pre-dating the contemporary critical approaches in this *New Casebook*; includes some reviews of professional productions.

R. V. Holdsworth (ed.), *Three Jacobean Revenge Tragedies: A Casebook* (Basingstoke: Macmillan – now Palgrave, 1990). Essays on *The Revenger's Tragedy, Women Beware Women* and *The Changeling*. In general, the collection does not reflect new critical approaches, although there is a useful essay by John Stachniewski on Calvinism and Middleton's tragedies.

Ian Jack, 'The Case of John Webster', *Scrutiny*, 16 (March 1949). Casts Webster as 'decadent', and argues that his plays are full of 'inconsistencies'. Representative of much criticism of the period. Reprinted in the Webster Casebook edited by Holdsworth (see above).

Robert Ornstein, *The Moral Vision of Jacobean Tragedy* (Madison and Milwaukee: University of Wisconsin Press, 1965). See brief discussion of this and Ribner (below) in the Introduction, pp. 6–7.

Eleanor Prosser, *Hamlet and Revenge*, 2nd edn (Stanford, CA: Stanford University Press, 1971). Like Campbell, above, good 'old historicist' account dealing with the complex detail of the morality of revenge.

Irving Ribner, *Jacobean Tragedy: The Quest for Moral Order* (London: Methuen, 1962). See Ornstein, above.

L. G. Salingar, 'Tourneur and the Tragedy of Revenge', in Boris Ford (ed.), *Pelican Guide to English Literature*, vol. 2, revised and expanded edn (Harmondsworth: Penguin, 1983), pp. 436–56. Another essay in the moralising tradition.

Michael Scott, *Renaissance Drama and a Modern Audience* (London: Methuen, 1982). Looks in some detail at revivals of plays such as *'Tis Pity* and *The Revenger's Tragedy* in the late twentieth century.

T. F. Wharton, *Moral Experiment in Jacobean Drama* (Basingstoke: Macmillan – now Palgrave, 1988). Like Brooke, a strong antidote to traditional views (Jack, Ornstein, Ribner) about the moral framework of these plays.

CONTEMPORARY CRITICISM: GENERAL

Catherine Belsey, *The Subject of Tragedy: Identity and Difference in Renaissance Drama* (London: Methuen, 1985). A key text in establishing cultural materialist approaches to the drama.

Celia R. Daileader, *Eroticism on the Renaissance Stage: Transcendence, Desire and the Limits of the Visible* (Cambridge: Cambridge University Press, 1998). Valuable discussion of Middleton and Webster in particular, heavily influenced by Derrida and deconstruction.

Alison Findlay, *A Feminist Perspective on Renaissance Drama* (Oxford: Oxford University Press, 1999). Chapter 2 includes a discussion of the ways in which revenge tragedies tap into fundamental male fears about women.

Wendy Griswold, *City Comedy and Revenge Tragedy in the London Theatre, 1576–1980* (Chicago: University of Chicago Press, 1986). A socio-cultural interpretation of these two genres in their own time, and at different points in the history of revivals of the plays.

James Hogg (ed.), *Jacobean Drama as Social Criticism*, Salzburg University Studies (Lewiston, NY / Salzburg, Austria: Edwin Mellen Press, 1995). Wide-ranging collection featuring essays on most of the issues and plays discussed in this volume.

Lisa Jardine, *Still Harping on Daughters: Women and Drama in the Age of Shakespeare* (Brighton: Harvester Wheatsheaf, 1983). See in particular chapter 3; an important book in the evolution of feminist approaches to the genre.

David Scott Kastan and Peter Stallybrass (eds), *Staging the Renaissance: Reinterpretations of Elizabethan and Jacobean Drama* (London: Routledge, 1991). A useful collection that provides general essays in part one, and studies of specific plays in part two (including all those covered in this volume except for *'Tis Pity She's a Whore*).

Kathleen McLuskie, *Renaissance Dramatists* (London: Harvester Wheatsheaf, 1989). Feminist reading of the plays, the theatre industry, and the context; see especially chapter 6.

Michael Neill, *Issues of Death: Mortality and Identity in English Renaissance Tragedy* (Oxford: Oxford University Press, 1997). Includes a chapter on *The Changeling*, with much of relevance in the general discussion elsewhere.

Karen Newman, *Fashioning Femininity and English Renaissance Drama* (Chicago: University of Chicago Press, 1991). Discusses plays other than those covered in this volume, but an important contribution to feminist and new historicist debates.

Gail Kern Paster, *The Body Embarrassed: Drama and the Disciplines of Shame in Early Modern England* (Ithaca, NY: Cornell University Press, 1993). Considers representations of the body in the drama of the period, in relation to gender and class structures in early modern society.

Robert N. Watson, *The Rest Is Silence: Death as Annihilation in the English Renaissance* (Berkeley, CA: University of California Press, 1994). Discusses early modern attitudes to death in a variety of texts.

Frank Whigham, *Seizures of the Will in Early Modern Drama* (Cambridge: Cambridge University Press, 1996). Focuses on the construction of the subject in a number of early modern plays, including *The Spanish Tragedy* and *The Duchess of Malfi*.

CONTEMPORARY CRITICISM: INDIVIDUAL AUTHORS AND TEXTS

The Spanish Tragedy

Barbara Baines, 'Kyd's Silenus Box and the Limits of Perception', *Journal of Medieval and Renaissance Studies*, 10 (1980), 41–51. Explores the play in the light of Renaissance scepticism, as touched on in essay 4 in this volume.

C. L. Barber, 'Unbroken Passion: Social Piety and Outrage in *The Spanish Tragedy*' in his *Creating Elizabethan Tragedy* (Chicago: University of Chicago Press, 1988), pp. 131–63. Draws on psychoanalytic theory as well as socio-historical perspectives.

G. K. Hunter, 'Ironies of Justice in *The Spanish Tragedy*', *Renaissance Drama*, 8 (1965), 89–104. Not from a contemporary critical perspective, but a very useful account of the way in which the action of the play interrogates traditional notions of justice.

James Shapiro, ' "Tragedies naturally performed": Kyd's Representation of Violence' in David Scott Kastan and Peter Stallybrass (eds), *Staging the Renaissance: Reinterpretations of Elizabethan and Jacobean Drama* (London: Routledge, 1991), pp. 99–113. Showing the influence of Foucault in its examination of the staging of punishment and execution in relation to state power.

Kay Stockholder, ' "Yet Can He Write": Reading the Silences in *The Spanish Tragedy*', *American Imago*, 47 (1990), 93–124. Freudian interpretation.

William L. Stull, ' "This Metamorphosde Tragoedie": Thomas Kyd, Cyril Tourneur, and the Jacobean Theatre of Cruelty', *Ariel*, 14:3 (July 1983), 35–49. Interesting for its use of Artaud and Brecht in analysis of violence in *The Spanish Tragedy* and *The Revenger's Tragedy*.

The Revenger's Tragedy
Scott McMillin, 'Acting and Violence: The Revenger's Tragedy and its Departures from Hamlet', *Studies in English Literature 1500–1900*, 24:2 (1984), 275–91. Some interesting reflections on the performative dimensions of the play, and its self-reflexivity.
Peter Stallybrass, 'Reading the Body: *The Revenger's Tragedy* and the Jacobean Theater of Consumption', in Kastan and Stallybrass (eds), *Staging the Renaissance*, pp. 210–20. Draws on theories of carnival via Bakhtin, as well as Freud and Kristeva.
William L. Stull, ' "This Metamorphosde Tragoedie": Thomas Kyd, Cyril Tourneur, and The Jacobean Theatre of Cruelty', *Ariel*, 14:3 (July 1983), 35–49. See under *The Spanish Tragedy*, above.
Martin White, *Middleton and Tourneur* (Basingstoke: Macmillan – now Palgrave, 1992). Includes lively, accessible debate of *The Revenger's Tragedy* and *The Changeling*, as well as an appendix on the authorship debates over the former play.

The Changeling
A. A. Bromham and Zara Bruzzi, '*The Changeling' and the Years of Crisis 1614–1624: A Hieroglyph of Britain* (London: Pinter Publishers, 1990). Argues that the play is riddled with hidden references to contemporary political events, including the planned Spanish marriage for Prince Charles – cf. Cristina Malcolmson's contribution to this volume (essay 7).
Mohammed Kowsar, 'Middleton and Rowley's *The Changeling*: The Besieged Temple', *Criticism*, 28 (1986), 145–64. Drawing on the work of Julia Kristeva, Kowsar interprets the castle in the play as an image of patriarchal power, under attack via the alliance of Beatrice-Joanna and De Flores.
Arthur L. Little, ' "Transshaped" Women: Virginity and Hysteria in *The Changeling*' in James Redmond (ed.), *Madness in Drama*, Themes in Drama no. 15 (Cambridge: Cambridge University Press, 1993), pp. 19–42. A sharp indictment of the play from a feminist perspective.
Martin White, *Middleton and Tourneur* (Basingstoke: Macmillan – now Palgrave, 1992). See under *The Revenger's Tragedy*, above.

The White Devil
Laura L. Behling, ' "S/he Scandles our Proceedings": the Anxiety of Alternative Sexualities in *The White Devil* and *The Duchess of Malfi*', *English Language Notes*, 33:4 (June 1996), 24–43. Analyses the threat posed to patriarchal order by the behaviour of women whose behaviour is 'politically and sexually masculine'. Useful parallel reading for Christina Luckyj's essay (9) on *The White Devil*.
Richard Allen Cave, *The White Devil' and 'The Duchess of Malfi': Text and Performance* (Basingstoke: Macmillan – now Palgrave, 1988). Detailed accounts of several major productions.

Kathryn R. Finin-Farber, 'Framing (the) Woman: *The White Devil* and the Deployment of Law', *Renaissance Drama*, 25, new series (1994), 219–45. New historicist study, examining how Vittoria's interrogation of the terms of legal discourse destablises the *modus operandi* of the patriarchy in the trial scene.

Charles R. Forker, *The Skull Beneath the Skin: The Achievement of John Webster* (Carbondale and Edwardsville: Southern Illinois University Press, 1986). Voluminous account of Webster's work, running to over 600 pages, from a more traditional literary critical perspective.

Dena Goldberg, *Between Worlds: A Study of the Plays of John Webster* (Waterloo, Ontario: Wilfrid Laurier University Press, 1987). Emphasis on state politics in *The Duchess of Malfi* and *The White Devil*.

Joan Lord Hall, *The Dynamics of Role-Playing in Jacobean Tragedy*, ch. 7: 'Acting and Self-Definition: *The White Devil*' (Macmillan – now Palgrave, 1991), pp. 136–56. A reading of the play in terms of its metadramatic aspects, challenging traditional readings of 'character' via an analysis of the text in terms of the different roles and *personae* inhabited by Flamineo, Vittoria and others.

Christina Luckyj, *A Winter's Snake: Dramatic Form in the Tragedies of John Webster* (Athens, GA: University of Georgia Press, 1989). A re-assessment of Webster, via *The Duchess of Malfi* and *The White Devil*, challenging the traditional criticisms of his dramaturgy.

'Tis Pity She's a Whore

Donald K. Anderson, Jr (ed.), *Concord in Discord: The Plays of John Ford 1586–1986* (New York: AMS Press, 1986). Along with Michael Neill (ed.), *John Ford: Critical Re-Visions* (see essay 11), this is the most important recent collection of essays on Ford.

Terri Clerico, 'The Politics of Blood: John Ford's *'Tis Pity She's a Whore*', *English Literary Renaissance*, 22:3 (Autumn 1992), 405–34. A cultural materialist reading which reconfigures the incest in the play as a class issue.

D. Gauer, 'Heart and Blood: Nature and Culture in *'Tis Pity She's a Whore*', *Cahiers Elisabéthains*, 23 (1987), 43–57. Draws on psychoanalysis and anthropology.

Lisa Hopkins, *John Ford's Political Theatre* (Manchester: Manchester University Press, 1994). Sets Ford in the context of some of the political and religious controversies of the time – including a discussion of *'Tis Pity* as an indictment of Protestant language and ritual.

Richard Marienstras, *New Perspectives on the Shakespearian World*, trans. Janet Lloyd (Cambridge: Cambridge University Press, 1985), ch. 8: 'Incest and Social Relations in *'Tis Pity She's a Whore* by John Ford'. Reading of the play heavily influenced by psychoanalysis.

Rowland Wymer, *Webster and Ford* (Basingstoke: Macmillan – now Palgrave, 1995). Particularly useful for the attention it pays to the play in performance.

OTHER GENERAL READING

The following books are not all directly related to study of the plays, but pick up on the themes of this volume and provide some starting points for research outside the immediate vicinity of the genre.

Antonin Artaud, *The Theatre and Its Double* (New York: Grove Press, 1958). Artaud mentions '*Tis Pity* in passing, but many of the issues raised (or ranted about) in this polemic are relevant to the revenge tragedy genre in performance.

Kate Aughterson (ed.), *Renaissance Woman: Constructions of Femininity in England* (London: Routledge, 1995). A sourcebook, with headnotes, of extracts from early modern documents covering such areas as theology, sexuality and motherhood, and proto-feminisms.

Francis Barker, *The Tremulous Private Body: Essays on Subjection* (London: Methuen, 1984: reprinted Ann Arbor: University of Michigan Press, 1995). A crucial text, cited in several of the essays collected here, focusing on the birth of the subject in early modern culture.

Anthony Fletcher, *Gender, Sex and Subordination in England 1500–1800* (New Haven and London: Yale University Press, 1995). A thorough examination of the workings of patriarchy during this period, with a number of references to the drama of the period.

Michel Foucault, *Discipline and Punish: The Birth of the Prison* (London: Penguin, 1991; first published in English 1977; first published in French 1975. An influential work for a number of the essays included in this volume; Foucault's theories are foundational to new historicist thinking.

John Kerrigan, *Revenge Tragedy: Aeschylus to Armageddon* (Oxford: Oxford University Press, 1996). Discussion of the genre is limited, as the scope of the book is as wide-ranging as its title suggests; but this is a masterly survey of the concept of revenge in Western culture.

Jonathan Sawday, *The Body Emblazoned: Dissection and the Human Body in English Renaissance Culture* (London: Routledge, 1995). Interdisciplinary study of the human body in early modern art and literature, but also pursuing the theme in religion, law, politics and medicine.

Laurence Stone, *The Family, Sex and Marriage in England 1500–1800* (London: Penguin, 1977). A milestone in socio-historical studies of the period, though many of its assumptions have been challenged in more recent years.

Notes on Contributors

Deborah G. Burks is Assistant Professor of English at the Ohio State University at Lima. She is author of ' "This sight doth shake all that is man within me": Sexual Violation and the Rhetoric of Dissent in Shirley's *The Cardinal*', *Journal of Medieval and Early Modern Studies* (Winter 1996). She is at work on a study of violation in early modern drama.

Karin S. Coddon has taught Shakespeare, critical theory and writing at the University of California, San Diego, and at Brown University. She has published widely in the field of Renaissance Drama, including essays on *Hamlet*, *Macbeth*, and *The Duchess of Malfi*.

Jonathan Dollimore is Professor in the Department of English and Related Literature at the University of York. Prior to that he was Professor at Sussex University, and he has been visiting Professor in Australia, the USA, South Africa and Canada. His books include *Radical Tragedy* (1984, 2nd edn 1989), *Political Shakespeare* (joint ed. with Alan Sinfield, 1985, 2nd edn 1994), *Sexual Dissidence* (1991) and *Death, Desire and Loss in Western Culture* (1998). He is currently writing about sex, art and evil.

J. W. Lever was Professor of English at Simon Fraser University, British Columbia, and also taught at Durham University. His other publications include *The Elizabethan Love Sonnet* (1966), an Arden edition of *Measure for Measure* (1965), *Sonnets of the English Renaissance* (1974) and a parallel text version of Jonson's *Every Man in his Humour* (1972).

Ania Loomba is Professor of English at the University of Illinois at Urbana-Champaign. Her recent publications include *Colonialism / Postcolonialism* (1998) and a collection of essays co-edited with Martin Orkin, *Postcolonial Shakespeares* (1998). Her research specialisms include early modern English contact with and representations of 'the East', and she is currently working on a book on Shakespeare, race and colonialism, to be published by Oxford University Press.

Christina Luckyj, Associate Professor of English at Dalhousie University, Halifax, Nova Scotia, Canada, is the author of *'A Winter's Snake': Dramatic Form in the Tragedies of John Webster* (1989) and the editor of the New Mermaid *The White Devil* (1996). She has also written on Volumnia in Shakespeare's *Coriolanus* and on women, silence and performance in Renaissance texts. Her book manuscript, '*A Moving Rhetoricke*': *Gender and Silence in Early Modern England*, is currently under review.

Cristina Malcolmson is Associate Professor of English and Chair of Women's Studies at Bates College in Lewiston, Maine. She is author of *Heart-Work: George Herbert and the Protestant Ethic* (1999), and editor of *Renaissance Poetry* (Longman Critical Reader, 1998). She has also contributed essays to *The Matter of Difference* (ed. Valerie Wayne, 1991) and *Enclosure Acts: Sexuality, Property, and Culture in Early Modern England* (ed. Richard Burt and John Michael Archer, 1994).

Katharine Maus is Professor of English at the University of Virginia. She is the author of *Inwardness and Theatre in the English Renaissance* (1995), which won the Roland Bainton prize for a distinguished book in Renaissance studies. She is also the author of *Ben Jonson and the Roman Frame of Mind* (1984), editor of *Four Revenge Tragedies of the English Renaissance* (1995), and co-editor of *The Norton Shakespeare* (1997), *The Norton Anthology of Renaissance Drama* (forthcoming), and *Soliciting Interpretation: Literary Theory and Seventeenth-Century Literature* (1991).

Michael Neill is Professor of English at the University of Auckland, New Zealand. His publications include the Oxford edition of *Antony and Cleopatra* (1994), *Issues of Death: Mortality and Identity in English Renaissance Tragedy* (1997) and *Putting History to the Question: Power, Politics, and Society in English Renaissance Drama* (1999).

Molly Easo Smith teaches at the University of Aberdeen and has taught previously at Ithaca College and Saint Louis University. She is the author of *The Darker World Within: Evil in the Tragedies of Shakespeare and his Successors* (1991) and *Breaking Boundaries: Politics and Play in the Drama of Shakespeare and his Contemporaries* (1998). She is currently working on a book tentatively titled *Literature and Culture in Early Modern England: Shifting Centres and Expanding Margins*, which will see publication in late 2001.

Susan J. Wiseman lectures in English at Birkbeck College, London University. She is the author of *Drama and Politics in the English Civil War* (1998) and *Aphra Behn* (1996), and contributed to the collection of essays *Renaissance Bodies* (1990).

Index